A
DEATH
IN THE
ISLANDS

A
DEATH
IN THE
ISLANDS

The Unwritten Law and the Last Trial Of Clarence Darrow

MIKE FARRIS

Skyhorse Publishing

Skyhorse Publishing books may be purchased in bulk at special discounts for sales promotion, corporate gifts, fund-raising, or educational purposes. Special editions can also be created to specifications. For details, contact the Special Sales Department, Skyhorse Publishing, 307 West 36th Street, 11th Floor, New York, NY 10018 or info@skyhorsepublishing.com.

Skyhorse® and Skyhorse Publishing® are registered trademarks of Skyhorse Publishing, Inc.®, a Delaware corporation.

Visit our website at www.skyhorsepublishing.com.

10 9 8 7 6 5 4 3 2 1

Library of Congress Cataloging-in-Publication Data is available on file.

Cover design by Rain Saukas
Cover photo credits AP Images, Robert Command

Print ISBN: 978–1–5107–1214–0
Ebook ISBN: 978–1–5107–1215–7

Printed in the United States of America

To Susan: *Mahalo* for your *aloha* and support.

Acknowledgments

It was many years ago, while on vacation in Hawaii, when I first stumbled across this tragic story. I knew then that I wanted to write about it, but as is so often the case, procrastination and inertia were my enemies. At long last, though, this book has become a reality. I want to thank my agents, Donna Eastman and Gloria Koehler, for their dedication to finding a publisher for this story. And I want to thank the great people at Skyhorse Publishing for their hard work, which has made this a better book: Joseph Craig, Stacey Fischkelta, and Ashley Vanicek. I also want to thank my "advance readers," Kelly Griffin, Jon Griffin, and Steve Baskind. And of course my wife, Susan, for her support, which included reading countless drafts of the manuscript along the way.

"UNWRITTEN LAW. See *LEX NON SCRIPTA*. A popular expression to designate a supposed rule of law that a man who takes the life of his wife's paramour or daughter's seducer is not guilty of a criminal offence."

—*Bouvier's Law Dictionary and Concise Encyclopedia* (1914)

"Of course, all the attorneys for the prosecution, and those for the defense, as well as the judge, knew that legally my clients were guilty of murder. Yet, on the island, and across the seas, and around the earth, men and women were hoping and praying and working for the release and vindication of the defendants. As in similar cases, every one was talking about 'the unwritten law.' While this could not be found in the statutes, it was indelibly written in the feelings and thoughts of people in general. Which would triumph, the written or the unwritten law, depended upon many things which in this case demand the most careful consideration."

—Clarence Darrow, *The Story of My Life*

Contents

Introduction

In the wee hours of the morning on Sunday, September 13, 1931, two events occurred nearly simultaneously in Honolulu which, although reported separately to the police, set in motion a series of events that included lies, deception, mental illness, racism, revenge, murder, and one of the greatest miscarriages of justice in United States history. It nearly tore apart the peaceful islands of Hawaii as it reverberated from the tenements of Honolulu to the hallowed halls of Congress, and right into the White House. And it ultimately left a stain on the legacy of one of the greatest legal minds of all time.

This is the story of the Ala Moana Boys, as they came to be known, and the last trial of Clarence Darrow.

I first became acquainted with this story more than twenty years ago while vacationing with my wife in our favorite vacation destination: Hawaii. We were in a small bookstore in downtown Hilo, on the Big Island, where I picked up a copy of a small paperback book that had a title that leaped out at me from the cover: *Rape in Paradise* by Theon Wright, published in 1966.

On the back cover, it contained this intriguing teaser:

A white woman claims she is raped by a gang of non-whites; white authorities attempt to push through a swift "justice." Ugly race hatred bursts out into open violence. The community divides into two angry factions, prompting the federal government to consider sending in troops to maintain order.

Alabama? Mississippi? No. *Hawaii in the early 1930s!*

Following that introduction to the events in Honolulu of 1931–1932, I became fascinated with the tragic story of five young men—the Ala Moana Boys—who I am convinced were innocent of the charges against them; the brutal murder of one of them; and the trial that brought the famous Clarence Darrow out of the retirement for one last tussle in a courtroom.

As a lawyer myself, I have long held Darrow in high esteem, as does virtually every lawyer in America. But after learning more about this particular story, I came to know that, as is so often the case, this hero had feet of clay. With his legacy solidly chiseled in American history as a champion of the underdog—the little guy—I was saddened to learn that he had been lured by a big payday to take the wrong side of history. If you had simply given me an overview of this story and then said that Clarence Darrow had come on the scene, I would have sworn that he had done so on behalf of the Ala Moana Boys. But that was not the case.

That doesn't mean, though, that there are no heroes in this tragedy. As I dug into the story and tracked down trial transcripts and court records, I discovered that there were at least two major heroes, and some minor ones. The major ones are Judge Albert Cristy and Honolulu prosecutor John C. Kelley. You'll read more about them in the pages that follow, but suffice it to say, my admiration for those two men stems from the fact that they were motivated, not by a big fee, as was Darrow, but by conscience and integrity.

What I hope to do with this book is present what is a relatively obscure story in a way that is easy to read, in the style of a novel, rather than in the academic style of a professor or the narrative style of a journalist. I also hope I have been able to add insights from my vantage point as a lawyer about some of the legal maneuvering and the events in the courtrooms.

Although I have obviously taken some liberties in setting some of the scenes and dialogue, I have tried to stay meticulously true to the historical record. Though some dialogue is invented, courtroom testimony and most of the police interrogations come verbatim from trial transcripts and police reports. I have, of course, done some editing to omit tangents and too much detail, but other than that, the words spoken in those settings came right out of the mouths of the participants; courtroom testimony is straight from the trial transcripts.

Ultimately, this story is a tragedy that can match anything fiction might offer, but it is painfully true. I hope that the reader will come away with a new appreciation for the law, as practiced by Judge Cristy and prosecutor John Kelley, as well as by the defense attorneys who represented the Ala Moana Boys in the original rape trial, and with an awareness that, although the potential for injustice can be great, all of us have a duty to ensure fairness for everyone, no matter their color or creed or station in life. In that respect, this is a cautionary tale that should never be forgotten or ignored.

—Mike Farris

PART ONE

THALIA MASSIE
AND THE ALA MOANA BOYS

Chapter One

The Woman in Green

"Are you white people?"

September 13, 1931
Approximately 12:50 a.m.

The young woman appeared like an apparition in the gloom.

Eustace Bellinger slowed his car and peered ahead into the darkness. His headlights illuminated a narrow path on an overgrown stretch of Ala Moana Road between Waikiki and downtown Honolulu, about one hundred yards prior to reaching the old animal quarantine station. The Bellingers and their friends, the Clarks, had spent the evening playing cards, and now they were on their way to an evening snack at the Kewalo Inn on Ala Moana. Eustace had just maneuvered his car beyond a row of squatters' hovels made of flattened tin cans and assortments of sheet metal, and then past a rubbish dump before entering this wild span of road that had once been a small airport. He never dreamed they would encounter anyone out here, much less a woman, alone.

She stepped into the beam of his lights and walked toward the car. She wore a green dress that stretched to her ankles, over which she wore a light green jacket with sleeves trimmed in fur. She had a strange way of walking, with a stooped, almost hunched posture. Light brown hair hung just above her shoulders, and her eyes had an odd bulge to them. She waved her arms to flag the car down.

"What the hell is she doing?" Eustace asked.

His tone brought conversation in the car to a halt. Eustace's wife, along with George Clark Sr. and his wife, sitting in the backseat, leaned forward to see what he was talking about. George Clark Jr., in the passenger seat, swung his head around to face front.

"Dear Lord," Mrs. Clark said. "Is that Ramona? She's supposed to be with friends this evening."

"That's not your daughter," Eustace said. "I don't know who it is or why in God's name she would be out here all by herself."

As the woman drew closer, injuries on her face became visible. A red scuff marked her cheek and she had a puffy, bloodied lip, but her dress bore no signs of distress nor were there any other visible marks.

Eustace slowed his automobile to a stop. The woman lurched to the passenger side, where she moved her lips, as if speaking. A faint whisper of a breeze, ripe with plumeria, filtered in, accompanied by the fluttering of palm fronds in nearby trees. The woman leaned forward and looked inside. She squinted, apparently having difficulty focusing. From up close, the mark on her cheek looked like it might have been made by a ring, perhaps caused by a punch. Her lip was bleeding, and blood dripped from her chin, proof that the injuries were recent.

"Are you white people?" she asked.

A damn strange question, Eustace thought. Wasn't the answer readily apparent? But her squinting told him she might be unable to see clearly. "Yes," he said.

"Thank God," she answered. Without invitation, she opened the passenger door, got in, and sat on George Jr.'s lap. The teenager seemed stunned, but he sat silently as the woman settled in and stared straight ahead.

"Please take me home," she said. "Twenty-eight fifty Kahawai Street in Manoa Valley."

Eustace looked over his shoulder at his wife, who nodded. He took his foot from the brake and shifted it to the accelerator, then swung the car in a tight U-turn and retraced the path he had taken along Ala Moana Road.

Mrs. Bellinger took a handkerchief from her purse and handed it to the woman. "What happened to you, dear?"

"Some Hawaiian boys did this to me."

"Did what?"

"I was with some friends at the Ala Wai Inn and went out for a walk, to get some air." She squeezed her eyes tightly shut. "I'm afraid I'd had a bit of a spat and needed to clear my head. I didn't even hear the car when it stopped beside me."

* * *

Approximately 12:00 a.m. (fifty minutes earlier)
Midnight, and the Ala Wai Inn, a rocking nightspot on Kalakaua Avenue, on the west bank of the Ala Wai Canal, was still hopping. Saturday night had become known as "Navy Night" since the two-story, cottage-like structure, built in the style of

a Japanese teahouse, had been discovered by haole (white) sailors from Pearl Harbor, who flocked there on weekends. There was no official policy limiting Saturday night attendance to whites-only, but other Honolulu residents, particularly those of color, simply exercised their judgment in avoiding the Inn on nights when it was filled by military personnel, many of whom were disdainful of the local citizenry, and who imbibed as if liquor were on the verge of extinction. The Ala Wai boasted a large dance floor and billed itself as having the largest open-air pavilion in Honolulu. Dinner and a dance cost a dollar fifty, and the dance typically ended at one o'clock. But the young woman in the green dress left early that night.

She crossed the canal, turned left on Kalakaua Avenue, then turned right on John Ena Road, across from Aloha Amusement Park, sometimes known as Waikiki Park. Another Saturday night dance, this one for locals, had just ended at the open-air dance hall, and patrons were making their exit as she headed makai, or oceanward, on John Ena. She paid no attention to the couple who crossed John Ena and got in their car just as she passed. She continued past a series of bungalows and small apartments that housed bachelor officers from nearby Fort DeRussey, a few small businesses in a single building—Kimoto's store, a barbershop, another store—then a saimin wagon in a vacant lot, which served a soup made with noodles. Head down, walking slowly, she didn't notice the woman in the front window of a store who watched her go by, nor the couple she had passed earlier who were now pulled into the lot housing the saimin stand, awaiting an order of noodles.

She crossed a narrow road, called Hobron Lane, and eased into a bend in John Ena, just prior to the turn onto Ala Moana Road. Waves from the nearby Pacific harmonized with the wind in the trees, and there was a fragrance of sweetness in the air from native flora that flanked her on both sides.

An automobile suddenly pulled to a stop beside her. She hadn't heard it approach, and its sudden halt startled her. Had someone come from the Ala Wai looking for her? Could it be her husband? She turned her head to see but, before she could identify the vehicle, two men sprang from the car. One grabbed her by an arm while the other covered her mouth. She tried to scream, but a dark hand muffled the sound. She sank her heels into the ground and tried to pull away, but one small woman was no match for two full-grown men. They dragged her to an open-topped convertible. More hands grabbed at her as the abductors forced her into the backseat where other men waited. She tried to scream again, but the hand clamped tighter over her mouth, killing the sound in her throat. Another hand covered her eyes. As the car pulled away, she heard a distinctive flapping sound, like a rip on the cloth top vibrating in the breeze.

Panicking, she struggled to free herself from the hands that held her. The more she struggled, the tighter they gripped. A fist slammed into her jaw and she stilled. Dazed, she tried again to cry out, but to no avail. Tears filled her eyes, blurring shapes and figures in the darkness of the night. Then there was a whirlwind of fists pummeling her. Pounding and pounding. No portion of her face was safe. Her nose, eyes, cheeks, mouth. She felt the warm stickiness of blood on her chin as it streamed from her lips.

A jolt suggested that the car left the road and pulled onto hard ground, where it came to an abrupt halt. Her heartbeat kicked up. This is where it would happen. And she knew it was about to happen. After all, why else would dark-skinned men on this God-forsaken island snatch a white woman from the streets? Savages all.

A door opened. She caught her breath, awaiting the inevitable.

Then hands pushed her out onto the jungle floor. She hit the ground hard. Wind rushed from her lungs as she rolled over and came to her hands and knees. To her shock, the door slammed shut and the convertible sped away, its torn top still flapping like a sail in the night air.

She squinted after the speeding car as it left her behind. All she saw were vague outlines and shadows. She tried to focus on the license plate, but to no avail; it was just a blur.

And then the car was out of sight.

* * *

An incredible tale. The car's occupants were stunned.

"What kind of car was it?" Eustace asked.

"I couldn't tell," she said. "Maybe a Ford or Chevrolet. They covered my eyes when they forced me inside, and it was too dark to see after they pushed me out."

Mrs. Clark cleared her throat. "Dear, did they—" She halted, and then continued. "Did they hurt you in any other way?"

The question hung in the air for an instant. Everyone knew what she was really asking. Then the woman said, "No, they just hit me."

The story defied logic to Eustace, but he had no facts with which to refute the storyteller. After all, her face bore marks of an assault, albeit not as much as one might expect from the horrific beating she described. Still, it rang false in his ear. He glanced at the woman, who stoically faced ahead. Her dress was immaculate. He slid his glance down at her shoes, alligator-skin pumps. Not a mark on them, even on the heels. Surely being dragged into an automobile and then tossed onto the jungle floor would have left some mark on her shoes or tear in the fabric of her dress. No, something was not right about this story.

From the rear seat, George Clark Sr. voiced Eustace's concerns, as if reading his mind. "Why would they pick you up just to beat you and then to let you go? Are you sure they didn't do anything else?"

"I said they just hit me." Her tone was firm, almost petulant, and brooked no disagreement.

"Did you know these men?" Clark Sr. asked.

"I didn't know them, and it was too dark to see. But I heard their voices. They were all Hawaiian."

"You're sure?"

"I've been here long enough to know what Hawaiians sound like."

"How many were there?" Eustace asked.

"I don't know. Five or six, I think."

"Do you know where they went?"

"One of them said something about going to Kalihi. That's the way they drove off."

Eustace knew Kalihi to be a squalid residential area teeming with tenements and poverty. "Did you see the license plate number on the car?"

"No."

"How long ago did this happen? Have you been waiting out here long?"

"Just a few minutes ago. You're the first car to come by."

"I think we need to take you to the police station," Mrs. Clark said. "They can't be too far away."

"No!" the woman snapped.

There was a harsh bite to her voice that took the car's occupants by surprise. No longer merely petulant, she now sounded angry. But as quickly as her temper flashed, it subsided. "I don't want to go to the police station," she said in a softer voice. "Please, don't ask me any more questions. My jaw hurts too much to talk. I think they may have knocked some teeth out. Just take me home, and my husband will take care of me."

Then she turned her face to the passenger window and stared silently into the darkness. This inquisition was over.

Chapter Two

The Ala Moana Boys

"Something terrible has happened."

September 13, 1931
Approximately 12:45 a.m.

Just moments before the Clarks and the Bellingers picked up the young woman in the green dress, Agnes Peeples, a sturdy Hawaiian woman, stormed into the Honolulu Police Department's temporary headquarters at King and Alakea Streets. She slapped a scrap of paper on the counter in front of Officer Cecil Rickard, the Honolulu Police Department's official radio announcer. The sound echoed throughout the building. Rickard looked at the scrap, on which Agnes had scrawled the numbers "58–895."

"Cecil, I want to file a complaint against this *kanaka* boy who assaulted me. Here's the license plate of the Chevrolet him and his *bruddahs* were in."

"Now hold on, Agnes. What do you mean he assaulted you?"

"He hit me. In my face. With his fist."

Rickard studied Agnes's face. A red mark on the left side certainly testified to some kind of blow.

"Where did this happen?" he asked.

"At King and Liliha Streets. Five or ten minutes ago. First they nearly crashed into us in their car then this crazy *kanaka* boy hit me. Look at my ear."

Sure enough, blood trickled from her left ear. Something had happened to it, all right.

"Okay, let's back up here, Agnes," Cecil said. "Tell me exactly what happened."

* * *

Approximately 12:35 a.m. (ten minutes earlier)

Agnes was a just a wee bit tipsy after she and her husband Homer had spent an evening drinking with friends. A little something to eat was what she needed to settle her down, so Homer pulled their 1924 Hudson out of the garage and they headed toward the center of Honolulu from their home on the *ewa*, or westward, side of downtown, where Ewa Plantation was located. They cruised King Street in search of an open diner. Despite the lateness of the hour, the town was remarkably alive. After all, it was a Saturday night, actually early Sunday morning, with weekend revelers spending paychecks and enjoying time off from their labors.

Homer tried to ignore his slightly intoxicated wife, who babbled in the passenger seat as he drove. Theirs was a mixed-race marriage, Agnes being a native Hawaiian—a *kanaka*—while Homer was *haole*, or white. It was also clear who wore the pants in the family, and she was sitting firmly in the passenger seat.

"I'm hungry," she said, for at least the fourth time.

"I know, Agnes." Homer sighed. "I know, I know. You keep reminding me."

The sound of an engine revving drew his attention to the left. A tan Ford touring car blasted down Liliha Street, toward the short dogleg on King, on to Dillingham Boulevard that led to the squalid part of town known as Kalihi.

Alarm tinged Homer's voice. "He's not going to stop."

He shifted his foot to the space between the accelerator and the brake pedal, ready to react either way, as needed, if the Ford ignored the protocol of intersections. The Ford kept barreling forward, by Agnes's estimate traveling at least forty-five miles per hour, and a collision on the driver side appeared inevitable. Homer blared his horn and accelerated. At the last second, the Ford slammed on the brakes just as Homer shot past. The Hudson jumped forward into the intersection, barely clearing the nose of the Ford, which screeched to a halt in the middle of the intersection, just to the rear of the Hudson's passenger side. Homer stopped the Hudson in front of the Ford. He heaved a sigh of relief and took a deep breath.

Agnes was not so placid. She screamed out the window at the Ford, which was occupied by four young men.

"Hey, what the hell you doing? Watch where you going!"

"Go to hell, you *pupule wahine*," a male voice said.

"What the hell you talking about? You driving crazy; you gonna kill us all."

A muscular *kanaka* man got out of the backseat of the Ford, and a diminutive, but solidly built, Japanese man exited from the driver's seat. Both appeared to be in their early twenties, and the larger man, nearly six feet tall, moved with the grace and ease of an athlete. The Japanese man seemed a little frightened, perhaps unnerved by the close call with his car, but the *kanaka* was itching for a fight. And Agnes was ready to oblige him.

"What's the matter? Can't you drive?" the *kanaka* said.

"You the one can't drive. You the one who's *pupule.* My husband drive just fine."

The *kanaka* kept coming toward the Hudson. He leaned over the passenger window and peered inside, past Agnes. She smelled alcohol on his breath, just as, most likely, he did on hers. His unsteady eyes settled on Homer's white face. His lips pulled back, exposing a canine smile, as if he had spotted prey.

"Get that goddamn *haole* out of the car, and I'll give him what he's looking for," he said.

Agnes saw panic on her husband's face as his hand fumbled beneath the driver's seat. She knew he was feeling for his tire iron that he always kept there. This was on the verge of getting ugly.

She opened the door and shoved it into the *kanaka,* forcing him back. She got out and planted herself in his path with her sturdy frame. He stepped forward. She shot out her hands and slammed the heels into his chest. He staggered back a step. His face registered surprise at the strength of this crazy *wahine.*

"You get in your car and get the hell out of here," Agnes said.

The *kanaka* regained his footing and stood still for a moment, as if unsure how to respond. Then he stepped forward and swung his right hand, fingers clenched into a tight fist. It slammed into the left side of Agnes's head, squarely on her ear.

But she didn't go down. With lightning fast reflexes, she slammed her hands into his chest again, then delivered a roundhouse blow of her own, with an open hand, to his face. He appeared stunned.

Homer stepped out of the Hudson and waved the tire iron. "You get away from her," he said.

The Japanese driver grabbed the *kanaka* by his arm and pulled him toward the Ford. "Come on, bruddah. Let's go."

They both turned and sprinted for the Ford. The *kanaka* jumped into the backseat, the Japanese slid behind the wheel, and the Ford squealed away toward Kalihi. Agnes squinted after the departing car, memorizing the license plate just long enough to write it down when she got back in the Hudson: 58–895.

* * *

After dutifully listening to Agnes Peeples vent her outrage, Officer Cecil Rickard checked the license plate number with the police department's traffic division and learned that it actually belonged to a Ford Phaeton touring car, not a Chevrolet. At 12:50 a.m., just as the Bellingers and the Clarks were picking up the young woman on Ala Moana road, Cecil broadcast an alert to patrol cars on duty.

"Be on the lookout for a Ford touring car, license plate number five-eight-eight-nine-five, wanted in connection with an assault on a woman at King and Liliha Streets, last seen headed in the direction of Kalihi."

* * *

Approximately 1:05 a.m.

Things were starting to wind down at the Ala Wai Inn. One of those still whiling away the night was Lieutenant Tommie Massie, who served as engineer of the diesel-powered submarine S-43. In his mid-twenties, Tommie was slightly built, standing not quite five-and-a-half feet tall. His brown hair was short and parted on the right side, and he typically wore a solemn, if not downright sad, countenance on his face.

With Tommie was his intoxicated friend, Lieutenant Jerry Branson. They were both dressed in white linen suits, both now disheveled. Their wives had already abandoned them, Jean Branson disgustedly leaving when her drunken husband climbed up on the bandstand and pretended to lead the band.

And as for Thalia Massie—well, it had probably been about an hour and a half since Tommie had last seen his sullen wife. Tommie and Thalia had met four years earlier, when Thalia was just sixteen and Tommie was a cadet at the Naval Academy. Then they were married a few months later at the Bethlehem Chapel of the National Cathedral. But things soon soured for this young man from Kentucky and his bride, a daughter of socialites Roly and Grace Fortescue. By the time they arrived in Honolulu, their marriage hung by a thread.

Thalia hadn't wanted to come that night in the first place. In fact, she rarely wanted to go anywhere with Tommie and his shipmates. She didn't much like his friends, nor did they care for her. Her fits of temper and moody sullenness had ruined many an evening for Tommie and anyone in the vicinity. Her reputation was already legendary among the submarine officers and their wives, including rumors of overnight male guests at their home in Manoa when Tommie was away on maneuvers. Thalia insulted and criticized others as if it were a sport, and she had been known at times to walk around the house, and even out in the yard, in various stages of undress. Once she physically attacked her husband in public, scratching and biting, while at other times she had stormed off and abandoned him to his companions.

Most of Tommie's friends wished that Thalia would never come along, and they welcomed her occasional disappearing act as a refreshing respite from the rancid atmosphere that usually enveloped her. Even Tommie would have preferred that she not come with them that evening, but naval wives had obligations, one of which was to accompany their husbands on social occasions so they didn't become third wheels when out with other married couples. And if Thalia didn't like it? Well, Tommie had her signature on a pact that reminded her that she was just one violation away from divorce court, a threat he held over her head like the Sword of Damocles.

So she had joined him that evening with his fellow officers and their wives, Lieutenant Jerry and Jean Branson, and Lieutenant Tom and Mary Ann Brown. Nobody really paid any attention when Thalia, in one of her moods, had left their party downstairs and joined others upstairs. The last time anyone recalled seeing her was about 11:30, when she threw one of her usual tantrums in front of three naval officers and their wives—Lieutenant Commander Miller, Lieutenant Stogsdall, and Lieutenant Fish. Thalia had dropped in on them in an upstairs room they occupied and almost immediately confronted an inebriated Stogsdall. The circumstances of their argument were unclear, but it ended with Thalia telling Stogsdall that he was "no gentleman," and Stogsdall responding that she was, in fact, a "louse"—and she retaliated by slapping him.

Nobody really knew for sure when Thalia actually left the Ala Wai Inn, nor did they care. Out of sight, out of mind. That's the way most of them liked it.

The Browns departed about midnight, leaving Tommie Massie and Jerry Branson on their own. In his drunken state, Jerry took to the bandstand where he led the musicians, then removed his shoes and, with a boisterous crowd cheering him on, returned to the dance floor to dance in front of the band. At last the music stopped and Jerry flopped on the floor on his back, exhausted.

Tommie approached and stood over him. "Come on, Jerry; enough. Let's go home."

Jerry extended his hand. Tommie grabbed and pulled, but felt only dead weight. From his prone position, Jerry looked behind Tommie, as if searching for someone.

"Where's Jean?"

"She left a long time ago. I suspect she was a little embarrassed by her husband."

Jerry smiled. "Yeah, that happens sometimes. Where's Thalia?"

Tommie's mood sobered. "I don't know. Gone home, I guess." He pulled Jerry to his feet. "Come on, let's go over to Red and Monte's and get something to eat. They're probably waiting for us."

On the way out, Tommie stopped at a telephone. While Jerry leaned against a wall, Tommie dialed the number for his house. After letting it ring for a long while, he slammed the phone down.

"Damn it! She's not home," he said. Jerry wisely kept his mouth shut.

By now, the time was 1:15 a.m.

Tommie guided Jerry to his car, a tan Ford touring model, which was still where he had parked it. Obviously Thalia hadn't taken it. Where the hell was she?

With Jerry flopped drunkenly in the passenger seat, Tommie steered his vehicle down Kalakaua Avenue to Beretania Street and then doglegged east and north toward Lieutenant James "Red" Rigby's house in the same Manoa neighborhood where he lived with Thalia. He arrived at the Rigbys about ten minutes after leaving the Ala Wai, and deposited Jerry on a couch on the front *lanai*. The party had clearly not moved to Red's, a fact confirmed by Red and Monte's sleepy maid, whom he awakened by banging on the front door. Maybe everyone had gone to the Massie house.

"Can I use the phone?" Tommie asked.

The maid nodded and ushered him inside. Picking up the receiver, he called home again. This time he was rewarded by Thalia's voice.

"Hello?"

"Thalia?"

"Oh, Tommie," she said. "Something terrible has happened." Then she began to cry.

Chapter Three

The Accusation

"A woman was assaulted by a man."

After initially broadcasting the license number of the Ford touring car involved in the altercation with Agnes Peeples, Cecil Rickard received three responses from officers on patrol, meticulously noting it all in his logbook. At 12:55 a.m., Officer Percy Bond, who was on patrol with Claude Benton in patrol car number 2, radioed from King and Kalakaua Streets that they had received the call. At 1:05 a.m., Detectives John Cluney and Thurman Black, in patrol car number 3, reported from Waikiki by telephone, and at 1:30 a.m., the officers in patrol car number 1, motorcycle officer William Furtado and Detective George Harbottle, reported from a call box at Beretania and Fort Streets.

Although there were plenty of acknowledgements, little, if any, action was being taken. A simple assault wasn't a high priority, and the officers made no serious effort to follow up other than merely being on the lookout.

Rickard then set about going through license plate files manually to determine the owner of the Ford with the number 58–895. If he could get a name and address, they no longer would have to rely solely upon the happy accident of spotting the car on the streets in order to make an arrest.

* * *

Captain Hans Kashiwabara, who had been with the Honolulu Police Department for seventeen years, making captain just two-and-a-half years earlier, had come on duty at 10:30 that night. After checking in, he went out onto the streets of Honolulu and finally returned to the station at 1:00 a.m. Sergeant Kamauha was working the duty desk when Kashiwabara entered, while Rickard focused his attention on a stack of documents in front of him.

"What's Cecil doing?" Kashiwabara asked.

"Looking at license plate files, Captain," Kamauha said. "We've had a report of an assault on a woman at King and Liliha. *Kanaka* boy punched a *kanaka* woman, but she got the license plate number. Cecil's trying to find out who owns the car."

Kashiwabara frowned. He was used to fights and drunks on weekends, but not assaults. Especially not on women. "Tell me exactly what happened."

"All we know for sure is two cars nearly crashed into each other at King and Liliha. Then this big *kanaka* gets out of his car and hits the woman in the head. Cecil said her ear was bleeding."

"What time did this happen?"

"About 12:45 is when she came in. It happened a little bit before that."

"This *kanaka* do anything else to her?"

"No. He just hit her once, then jumped in his car and drove off. Japanese boy was driving, and there were others in the car. We got a plate number—fifty-eight eight ninety-five. Cecil's trying to find out who owns it now." He paused, then added, "Cecil said he could smell liquor on the woman's breath."

Kashiwabara shook his head as he moved to the desk. Now it made sense. Sounded, in fact, like a fairly typical confrontation between drunken drivers on a weekend night. Didn't sound like anyone really got hurt, though. They'd pick up the car soon enough and then they could sort everything out. He turned his attention to some paperwork that had piled up on the front desk, and time passed uneventfully until the telephone rang at 1:48 a.m. He picked up. "Police department."

A man on the other end of the line, speaking very calmly, said, "Will you please send a police officer to twenty-eight fifty Kahawai Street in Manoa. A woman was assaulted by a man."

The words sent a chill down Kashiwabara's spine. He had already heard eerily similar words earlier. What were the odds of two unrelated assaults on women occurring on the same night? It sounded like a spree was in the works. What made it even more frightening was that this second call didn't just involve a confrontation between drunken *kanakas*, but had apparently occurred in Manoa and, from the sound of the caller's voice, may have involved an assault on a *haole* woman.

Manoa was a neighborhood of middle- and upper-class homes in the very lush Manoa Valley, running from King Street on the *makai*, or ocean, end to Manoa Falls on the *mauka*, or mountain, end. Although the homes located farther up the valley were more exclusive, those on the lower end, where the address the caller had given was located, were modest but well-tended bungalows on small lots bursting with native flora, and they were popular rentals for military personnel. God help us if a *haole* navy wife was assaulted by a *kanaka*, Kashiwabara thought. Or, worse yet, by a gang of *kanakas*.

"Can I have your name, sir?" Kashiwabara asked.

"Just come quickly." Then the calm-voiced man hung up.

Rickard must have sensed something in his captain's tone because he stopped his work, turned, and stared at him.

Kashiwabara picked the phone back up from its cradle and called to the detective bureau upstairs. "Detective, we've got another assault on a woman," he said. "In Manoa."

The man on the other end said, "I'll be right down," then disconnected.

A minute later, Detective John Jardine, who was in charge of the night shift of detectives, descended the stairs. Only twenty-eight years old, Jardine had joined the Honolulu Police Department eight years earlier, and was promoted to detective less than two years later. His closest brush with fame had been working with his colleague in the detective bureau, Chang Apana, after whom novelist Earl Derr Biggers had modeled the fictional detective Charlie Chan.

"Are you telling me we've got some kind of gang going around attacking women tonight?" Jardine asked.

"We don't know it's a gang," Kashiwabara said. "The man who called said that the woman had been attacked by one man."

"One man? You're sure of that?"

"He said 'a woman was assaulted by a man.'"

"That doesn't necessarily mean it wasn't more than one. What else did he say?"

"That's it. He gave an address in Manoa, twenty-eight fifty Kahawai Street."

"Manoa." It wasn't a question, but a statement. They all knew the implications of that neighborhood. "He give a name?" Jardine asked.

Kashiwabara shook his head. "Sounded *haole*, though."

"So that's two women attacked tonight. That can't be a coincidence." Jardine turned to Rickard. "Call Furtado and Harbottle and send them to that house. And find out who owns that car with the license plate."

"I'm working on it now," Rickard said.

"Send Cluney to pick up the owner as soon as you find out who it is. Top priority. I'm betting if we find who was driving that car, we find our attackers in both cases."

* * *

Lieutenant Jerry Branson awoke to find himself alone on a couch on the front *lanai* of Red and Monte Rigby's house. Where the hell was Tommie? He pulled himself together and struggled to his feet. Looking to the street, he saw that Tommie's car was also missing. *No big deal,* he thought, probably gone home to see if Thalia was there. Only God knew why Tommie would care, though. As far as Jerry was concerned, Tommie was better off without her. She wasn't good for much, other than the obvious, and she shared that with anybody and everybody when Tommie was away on maneuvers. It was the worst kept secret at Pearl. Even Tommie knew, which is why there were always storm clouds brewing around the couple.

He staggered off the *lanai* and headed *mauka*, uphill toward the Massie house. The more he walked, though, the more his full bladder jolted with each step. He wasn't sure he could make it to Tommie's house without wetting himself, so he made his usual drunk's choice: he veered over into the yard of a darkened house and opened his pants. He had just finished watering the flowers when a light fell across him from behind, and then he heard the opening and closing of two car doors. He turned and looked over his shoulder at a police car and its occupants, who were heading his way. They weren't smiling.

"Hello, officers," he said. He knew his speech was slurred, but he couldn't help himself. He tucked himself back into his trousers, then turned around, pants still open. "Nice night, isn't it?"

"Sir, we need you to come with us," one of the policemen said.

* * *

Detectives George Harbottle and William Furtado, in patrol car number 1, had received the earlier call about the assault on Agnes Peeples, and although Furtado made a note of the license plate number—58–895—in his notebook, there really wasn't anything else they could do. Without a name and address, their options were few.

But the second call that came in at 1:50 a.m. seemed to have a bit more urgency to it. They were on their way to a burglary call on Jack Lane when they got the report about another assault on a woman, this one in Manoa, and a specific street address not far from their current location at Alapai and Punchbowl. After they radioed in from a police box, they headed to the address at 2850 Kahawai Street. Like Jardine and Kashiwabara, they operated under the assumption that they were looking for the same suspects in the two assaults. Police officers hated coincidences; some might say they didn't believe in them.

As they drove up Kahawai, they pulled over beside a patrol car sitting in front of a house just a few doors down from the address they sought. The driver of the other car was patrol officer William Simerson. With him were William Gomes, from a merchant patrol, or private security, detail, and a *haole* male in the backseat with mussed hair and a sloppy grin on his face.

"What have you got?" Furtado asked.

"This guy was taking a leak in a yard," Simerson said. "Or maybe he's a flasher. Can't be sure. All we know is his trousers were open when we found him in the yard."

"We just got an assault report from up the street," Furtado said.

Simerson glanced in the rearview mirror at his prisoner, who met his eyes and kept grinning. "Seems to me a man with his trousers open might know something about that." The prisoner's grin stayed in place, as if he didn't comprehend that the discussion might be about him.

"We're on our way now to take a statement," Furtado said. "Twenty-eight fifty Kahawai."

"The Massie house?"

Harbottle and Furtado exchanged looks. They thought they had been the only ones to get this call. "You know about it?" Harbottle asked.

"Don't know anything about the call, but I know plenty about the Massies. I've been there before. They're loud drunks. She's a bit of slut and he's a hitter. I guess that's fair, though; she's a biter."

"Well, why don't you come on along? And bring the trousers-guy with you."

"Might as well. They're always good for free entertainment."

* * *

It was roughly 2 a.m. when Harbottle and Furtado reached the Massie house, with Simerson and Gomes trailing behind. The bungalow was modest, but well kept, on a street full of modest, well-kept bungalows. There was nothing to make it stand out in this neighborhood except for an agitated man in a white linen suit pacing in front. The man rushed to the car as they exited.

"She's inside."

"You Mr. Massie?" Furtado asked.

"Lieutenant Massie. Hurry."

Massie hadn't said much, but what little he did say gave away a slurring of his speech, as if his mouth had been numbed by a dentist. Both detectives took note of the fog of liquor on his breath and his unsteady gait as he led them inside. Both also took note of his rebuke—making it clear that he was *Lieutenant* Massie, not Mister Massie, with all the superiority over them that distinction probably created in Massie's mind.

They followed Massie to a darkened living room, where a young woman in a nightgown lay on a couch. She was not unattractive, but neither could it be said that she was attractive. She was slightly pudgy—not overweight, exactly, but soft—and there was a noticeable bulge to her eyes. A lamp on an end table was turned on, but it shed little light. At the base of the lamp lay a pair of eyeglasses, although the young woman never touched them during the interview.

There were marks on her face and neck—a cut on her lip, a bruise under her eye, a swollen jaw, and a black and blue mark on her neck—but no other obvious injuries. She was crying, though to Furtado it seemed strangely unemotional, almost as if she had summoned the tears on cue. And she appeared nervous, which was not surprising. Most people who talked to police detectives were nervous, even the innocent ones. As with her husband, they smelled liquor on her breath, but while he was clearly drunk, she seemed only slightly lit.

"That's my wife Thalia," Massie said. "She was raped by a bunch of thugs."

Thalia glanced up at the officers, then at her husband, as if seeking approval to speak to the police. Furtado sensed uneasiness between the two of them, but under the circumstances, who could blame them? He took a small notebook and pencil from his pocket and approached the couch. Harbottle stood back as his partner began questioning the woman.

"Mrs. Massie, can you tell me what happened?"

"I was attacked by a gang of men," she said.

* * *

Thalia struggled with her captors in the backseat, her eyes blurred with tears as fists continued to batter her face. A jolt suggested that the car left the road and pulled onto hard ground, where it came to an abrupt halt. A door opened. She caught her breath, awaiting the inevitable.

Hands pushed her out onto the jungle floor. She heard sounds of doors opening and closing, then footsteps. More hands grabbed her, dragging her toward the trees. Muted voices and laughter barely registered, as if the sound were underwater. Someone forced her onto her back, another pinned her arms to the ground, spread out above her head. Another yanked her dress up and tried to pull her underwear down. She struggled to lock her knees together but she wasn't strong enough.

She closed her eyes and tried to pretend this wasn't happening.

* * *

All Furtado and Harbottle had been told about the original call was that "a man" had assaulted a woman. Now it was more than one, just like Agnes Peeples had run up against, and now it was rape and not just a simple assault.

"Where did this happen?" Furtado asked.

"They picked me up on John Ena Road."

Furtado made a note of the location. It hadn't happened in Manoa but closer to Waikiki. He knew of John Ena Road and its sketchy reputation. All police officers did.

"Can you identify the boys who did this?"

"It was too dark. I didn't see their faces, but I could see that they were dark-skinned. All I know for sure is that they were Hawaiian."

"How can you be sure of that?" Furtado asked. "If you couldn't see their faces, how can you be sure they weren't Japanese or Chinese? Or Filipino?"

"From their voices. I'm positive they were Hawaiians because of the way they spoke. I know Hawaiians when I hear them."

She spoke the last words with attitude, offended at being doubted. Still, it was a fair point. After all, most Hawaiians had a distinct way of speaking, with their pidgin English and lilting tone that differentiated them from the Asians in the islands.

"Okay, let's go through this again from the start," Furtado said. "What way were you going on John Ena?"

"Toward the ocean. I—my husband and I had been at the Ala Wai Inn, and I went out for a walk."

"By yourself?"

"I needed some air." She sounded petulant, her tone sharp. "I often walk by myself when I need some air."

A glance at Massie revealed a look on his face that might have been skepticism. Could it be that he didn't believe her?

"Then what?"

"I heard a car behind me, then two men jumped out and grabbed me. They started hitting me for no reason. I tried to resist and one of them hit me under the mouth. I felt a little woozy, so I'm afraid I couldn't do much to fight them off after that. They dragged me to the car and threw me in, then drove off."

"What kind of car was it?" Furtado knew that the car the police were looking for in the Peeples assault was a Ford touring car. He hoped it was the same car. If so, with the license plate number they already had, it was just a matter of time before they made an arrest and solved two cases.

"It was a Ford, I think. Or a Dodge. I don't know. It was too dark to tell. All I know for sure is that it was an old car, with the top open. And I think the top was torn, because I could hear it flapping in the wind."

"What happened next?"

"They took me into the jungle on Ala Moana Road, near the animal quarantine station. That's where they did it. I don't know how many times. All of them took a turn."

She continued to cry throughout her recitation, but Furtado was struck at how devoid her voice was of emotion. He snuck another look at her husband, who wore the same look he had worn earlier, and he seemed just as emotionless. Skepticism? Or was he just too drunk to understand what his wife was saying?

"After they finished, they pointed to where the road was and then got back in their car and drove off."

"Could you see the car when it drove away?"

"It was too dark."

"How about the license plate? Could you see it?"

"No. It was too dark, I tell you."

"Local Honolulu cars have five numbers," Officer Simerson said. Furtado hadn't seen him come in, nor had he seen Harbottle leave. Gomes, with the private security patrol, wasn't with Simerson, so Furtado assumed that he was guarding the *haole* in the patrol car and that Harbottle had gone out to help when Simerson entered.

"Can you maybe remember at least two numbers, the first two or the last two?" Simerson asked. "That would be a big help if you could."

And if she came up with five-eight or nine-five as the first or last two, it might close the books on this case quickly.

A hint of anger slipped into her tone, much like her earlier resentment at being questioned about the race of her assailants. "I already told you it was too dark."

"And you're sure you can't identify the boys?" Furtado asked as he took over the questioning again.

"By their voices, maybe. But only by their voices. All I could tell for sure is that they were Hawaiian."

"Did you hear any names? Maybe they were talking to each other and someone said a name."

"No, no names." She paused, then added, "Well, one of them, I think, was called 'Bull,' or something like that."

That wasn't much help. Bull was a fairly common nickname among the Hawaiians, similar to whites calling each other "Mac" or "Buddy." Still, it was at least something.

"Is there anything else you can remember about the car? If we can just identify the car, then we can pick somebody up."

"Only what I already told you. It was an old car, a Dodge or a Ford. The top was open, and I could hear it flapping when we were driving."

"And you can't remember the license plate number?"

"I told you already," she snapped, the edge returning to her voice. She had a way of turning the anger on and off at will. This was a woman who did not like being doubted. "It's not that I can't remember it; I couldn't see it. It was too dark."

Furtado looked at his notes then turned to Massie. "Lieutenant, may I use your telephone?"

Massie nodded and led Furtado to a telephone in the near corner of a bedroom adjacent to the living room. Close enough that he could be heard in the living room when he picked up the receiver, dialed, and spoke to Detective Jardine at headquarters, so he lowered his voice.

"We've got a serious case up here," Furtado said. "This isn't just punching a woman. She was raped."

"Raped! Does she know who did it?"

"No. But it was a gang of them, not just one man like we thought at first. How are you coming on tracking down that car?"

"We've got a line on it. The owner lives in Cunha, and Cluney's on his way out there now."

Cunha was on the edge of what was known as Hell's Half Acre, filled with tenements and poverty. Poor people packed into a dense area of deterioration and decay, boiling with resentment of the *haole* elite and the ever-present military, who lorded their superiority over the native and Asian population just as Massie had earlier lorded his naval rank over the police officers. This was sounding more and more like a racial attack on an island already smoldering with racial hostility. Furtado worried that it could be the spark to set off a conflagration.

"I think you need to come up here, detective."

"I'm on my way," Jardine said. "I also sent Nakea and Bettencourt. They should be there by now." Then he hung up.

Furtado turned and came face-to-face with Massie, who had lingered just outside the doorway, listening to his call.

"What car?" Massie asked.

"What do you mean?"

"I heard you say something about tracking down a car. What car?"

"We had another report of an assault on a woman earlier tonight by a car full of boys. The victim got a license plate number."

A spark flashed in Massie's eyes, as if something had infiltrated the haze of drunkenness about him. "It's the same ones."

"It's sure looking like it."

"Do you have the car?"

"Not yet."

"We can get navy personnel to help look for it. What's the plate number?"

Furtado glanced at his notebook. "Fifty-eight eight ninety-five. But we've already tracked down the owner and we're going to pick him up, so we don't need navy help." Nor did the police want navy help. This was police business, not navy business. The last thing he or any other policeman wanted was a bunch of *haole* sailors on the prowl looking for *kanakas* in a city that was already a racial tinderbox.

As he broke off the conversation with Massie, Furtado heard new voices in the living room. Returning, he saw that Simerson had left, ostensibly to help Gomes guard the prisoner in the car, and Harbottle had returned, but additional detectives, George Nakea and Frank Bettencourt, had also arrived. Before Furtado could resume his questioning of Mrs. Massie, one of the new arrivals, Nakea, took over the questioning, rehashing and confirming what had already been discussed earlier.

"Tell me what happened," Nakea said.

Mrs. Massie, who was now holding a damp cloth over her lip, said, "I've been assaulted. By some Hawaiian boys, after I left the Ala Wai Inn. I've already told this to these other policemen."

"Sometimes it helps to go through it again. Helps to jog your memory."

She nodded but didn't say anything.

"If we pick these boys up and bring them in, could you identify them?"

"No. All I know is that they were Hawaiian boys."

"Do you know the car number?"

Furtado could swear that, upon hearing Nakea ask that question, Massie seemed to be trying to get his wife's attention, but she ignored him. He wondered if he had made a mistake by telling it to him.

"No. I couldn't see it."

"Why did you leave the Ala Wai?" Detective Bettencourt, the other new arrival, asked.

"I was bored and just wanted to go out for a walk. To get some fresh air."

"Alone?"

The edge, which always seemed to linger close by, returned to her voice. "Yes, alone. All by myself. Just me."

Furtado noticed that, after answering, she looked at Massie, who dropped his gaze. The question had touched a raw nerve, just as it had earlier. Why had she left alone? Or had she left alone? And what really happened after she left the Ala Wai? A fist knotted up in Furtado's gut. She was lying about something. The question was what?

Chapter Four

The Physical Examination

"Clean as a new pin."

September 13, 1931
2:20 a.m.

A number of cars were parked outside the Massie house when Detective Jardine arrived, accompanied by patrol officer William Seymour. Just prior to leaving the station, alarmed by his telephone conversation with Furtado, Jardine had instructed Cecil Rickard to summon Captain John McIntosh, chief of detectives, from home. If this thing was about to get out of hand, he wanted the top man involved.

As Jardine and Seymour exited their patrol car, they noted a scattering of people standing in clumps in yards, many dressed in nightclothes, obviously neighbors drawn like moths to the flame of the ruckus in their nice little neighborhood. Jardine feared this was about to get even uglier and reassured himself that he had done the right thing by summoning McIntosh away from his comfortable bed.

Furtado met Jardine at the door and filled him in on what Mrs. Massie had reported.

"Nobody said anything about rape before you called me," Jardine said. "The man who called in the complaint didn't say anything about it. What's going on?"

"We didn't know until we got here, but that's what she says."

Jardine turned and gestured at the patrol car in front of the house on Kahawai Street, guarded by merchant patrol officer Gomes, with its *haole* occupant in the back street. "What's he got to do with it?"

"We don't know," Furtado said. "Simerson said they found him up the street, walking around with his pants open. Seems like an unlikely coincidence."

"It sure does." He peered at the man in the backseat, who seemed to smile back. "Who is he?"

"Says he's navy."

"Oh, that's just great." Jardine took a deep breath and nodded. "Okay, let's go in."

Upon entry to the house, where Mrs. Massie still lay on a couch, sobbing, with a cloth covering her mouth, Jardine could see that things were not going well. An angry and agitated victim, a drunk husband, an unbuttoned navy man outside, and four very frustrated cops were not the ingredients for an effective investigation. He took a quick assessment and decided that additional questioning wouldn't serve any purpose, not with the condition she was in. And with the new allegation of rape that had surfaced, he was concerned about any further delay before she could be examined physically.

"Mrs. Massie, I'm Detective John Jardine," he said. "I believe we need to get you looked at by a doctor. Would you please come with me to the hospital?"

It was as if a switch had been flipped. Mrs. Massie transformed from agitated to half-hysterical, her voice shrill and shriek.

"I don't want to go!" she shouted. "I don't want to go! I won't go!"

Her strong reaction took Jardine aback. She seemed more afraid of going to the hospital than traumatized by what she told the officers had happened to her.

"Mrs. Massie, please—"

"I won't go, I said." Her sobs grew more desperate as she turned to her husband. "Tommie, don't let them make me go."

For his part, Lieutenant Massie seemed almost indifferent to her pleas, his senses deadened by the haze of alcohol that enshrouded him. Jardine took him by the arm and pulled him aside. Speaking in a low voice, he said, "Lieutenant, do you understand how important it is to have her examined? She's made an allegation of rape, and we've got to get evidence. We've also got to make sure she hasn't been harmed, physically. You know, her woman parts. Can you help us out?"

Massie exhaled a boozy breath and nodded.

"Thalia, you've got to go," Massie said. "We have to make sure you're all right. Now come on, don't make a fuss."

Her sobs subsided as she appeared to be weighing her options. After a moment, she stood. Lieutenant Massie took a blanket from the end of the couch and wrapped it around her shoulders.

"Is it all right if she rides in the car with me?" Massie asked.

"Sure," Jardine said. "You can follow me."

After leaving the house, Jardine led the Massies to an automobile parked on the street. By now the crowd of onlookers had grown, including other navy personnel, recognizable by their white suits that seemed to match that of Lieutenant Massie. As they walked past Simerson's patrol car, the passenger in the backseat, Lieutenant Jerry Branson, smiled out the window at them. Thalia's tears suddenly switched off, and her voice took on a more normal, although completely surprised, tone.

"Why, Jerry, what are you doing here?"

"Just going where they take me."

"Everything's all right, Jerry. Don't worry."

Lieutenant Massie turned to Jardine. "Why is he in that police car?"

"We need to ask him some questions about tonight."

"He was with me all night. He didn't have anything to do with this."

"Well, we'll sort it all out when we get to the station," Jardine said. "But first, let's have your wife looked at by a doctor."

* * *

2:35 a.m.

Dr. David Liu and graduate nurse Agnes Fawcett knew they had to be prepared on weekend nights, because you never knew who would darken the door of Honolulu's Emergency Hospital during those hours. During the weekdays, they often saw victims of accidents, usually plantation workers, but on weekends, drunken brawls produced their own particular kind of victims. He and Nurse Fawcett weren't prepared, though, for the parade of police and other cars that approached the hospital early Sunday morning.

The hospital's time card showed the admittance of Mrs. T. H. Massie at 2:35 a.m. The victim was a young woman who said that she had been raped. She had obviously been beaten as well, judging from her bruised and swollen jaw. As was protocol, the initial examination was handled by Agnes; then Dr. Liu would follow with his own.

As Agnes performed a visual vaginal examination on the victim, who said her given name was Thalia, Agnes was struck by what she deemed a noticeable lack of trauma. Rape was usually not a crime of passion, but rather one of rage and anger, yet Thalia's private parts struck Agnes as being "clean as a new pin," as she later described them to investigators. No bruising on her thighs, no tearing or ripping of the vagina, and no blood.

"What happened to you, Mrs. Massie?" Agnes asked. She wondered if she had been misinformed, and she wanted to hear the story straight from the victim's lips.

"Some Hawaiian boys took me in a car and raped me."

"Oh, dear Lord. You said 'boys'; how many were there?"

"Six."

"And they all raped you?"

"Yes, all of them."

How odd, Agnes thought. A gang rape, yet not a single trauma to her vagina. Was that possible? Agnes was no expert on sexual assault, but it certainly seemed unlikely.

The door opened and in walked Dr. Liu. Although Thalia was lying in an exposed position on the examining table, she showed no sign of embarrassment and made no effort to cover herself. It was as if it was a regular occurrence for her private parts to be exposed to strangers.

"Mrs. Massie, I'm Dr. Liu," he said. "I know Nurse Fawcett has already examined you, but I'd like to examine you as well. Then she and I can compare notes."

"That's fine, doctor." She spoke the words without a shred of emotion, and again Agnes noted the inconsistencies between her condition and what she said had happened.

Like Agnes, Dr. Liu was also struck by the lack of injury that would normally have accompanied even a single rape, much less a gang rape. There was no tearing of her vagina, no seminal fluid, nothing other than the swollen jaw and marks on her face, along with a few bruises on her arms and legs, to suggest that anything out of the ordinary had happened to her. But a beating was not the same thing as rape.

"Mrs. Massie, I know you have already told all this to the police, but can you tell me what happened?"

"Isn't that a police matter?" she asked. "Why do you need to know?"

"It will help me in my examination. If I know what happened, then I know what to look for. I know this has been difficult, and I don't mean to belabor your troubles, but please, tell me what happened. I may need to examine you again based on what you tell me."

Thalia took a deep breath, steeling herself to repeat the tale she had already told numerous times. "I was walking along John Ena Road when a car came up behind me. Two men jumped out and grabbed me and dragged me into the car, then they drove to an isolated place and raped me. They all took turns."

"How many?"

"I don't know for sure. Four or five. Maybe six or seven."

"And they all raped you?"

"Yes. All of them."

Dr. Liu looked at Agnes, his eyebrows raised. She knew what he was signaling to her: Do you buy that? She shook her head.

"You know, things look very clean down here," Dr. Liu said. "When did this happen?"

"About two hours ago. I douched myself when I got home, so that's probably why you can't find anything."

But did she miraculously heal herself? Douching could explain the lack of seminal fluid, but it couldn't remove the violent traces of sexual assault by a gang of men. This did not make sense.

* * *

2:50 a.m.

Detective John Cluney, who had been a used car salesman in an earlier life, took the radio call from Cecil Rickard with a license plate number and an address, and turned his patrol car in the direction of a desperately poor part of town known as Cunha Lane. Between him and his partner, Thurman Black, a former employee of Matson Navigation Company, the two detectives had less than two years of experience on the job. Little did they know they were about to be ensnared in a morass that would tarnish their reputations, along with the reputations of the entire police force and the Territory of Hawaii itself, as they unsuspectingly headed toward the address Rickard had given them, which was the home of a Japanese family called the Idas.

While the physical address was actually on Cunha Lane, the entire neighborhood on the west side of downtown was called Cunha Lane. It was one of several sections of Honolulu that had festered over the decades in an area where two traditional districts merged. Those districts were historically known as A'ala, the Hawaiian word for fragrant, and Palama, which designated a sacred site. Now this part of town was anything but fragrant or sacred.

A'ala was the poorest and most crowded area in Honolulu. Nearly a third of the city's population was crammed into hovels and tenements, gambling establishments, opium dens, and unregulated whorehouses. Its residential neighborhoods, filled with the impoverished, almost exclusively native Hawaiian or Asian underclass, bore names like Hell's Half Acre, Tin Can Alley, Mosquito Flats, and Blood Alley.

Thurman Black pulled in front of the address they had been given—1408 Kunawai Lane—and Cluney got out, leaving Black behind the wheel. *God, it must be miserable to live like this*, Cluney thought. Rotting cottages, originally built as housing for field workers and crammed right next to each other, marked this neighborhood. The fairly new Ford touring car parked alongside the Ida cottage seemed sorely out of place, as if its owner had gotten lost and then, fearing for his or her life, abandoned the automobile.

Cluney shined his flashlight on the Ford and saw the license number he expected to see: 58–895. He drew closer and carefully examined the car. A 1929 model, tan in color, convertible top unripped or unscarred in any respect. He hadn't heard the description of a flapping top, so the absence of a tear aroused no suspicion. He placed his hand on the hood, near the radiator. Heat. It had recently been driven.

He approached the front door and knocked. After a brief moment, he heard voices inside. Female voices, speaking Japanese. He rapped on the door again with his knuckles.

"*Tantei*," he called, using the Japanese word for detective.

The female voices continued, more excited now but in hushed tones.

"*Tantei*," he called again.

The door opened. Two young Japanese women in nightgowns stood in front of him, one still with her hand on the doorknob, the other standing close by her side. Behind them, an elderly Japanese woman waited. All three seemed frightened—not surprising given the lateness of the hour and the appearance on their doorstep of the police. It was never good for the residents of this neighborhood when the police arrived.

"It is late," the woman who opened the door said.

Cluney pointed toward the side of the house. "I'm sorry to wake you so late, but I need to talk to the driver of that car. Is that yours?"

"Yes, it is," the woman who opened the door said.

"Are you Haruya Ida?"

"Yes, I am Haruya. This is my sister, Chiyono. What is wrong?"

"Was there a boy driving this car earlier tonight?"

"Why do you ask?"

"I just need to know if there was a boy driving this car tonight. I need to talk to him."

"It is very late. It is nearly three o'clock."

"I know what time it is, but I still need to see the boy who was driving this car tonight."

"Wait here, please."

She whispered something to her sister then hurried to the rear of the house. Cluney waited on the porch while the other two women watched him carefully, fear palpable on their faces, especially on the countenance of the elderly woman. After a moment, Haruya returned, followed by a boy who appeared to be little more than a teenager, or possibly in his early twenties. He was a small man in stature, not unlike many of the Asian males in Honolulu. His black hair was mussed, his eyes barely open, looking as if he had just been awakened from a sound sleep.

Cluney looked at his watch: almost 3 a.m. The first report had come in at 12:45 a.m., the second at 1:48, but the latter was an assault that had occurred more than an hour prior to the report, so it was certainly possible, if not likely, that one of the perpetrators would be asleep two hours later.

The boy wore a white t-shirt and pinstriped trousers that he was still buttoning as he approached the door. "What is the matter?" he asked.

"What's your name?" Cluney replied.

"I am Shimotsu Ida. Most people call me by my *haole* name, Horace. Or my nickname, Shorty. Now please tell me what is going on. It is late and you have awakened my mother and my sisters. You have frightened them."

The three women huddled in the background as Horace spoke with Cluney. They clearly didn't know what was going on, and, for that matter, Ida didn't seem to either. Either he was a very good actor or maybe Cluney had been given a wrong license number.

"Were you driving your sister's car earlier tonight?" Cluney asked.

Suddenly the look of ignorant innocence vanished from Horace's face. "No, I loaned it to a friend. A Hawaiian boy."

Cluney knew instantly that Horace was lying. "Oh, really? What's this boy's name?"

There was a slight pause then Horace said, "I don't know."

"Are you telling me you loaned your sister's car to someone you don't know?"

"I know him, but I don't know his name."

"Who else was in the car?"

Horace paused again. Cluney could almost hear the wheels spinning as the boy searched for his next answer.

"There were four other boys, but I don't know their names."

Cluney heaved a deep sigh of exasperation. "Okay, if that's the story you want to go with, I'm going to have to take you downtown."

"Please, *tantei*," Haruya said, "my father is no longer living, and my brother is the only man of the house. It will break our mother's heart if he is in trouble with the law."

"I can't help that," Cluney said. "I have to take him to the station to answer some questions. You can come along if you like. You'll need to get dressed first, then drive your car and follow me. I'll take your brother in my car." He looked at Horace and said, "Go on and finish getting dressed. In the meantime, I need to use your telephone."

Horace nodded and pointed to the wall where it was located, then retreated to the rear of the house again, followed by his sisters. His mother, still frightened, scurried away as Cluney entered her house. It took only a few minutes for him to call the station and announce that he and Black would soon be bringing in the suspect who had been driving the car with license plate number 58–895. By the time he hung up, the Ida sisters had returned, dressed, and Horace reappeared after putting on his shoes, wearing a brown leather jacket over his t-shirt.

They followed Cluney out of the house, leaving the elderly Mrs. Ida alone and panicky.

* * *

The number of people gathered on the *lanai* outside the hospital examining room's louvered windows swelled as word made its way through the ranks of personnel at Pearl Harbor. Two police patrol cars sat idle on the street nearby, windows open, staticky radios periodically crackling with life, audible to those on the *lanai*. Furtado and Harbottle remained beside their vehicle and idly chatted, while a handful of police detectives moved among the sailors on the *lanai*, asking questions. All talking stopped periodically when Cecil Rickard broadcast updates on the search for the driver of the vehicle bearing license plate number 58–895, a number he articulated at least two or three times by Furtado's count.

Away from the crowd, Detective Jardine talked with Tommie alone. "Like I said before," Tommie said, "Lieutenant Branson was with me tonight. All night. Right up until the time I called Thalia at the Rigbys, and she asked me to come home. You've got the wrong man."

"You can see why I have to ask, though, don't you? Your wife says she was raped and we find a man with his trousers open just a few houses away."

"I understand, but he had nothing to do with it. You heard Thalia say it was Hawaiian boys. Five or six of them. She knows Jerry Branson, and he certainly isn't five or six Hawaiian boys."

Jardine nodded just as, at about 3:00 a.m., the radios in the cars on the streets came to life again, and talking ceased. "Detectives Cluney and Black picked up vehicle number 58–895 and have the driver in custody."

* * *

Inside the examining room, Dr. Liu and Nurse Fawcett were completing their examination of Thalia Massie, still unable to find sufficient trauma to suggest rape by even one man, much less a gang. Dr. Liu had noted lacerations of her hymen at the five and seven o'clock positions, but they were old, definitely not made that night. There were no other abrasions or contusions that he could see. Of course, as Liu noted to himself, she was a married woman, so it was *possible* that she could have had sex with four or more men and not shown any sign of it. Possible, but at best only remotely possible. And remotely possible didn't mean probable.

As he made notes in his file, he caught the last part of yet another broadcast on a patrol car outside about car number 58–895, but he paid it no mind, as it was of no consequence to him. He noted, however, that Mrs. Massie cocked her head to the side, listening to the broadcast.

"Mrs. Massie," Liu said, "I know you've been asked this before, but I'm sure the police will want to know if we've had any conversation, so I have to ask. Did you see the license plate on the car?"

"It was too dark. I couldn't see anything."

"Would you be able to recognize the men who did this if you saw them again?"

"No. Like I said, it was too dark and I couldn't see anything. I just know they were Hawaiian."

"Are you sure they weren't Filipino or something else?" Agnes asked.

"I know Hawaiians when I see them."

"Even though it was dark?" Dr. Liu asked.

"I'm telling you I know the difference. They were Hawaiian."

Liu exchanged looks with Agnes, who wore the same skepticism that he felt, but hoped he kept from his face.

"And the car?" Liu asked.

"All I know is that it was old and dark-colored. And it had a torn roof. I know because I could hear it flapping as we drove."

"All right, then," Liu said. "I'm through with my examination. I believe you can go now."

Without another word, she got up as if she had experienced nothing more than a routine exam, put her clothes on, and then walked out the door.

Chapter Five

Thalia's Statement

"Now look at your beautiful work."

3:05 a.m.

Detectives Cluney and Black arrived at the police station with Horace Ida in tow, followed by Haruya and Chiyono Ida in the Ford touring car. The women were outright scared, but Horace, though a bit fidgety, wasn't overly concerned. He assumed this all had something to do with the *kanaka* woman Joe Kahahawai had punched in the head near downtown, but it had been Joe, not he, who had thrown the punch. Well, not even a punch, really; just an open-handed slap. Or had it been a closed fist? Did it really matter? At most, this was going to be a minor inconvenience—some lost sleep, maybe, but he knew it would get straightened out soon enough, and he would be back at home and in bed before he knew it.

His sisters, on the other hand, were clueless. They knew nothing about the confrontation with Agnes Peeples, but they did know that their brother had lied to the detective about loaning Haruya's car to someone else. The detective had been close-mouthed at the house, and he was sure his sisters' minds reeled with the possibilities of what kind of trouble he might have gotten himself involved in that would necessitate his willingness to lie to the police. When he got home later, they would be mad at him, but they would get over it soon enough.

The detectives exited their car with Horace in tow. Detective Cluney approached the open driver's window of the Ford. "Go park your car and then wait inside, downstairs," he told Haruya, who was driving.

She looked at Horace for guidance. He nodded for his sister to do as she was told and smiled, as if to reassure her that all would be okay. Because, of course, it would. Cluney grabbed Horace by one arm and Black grabbed him by other. Together they roughly led him inside the building. Horace's sisters could only watch in shock. After her brother had disappeared from sight, Haruya pulled away and headed for the nearest parking area.

* * *

Twenty-four-year-old Horace Ida had been born on Maui, the son of plantation workers who had immigrated to Hawaii from Japan. The family later moved to Honolulu, where Horace's father worked on a fishing boat, while his mother stayed home and took care of Horace and his four sisters, who were born in Honolulu. Horace had been a bit of a troublemaker in school—nothing too serious, just a bit of mischief—but he had tried as best he could to help out around the house, working odd jobs to bring in additional money.

In 1927, at the age of twenty, he had packed up and moved to Los Angeles, to make his fortune on the mainland. But when his father and the entire crew of their sampan were lost at sea a year after he left, Horace had become the man of the house. That wasn't a position he could handle from afar, although he tried, sending gifts when he could, but very little money. And so, only a few weeks earlier, he had returned to Honolulu, though he still had plans to return to California.

He would have to put those plans on hold.

* * *

Once inside police headquarters, Cluney and Black led Horace upstairs to the detectives' assembly room, where Cecil Rickard was keeping vigil. "Is McIntosh here?" Cluney asked.

"I haven't seen him in a while, but he's here somewhere," Rickard said. "The Massies are on their way, so he may be setting up in his office to talk to them."

"Watch this one for a minute," Cluney said, letting loose of Horace. "I'll go find him."

Joined by Black, Cluney set out on a room-to-room search for the captain, while Rickard stood guard over their prisoner. Horace fidgeted nervously under Rickard's laser-like gaze. This all seemed like a lot of trouble for one little slap—that he hadn't even done.

After a few minutes of awkward silence, Rickard asked, "Did you attack that white woman?"

Surprise registered on Horace's face. That was the first he had heard from anyone about a white woman. It also explained why all these white policemen were so hostile. "What white woman?"

"You know the one. On Ala Moana."

"We weren't on Ala Moana," Horace said. There had obviously been some kind of misunderstanding, and he needed to clear it up right away. "My friends and I were driving around after we left the dance at Waikiki Park, but we were not on Ala Moana. I nearly had a wreck with a car at King and Liliha, but it was a Hawaiian woman in the other car, not a white woman."

"I know about that," Rickard said. "But I'm not talking about the *kanaka*. I'm talking about the *haole* woman."

"There wasn't no *haole* woman. Just a *kanaka*. She had a *haole* man with her, but no woman. She pushed Joe, and Joe slapped her, but she was Hawaiian, not a white woman."

"Joe who?"

"Joe Kalani. Sometimes people call him Joe Kahahawai."

"Look, we know you boys did it. There's no point in lying about it to me. And if you lie about it to Captain McIntosh, things won't go good for you, I can tell you that for sure."

"I am not lying." Horace felt himself growing panicky. His breath came in gasps and tightness squeezed his chest. He didn't know what he had gotten himself in the middle of, but he could see that it was headed toward big trouble unless he could stop it now. "I am telling the truth."

Footsteps interrupted their conversation. Rickard glanced over Horace's shoulder at Cluney and Black, who had returned. "Did you find McIntosh?"

"Yeah, in his office," Cluney said. "We're going to take this one there so he can ask him some questions. Let us know when the Massies get here."

Cluney and Black each grabbed Horace by an arm and led him down a narrow hallway. Horace stumbled as he walked, as if in a daze. He was not the slightly fidgety, but seemingly unconcerned, young man of just a few minutes before. Now he appeared to be as frightened as his sisters had been. Maybe more.

"I don't know anything about a white woman," Horace blurted out. "I just know about the Hawaiian woman."

Black cut a look at Cluney. The question raised by Horace's outburst was how he would know about a white woman unless he had been there. You don't just suddenly bring up a white woman in conversation unless there was, in fact, a white woman to bring up. Of course, neither detective had been privy to Cecil Rickard's conversation with Ida and his prior question about the white woman. If they had, it might have put Horace's comment in a different light.

The door to McIntosh's office was open, but no one was inside. Cluney and Black pushed Horace in. Cluney pointed at a hard wooden chair. "Sit there. Captain McIntosh has some questions for you."

The office was small and spartan, furnished with only a couple of rigid chairs, a small wooden desk and desk chair, and a low bookshelf. Horace sat in the chair he had been directed to, while Cluney stood beside him. Black left the men alone and disappeared down the hall. A moment later, Captain John McIntosh entered the office. He walked around to the front of his desk and sat on the edge. He was taller than Horace to start with, but sitting on the desk made him appear even taller. Looking down on the diminutive Japanese man, he clearly had the upper hand. Horace's anxiety level ticked up a notch or two—or five.

"Let's start at the beginning," MacIntosh said. "Tell me where you've been tonight. I want to know everywhere you were and when you were there."

"I was there when Joe slapped the Hawaiian woman. On Liliha Street. We were going home from a luau at Correas' house. It was after 12:30."

"I'm talking about before that. I'm talking about the white woman on Ala Moana."

"I don't know nothing about that. I wasn't on Ala Moana."

"That was your sister's car, though, wasn't it?"

"I was in Haruya's car when we saw the Hawaiian woman. I don't know where it was before that."

"What do you mean you don't know where it was before that?"

"I loaned it to Bennie and Joe earlier. Then they picked me up again later."

"Who are Bennie and Joe?"

"I don't know their last names. I just know them as Bennie and Joe." Horace's face betrayed the truth of his statement, as did the logic of what he had said. At least this time, unlike earlier, he was able to come up with some first names, if not last names.

"So you're telling me you're in the habit of loaning your sister's car to boys you don't even know well enough to know their last names?" McIntosh's tone, as much as his question, made clear his skepticism.

Horace opened his mouth to speak, but no words came out. A loud laugh from downstairs cut through the silence, then more laughter was followed by a buzz of male voices, along with enough footsteps for a marching band. Loud conversation. Maybe even drunken conversation.

"That must be the Massie party," Cluney said.

"Take this guy to an empty office and stay with him," McIntosh said. "If you see Bond and Benton in the dayroom, tell them I want to talk to them. And have someone bring Mrs. Massie up here. I want to talk to her first before I finish with Ida, then I'll come back and deal with him later."

"You want me to do anything with him?"

"Just sit on him until I'm ready."

Horace didn't move, almost frozen to his chair. Cluney grabbed him by the arm and jerked him roughly to his feet. "Come on, boy."

Cluney dragged Horace out of the office and closed the door behind him. McIntosh sat behind his desk and leaned back in this chair. He reflected on what he had heard thus far. That bit about loaning his sister's car to people he barely knew? That didn't make any sense. At the same time, the story he had gotten from his detectives was that Mrs. Massie claimed to have been raped by Hawaiian men, not Japanese. And Ida was clearly very Japanese.

This was the strangest set of circumstances he'd ever come up against in his years in law enforcement, and he'd seen plenty. Born a half-century earlier in Ireland, McIntosh's career had included serving in the British colonial forces in South Africa near the end of the Boer War as part of the South Africa Constabulary. He later spent more than a decade as a policeman in New Zealand before coming to Oahu in 1921, where he was hired as a plantation field overseer at Ewa Plantation. When Honolulu's sheriff got word of McIntosh's law enforcement background, he hired him away from the plantation. McIntosh quickly rose through the ranks before being promoted to captain and named to head of the detective bureau, his current job.

And now here he was with two women assaulted in one night, one of whom was the wife of a naval officer. The military controlled the Territory of Hawaii, whose economy depended heavily upon dollars spent by enlisted men and officers alike. There was already plenty of racial tension in the Islands between the natives and the whites, considered by many natives as interlopers who had stolen their land. The last thing he needed was for the rape by locals of a navy wife to go unpunished, or even unsolved. What he needed was a quick arrest and fast conviction.

A knock at the door interrupted his thoughts. "Enter," he said.

Officers Percy Bond and Claude Benton entered. "You wanted to see us, Captain?" Bond asked.

"I need you two to drive out to Ala Moana, around the old quarantine station. I understand Mrs. Massie was picked up near there, so the crime scene has to be close by. See what you can find."

"Are we looking for anything in particular?" Bond asked. "Or just looking in general?"

"If this woman was beaten and raped there, like she says she was, there has to be something. You'll know it when you see it."

"Yes, sir."

"This man I was just talking to says he wasn't there. But he was involved in another assault on a woman tonight, and I don't believe in coincidences. See if you can find any evidence that he really was there, or that his car was there."

"Yes, sir."

"Be thorough, but be quick. Bring me whatever you find right away."

He dismissed the two officers just as voices in the hallway announced his next set of visitors, Detectives Jardine and Nakea ushering in Tommie and Thalia Massie. As far as McIntosh was concerned, this was the main event.

"Mr. Massie, I'm Captain McIntosh," he said and extended his hand.

Tommie took it limply. "That's Lieutenant Massie."

"Yes, of course, Lieutenant. My apologies." He turned to Thalia. "Mrs. Massie, won't you have a seat?"

"Thank you, Captain."

McIntosh was immediately struck by two things as he surveyed his guests. The first was the bruising on Mrs. Massie's face, which was consistent with her report of a beating. But it was not necessarily consistent with having been beaten by five or six men. The second was the telltale whiff of liquor he detected on Massie's breath. The man wasn't drunk, exactly, but certainly might have been earlier. And, judging by his correction of McIntosh as to his rank, he carried a chip on his shoulder.

"First, let me say how sorry I am about what has happened to you tonight, Mrs. Massie. We're doing everything we can to find the men who did this to you and lock them up. But in order to do that, I need your help. I need to ask you some questions. Do you feel up to that?"

"I do," Thalia said. "Just please don't be too long. I'm in a great deal of pain and would like to go home as soon as possible."

McIntosh shifted his attention to Massie. "Lieutenant, I'd like to speak to your wife alone, if I may."

"Why can't I be here?" Massie asked. "I don't want to leave her alone after what's happened."

"I can certainly understand that, but I need to get your wife's story directly from her. I don't want her to feel pressured or embarrassed by your presence, and maybe omit some details that might be of importance."

Massie remained silent. He clearly didn't like being asked to leave, but McIntosh couldn't quite figure out why. A perfect solution would be to find something for Massie to do. Something useful. Something that would take him away for a while.

"Lieutenant, while I talk with your wife, I'd like for you to accompany Detectives Nakea and Jardine back to your home to retrieve the clothes Mrs. Massie was wearing tonight when she was assaulted. We need to have each garment examined by our professionals for any evidence that we might find on them."

Like blood. Or semen.

Massie stared sullenly at McIntosh. It was hard to tell exactly what was going on behind those blank eyes. He seemed to be weighing his options—but to what end?

"Will you do that for me, Lieutenant? It will be an enormous help if we can get that done as quickly as possible. After all, we want to catch these men as badly as you do. If they did this once, they might do it again, and we need to get them off the streets."

"All right." Massie turned his attention to his wife. "Tell him exactly what you told me," he said. He focused squarely on her eyes and added, "Don't leave anything out."

McIntosh looked at Nakea and Jardine. Hard to tell if either of them had picked up on the nuance of what Massie had just said. Not "tell the truth," but rather "tell him what you told me." And what was that last little bit about not leaving anything out?

"Anything else you need from us, Captain?" Jardine asked.

"Just the clothes for now. If I think of anything else, I'll let you know."

Massie stood by his wife for a moment. He placed his hand on her shoulder, but said nothing. Then he left, followed by Detectives Jardine and Nakea.

As soon as they left, McIntosh closed the door to the office and took a seat behind his desk, directly across from Thalia. "Now, Mrs. Massie, I know this is uncomfortable for you, and I know you've been through your story before, but if you don't mind, will you please tell me what happened tonight? Start at the beginning, please."

Thalia took a deep breath, then launched into the same tale she had already told several times that night. Just as she began to recount the rape, McIntosh interrupted her. "Mrs. Massie, if you don't mind, I'd like to make this a little more formal. I'm going to be taking some notes and asking you some questions, and I want to make sure I get down exactly what you say. When we're finished you can review it and, if it looks correct to you, I'll ask you to sign it. Is that alright?"

"Yes, that's fine."

He took a small notebook from his desk, glanced at his watch, and wrote at the top of the first page, "Statement of Mrs. Tommie Massie given to John McIntosh, Inspector of Detectives, at 3:30 a.m., September 13, 1931."

"Now, Mrs. Massie, are you ready?"

"I am."

"Okay. I'm going to start out with a few background questions first. What is your full name?"

"Mrs. Thalia Hubbard Massie."

"Where do you live?"

"Twenty-eight fifty Kahawai Street."

"Are you married?"

"Yes. My husband is Lieutenant Thomas Massie. He's in the United States Navy, stationed at Pearl Harbor."

McIntosh jotted down the answers then moved to the heart of the questioning. "Will you relate what happened to you tonight?"

She took another deep breath and started in on her story once again. "I left home about 9:00 p.m. with my husband to go to the Ala Wai Inn. In our party were Lieutenant Branson, Lieutenant Brown, and their wives. They had been to our house and followed Mr. Massie and me to the Ala Wai Inn in their own cars. When we got to the Inn, the six of us took a table together. Around twelve midnight I decided to go for a walk and some air. me walked along Kalakaua Avenue and crossed the canal and turned down John Ena Road and walked a block or so down John Ena Road. A car drove up behind me and stopped. Two men got off the car and grabbed me and dragged me into their car. One of them placed his hand over my mouth. When they got me into the backseat of the car, they held me down between them. They were Hawaiians."

She paused, as if waiting for McIntosh to catch up in his note taking. He nodded at her to continue her story.

"I begged and pleaded with them to let me go," she said. "I struggled to get off the car and away from them, and they kept punching me on the face. I offered them money if they would take me back to the Ala Wai Inn. They asked me where the money was. I told them it was in my pocketbook. They grabbed my pocketbook and found I had no money in it. They were driving along Ala Moana Road all this time, heading towards town. I really don't know how far they drove me—maybe two or three blocks. They drove the car into the underbrush on the right hand side of the road, dragged me out and away from the car into the bushes, and assaulted me. I was assaulted six or seven times."

McIntosh looked at her, gauging her reactions and emotions. They were now getting to the crux of the assault, and he anticipated that she might be fragile, emotionally, when talking about it. "You mean they raped you?"

"Yes." Her answer was matter-of-fact, completely devoid of emotion.

"How many men were in the car when they stopped and picked you up on John Ena Road?"

"At least four; two in front and two in the backseat."

"What nationality were they?"

"Hawaiians, I would say."

"What make was the car which they had?"

"It was a touring car. I can't say what make it was, but I think it was a Ford."

"What color was it?"

"I don't know."

"What was the license plate number, do you know?"

She closed her eyes and put her head back, as if trying to remember. Trying to visualize what had happened to her.

* * *

Thalia struggled with her captors in the backseat. Her eyes blurred with tears as fists continued to batter her face. A jolt suggested that the car left the road and pulled onto hard ground, where it came to an abrupt halt. A door opened. She caught her breath, awaiting the inevitable.

Hands pushed her out onto the jungle floor. Other doors opened and closed, and then there were footsteps. More hands grabbed her and dragged her toward the trees. Muted voices and laughter barely registered, as if the sound were underwater. Someone forced her onto her back, another pinned her arms to the ground, spread out above her head. Yet another yanked her dress up and tried to pull her underwear down. She struggled to lock her knees together, but she wasn't strong enough.

She closed her eyes and tried to pretend this wasn't happening. But it happened, one right after another.

When they were finished with her, they piled into the car and sped away, leaving her sprawled in the dirt. She squinted after the dark-colored, older car as it left her behind. Its torn top flapped in the night air. At first, all she saw were vague outlines and shadows. She tried to focus on the license plate, but to no avail.

But then vague lines sharpened and shadows dissipated. And then, for one brief second, there it was.

* * *

"I think it was 58–805," Thalia said. "I would not swear to that being correct. I just caught a fleeting glimpse of it as they drove away."

McIntosh wrote the number on the blotter on his desk and stared at it for a long moment. Up until this point, her story had been consistent with the story that had been reported to him by his detectives. According to them, she had steadfastly stuck to her story that she had not seen the plate number because it had been too dark. But now he had it.

"Excuse me a minute, Mrs. Massie." McIntosh went to the door, opened it, stepped into the hallway, and closed the door behind him.

"Cluney!"

Detective Cluney stuck his head out from a room down the hallway. "Yeah, Captain?"

"Come here a minute."

Cluney approached. McIntosh lowered his voice. "What was the plate number of the Ida car?" McIntosh asked.

"It was—"

"Don't say it out loud. I don't want Mrs. Massie to hear."

"Well, I wrote it down here somewhere," Cluney said. He patted his coat pockets until he found a crumpled piece of paper in his side pocket. "Here it is."

He took it out and uncrumpled the paper. The page contained the name of Haruya Ida, her address, and the make and model of the car. And the license plate number: 58–895.

"Don't say anything, but come in here for a second."

He led Cluney to his desk then pointed to the number he had written on the blotter. McIntosh held his own page next to the blotter. Cluney's page said 58–895; the blotter said 58–805.

McIntosh motioned for Cluney to follow him back out into the hall. "She said she just got a quick look," McIntosh said, "but that's close enough for me."

"Me, too."

"Give me about ten minutes, then bring Ida back down here."

While Cluney went to fetch Horace Ida, McIntosh reentered his office and resumed his place behind his desk. "I apologize for the delay, Mrs. Massie. Just a few more questions, then I promise I'll be finished."

"My jaw hurts very much, and it's difficult to talk. I just want to go home, Captain, so please hurry."

"Yes, ma'am." He shifted his notebook back in front of him on the desk, covering the number on the blotter, and continued. "Where were the others of your party when you started out for this walk?"

"They were all at the Ala Wai Inn."

"After these men assaulted you, what happened? Did they drive away and leave you there?"

Thalia pursed her lips and looked at the ceiling. Organizing thoughts in her head. "One of them told me which way to go to get back on the road. Then they bolted for their car, got into it, and drove away. I managed to get back on the road and stopped a car coming from Waikiki and heading towards town. I told the occupants of the car what had happened to me—that I had been assaulted by some Hawaiians—and asked them to take me home. They wanted to bring me to the police station, but I asked them to take me home, which they did."

"Who were those people?"

"I don't know. They were white people. There were two men in the front seat and two women and a man in the backseat. I sat in the front seat and they took me home in Manoa. After I got home, Lieutenant Massie called me on the phone from a friend's house. I told him to come home at once, which he did, and I told him what had happened to me. He immediately called for the police."

McIntosh circled back around to the car. He understood that she had previously denied seeing the license plate or being able to even recognize the car. But he also knew, from long experience, that traumatic events can repress memories and that, if taken back through the events often enough, those repressed memories can resurface. It was a standard practice in police investigations to ask the same questions repeatedly, sometimes in different forms, and sometimes simply having them asked by different detectives, to jog memories and dredge up incomplete or missing portions of a story. That had already worked with the license plate number. Now it was time to focus on the car itself.

"Would you know the car which they were in if you saw it again? I mean the car in which your assailants rode."

"I think I would if I saw a rearview of it and saw the backseat."

"When they dragged you from the car, how far did they take you away from it?"

"Not very far."

"Did you hear any names mentioned?

"I heard the name 'Bull' used several times and some common name like Joe or likened to that."

That was not all that helpful. "Bull" was a common term thrown around by these Hawaiians. The name "Joe" might be helpful, although that was also a very common name in Honolulu. Still, hadn't Ida mentioned a Joe?

"Do you think you could identify these men, Mrs. Massie?"

"I don't know."

"You were taken to Emergency Hospital before coming here, weren't you?"

"Yes. I was taken there and examined."

"What colored dress or gown did you wear tonight at the Ala Wai Inn?"

"A green dress."

"Where is that dress now?"

"At home."

"Was it torn at all?"

"I don't think it was."

That would be odd, McIntosh thought, especially given the brutal nature of the attack Mrs. Massie had repeatedly described. He was just about to pursue that when a knock on the door interrupted him.

"Come in."

Cluney opened the door and ushered in Horace Ida. McIntosh stood abruptly and glared at Horace. He pointed at the bruises and the swelling on Mrs. Massie's face. "Now look at your beautiful work," he said.

Ida seemed to shrink back toward the doorway, as if frightened. Thalia squinted at him. She dropped her gaze, looking at his brown leather jacket, and then shifted it back to his face. The squint deepened. Time slowed to a crawl as she appeared to struggle to focus.

Finally, she nodded at McIntosh. Just a slight bob of her head, up and down twice. McIntosh interpreted that as a positive identification.

She shifted her attention back to Ida. "Where are the other boys?" she asked.

Ida looked like he had been touched with a live electrical wire. He turned to McIntosh, his voice a pleading whine, more of a whimper. "I didn't do it. I didn't see this woman. I didn't do nothing to her."

"Do you know someone named Bull?" Thalia asked.

Ida shook his head. He looked at McIntosh, as if to ask, "Why does this woman get to question me?"

"Okay," McIntosh said to Cluney, "get him out of here."

Just as Cluney left with Ida, Officer Claude Benton entered, carrying a small cardboard box. It didn't seem as if he had been gone very long, hardly more than enough time to drive to Ala Moana and back, but he arrived bearing fruits from the search he and Percy Bond had conducted. He mollified McIntosh by telling him that Bond was still on the scene, but that he had wanted to bring the evidence they had already found back to the station as soon as possible in case McIntosh needed it for his questioning.

Once McIntosh was satisfied that the search was ongoing, he asked, "Okay, what did you find?"

"There were some tire tracks near the old quarantine station," Benton said as he set the box on the desk. "They looked pretty fresh. And we found this. Like I said, Bond is still out there looking."

Thalia leaned forward expectantly, interested to see what was inside. One by one, Benton took out the contents and lined them up on McIntosh's desk: a small mirror with an orange back; a handkerchief; an empty ginger ale bottle that reeked of homemade Hawaiian booze known as *okolehao*, usually just called *oke;* two books of matches; and three packages of cigarettes—two Lucky Strike and one Chesterfield.

Thalia squinted at the items. "That's my mirror," she said. She pointed at one of the cigarette packages. "And I had a pack of cigarettes in my pocketbook. My brand is Lucky Strike."

McIntosh smiled. It had been a bad night on the streets of Honolulu, but a good night for police work. Barely four hours since two assaults had happened on the streets of Honolulu, but he had spearheaded an investigation that yielded the car involved in both assaults, a positive ID of one of the assailants—if you could count a head bob as an identification—and concrete proof that Thalia Massie had been on Ala Moana Road where she said she was assaulted. The investigation was moving quickly, and McIntosh was confident they had one of their men. All that was left to do was to break Ida and get him to identify his compadres. Maybe he'd be able to wrap this all up in a nice, neat little package before the weekend was over.

Chapter Six

Rounding Up the Boys

"It was a car like that."

After the identification of Horace Ida by Thalia Massie, McIntosh formally placed Ida under arrest. The interrogation by police then continued, led by Detective John Jardine, who had been at the Massie house earlier. McIntosh joined him and together they hammered at Horace for several hours.

At first, Horace told a story of having been in the car with Ben Ahakuelo and Joe Kahahawai—the Bennie and Joe he previously said he had "loaned" his sister's car to—at the time of the near collision with Agnes and Homer Peeples, but persisted in denying any involvement with the assault on Thalia Massie. The detectives knew that was a lie because Thalia Massie had given them a license plate number that varied by only one digit from the number of the car Ida had been driving—close enough for police work—and she had also positively identified Ida.

Then he changed his story and said he had been in the car earlier, rather than loaning it, but that he had attended a luau at the home of his friends Wilhelmina and Sylvester Correa, brother and sister, and children of city supervisor Sylvester P. Correa. According to this new account of the evening, Ben Ahakuelo, a handsome, athletically built Hawaiian, walked home from the Correa house. David Takai, his features clearly identifying him as Japanese, had left with Ida, as had Henry Chang, of Chinese-Hawaiian descent, and Joe Kahahawai, a Hawaiian. Henry and Joe were with him at the time of the Peeples incident, though he couldn't remember if he had already dropped off David Takai at home, or if Takai got out of the car at King and Liliha, which was close to his house, and walked home from there. Takai didn't interest the detectives, but Chang and Kahahawai did. The number of Hawaiians in this story was quickly starting to mount.

These young men had been friends for quite some time, so it made sense that they would band together for their mischief. Ida had known Chang since the Ida family first moved to Honolulu. While attending Kauluwela Grammar School, Ida also befriended Joe Kahahawai, David Takai, and Ben Ahakuelo. All five had attended Catholic Sunday school together, but little knew then the fate that would befall them a few years later on that eventful September night in 1931.

With the names given by Horace Ida, the police moved quickly on Sunday morning to round up Joe Kahahawai, Ben Ahakuelo, Henry Chang, and David Takai. Ahakuelo and Kahahawai were well known in Honolulu for their athletic prowess, starring in barefoot football and also as boxers, with Kahahawai boxing under the name Joe Kalani. Of the two, Ahakuelo was the more accomplished football player and was often prominently mentioned in the sports pages of the Honolulu newspapers.

Detective Luciano Machado, a homegrown cop, knew that the most likely place to locate them, all of whom he knew personally, on an autumn Sunday morning, would be at the Kauluwela School athletic field. When he arrived there around mid-morning, he found Joe, Henry, and David, but not Ben. Joe had been playing barefoot football, and Henry and David had been mere spectators, watching Joe star in the game. Because the men knew Machado, they quickly came to him when he motioned them over. Ben's team didn't have a game, they told Machado when he asked, but he was practicing at another field across town.

"I need to take you boys in for questioning about an incident with a woman named Agnes Peeples last night," Machado said.

They didn't seem surprised, or at least Joe wasn't. This wasn't Joe's first run-in with the law and, as with the slap of Agnes, it was his temper and his hands that usually got him in trouble. He once broke a man's jaw for kicking a dog and was also once charged with robbery and assault, an incident that involved his efforts to collect a debt by punching the debtor. He hadn't been arrested in the first incident, and as for the second, he was acquitted of the robbery charge in a jury trial but convicted of assault. The conviction earned him a thirty-day suspended sentence.

Henry had had his own problems with the law, but his were a bit more serious. He, along with Ben Ahakuelo and several others, had been previously charged with gang-raping a Chinese girl named Rose Younge. The evidence at trial revealed that the sex with all of the defendants had been consensual, with the "victim" admitting that she had made up the story because of rumors that circulated about her easy virtue. Apparently the rumors were true. The jury acquitted the defendants, including Ben and Henry, of rape but convicted them of the lesser offense of "assault with intent to ravish," and recommended leniency. Judge Albert Cristy, who presided over the trial, sentenced them to four months, and they spent three months in the territorial prison before being released.

David Takai, on the other hand, had no real history with the police. He had been raised by a single father with his two sisters, and the extent of his legal troubles had been two appearances in juvenile court—once for truancy and "disobedience to his sister," and on another occasion for fighting, which cost him a five-dollar fine. As an adult, though, his record was clean.

"You can't keep your temper, can you, Joe?" Machado asked.

Joe shook his head. "I know, Luciano. But I been drinking and this big *kanaka* woman been drinking. We were both maybe a little drunk. Besides, she pushed me first. Then I pushed her back, and I guess I might have slapped her a little. But that's all."

"She said you hit her with your fist. She's pressing charges, so I've got to take you in for questioning."

"Maybe it was my fist. I don't know. It wasn't hard, though. And David and Henry didn't have nothing to do with it. David wasn't even there. He got out and went home when we stopped. So it was just me and Shorty and Henry, and Henry never got out of the car. The whole thing didn't take but a minute or two."

"I'm sure we can get it all sorted out back at the station. Get in the car and I'll take you. I'll bring you back later when we're finished."

The four men crossed the street to where Machado had parked his radio car. They seemed to think it was a big joke, and they laughed and cracked wise about Joe and his temper as they walked. They got in the backseat of the car and Machado headed for police headquarters.

The mood was still light-hearted as they drove. Then Machado looked in his rearview mirror at Joe and asked, "What about that *haole* woman?"

Joe laughed. "I told you, it was a *kanaka*. What's the matter, you can't hear so good?"

"I'm not talking about her. I'm talking about the white woman on Ala Moana." Machado's tone suggested a seriousness to the question that the men had not sensed when he had been talking about the fight with Agnes Peeples.

Joe stopped laughing. He made eye contact with Machado in the mirror. "We weren't on Ala Moana. It was on King Street. And it wasn't a *haole*. It was a *kanaka* woman."

"We've got a white woman who says you picked her up on Ala Moana, and you assaulted her. She gave us the license plate number to the Ida car, so there's no mistake."

"Yes, there's a mistake," Joe said. "A big mistake."

He glanced at Henry and David, neither of whom was smiling now, though they had been laughing just moments earlier. The mood had turned somber like the flip of a switch. It now seemed that they had made a mistake of their own, allowing themselves to be lured into the police car.

David appeared totally befuddled. "Like Joe told you, I wasn't even there for the *kanaka* woman," he said. "And I sure wasn't there for any *haole* woman."

Machado pulled up in front of the police headquarters building and turned off the car. He turned around and placed his arm across the back of the seat. "Shorty Ida told us you were there. How do you think we knew who to look for? And we've got evidence. It will go a lot easier for you if you tell me the truth now, before we get inside. Once Captain McIntosh gets involved, there won't be anything I can do to help you."

* * *

Tommie Massie had tried to reach his commanding officer, Captain Ward Wortman, the night before, to tell him what happened to Thalia, but Wortman hung up on the obviously drunken lieutenant who had interrupted his sleep. Tommie also called the commander of his submarine, Leo Pace, but Pace's wife stiff-armed him as well, refusing to awaken her husband for his drunken subordinate.

The next morning, while Detective Machado was out looking for the four men whom Horace Ida had named, Tommie tried calling Pearl Harbor again to reach Leo Pace. Successful this time, he filled his skipper in. Horrified, Pace promised that he and his wife would be right over to assist in whatever way they could. Tommie also placed a call to Lieutenant Commander John Porter, a Navy doctor who had been the Massies' physician ever since Thalia's miscarriage earlier that year, during the summer. Tommie was worried about Thalia's injuries, he said, but he was also worried about her mental condition. Porter assured Tommie that he was on his way.

Leo and Peggy Pace arrived shortly after being called, and Tommie and Leo immediately left to report the incident to Captain Wortman at Pearl Harbor and to send an important cable back to the mainland, leaving Thalia under Peggy's care. Lieutenant Commander Porter, who had been a licensed physician in the United States Navy since 1915, arrived around ten o'clock, and Peggy quickly ushered him into the bedroom, where Thalia sat up in bed, wearing a nightgown. Porter was shocked at her appearance. Her right eye was practically closed from the swelling on her cheek, which had turned purplish with bruising. He tried to put on his professional persona, rather than give way to his emotions.

"Well, Thalia," he said. "Are you in any pain?"

"My jaw hurts quite a bit, Commander Porter." It was difficult to understand her as she spoke through the injury.

"Is it bearable?"

"Can you give me something for it?"

"Of course. But let's have a look at you first."

Wordlessly, Thalia slid to a reclining position. She knew the drill.

Porter set about his examination with professional efficiency. He noted on a pad the bruises on her face and arms, as well as some smaller bruises and abrasions on her legs. None of the injuries to her extremities appeared serious, but her face was another matter. Her jaw was likely broken, although X-rays would be necessary to confirm. It and the bruises certainly indicated that she had been manhandled by someone. Whether it was by five or six men, though, he had no way of knowing.

"Okay, Thalia, now I need to check for other injuries."

He lifted her nightgown, exposing Thalia's vagina. She again knew the drill, and spread her legs. Porter was struck by the lack of any recent trauma. Prior injuries from her miscarriage the previous summer had healed, leaving scars, but there was no new tearing, nor was there any particular bruising in or around her vagina. While she certainly showed signs of having been beaten about the face, it didn't appear to him that she had experienced violent rape, as he had been led to believe. And certainly not six or seven times, as it had been reported. But he kept those thoughts to himself, rather than add them to his notes on the pad.

A noise from the front part of the house let Porter know that Lieutenant Massie had returned. Tommie entered the bedroom just as Porter was finishing his exam. He dismissed Peggy Pace to rejoin her husband, who was waiting in the living room.

"What do you think?" Tommie asked Porter.

"She appears to be in a great deal of pain, which is not surprising. I'm going to give her some opiates for the pain, but that's going to knock her for a loop, and she's not going to know which end is up. I think you need to check her into Queen's Hospital as soon as possible."

"Is that really necessary?"

"I'm worried about that jaw. It looks like it's broken and, if that's the case, the break needs to be set right away. It looks like there's a wisdom tooth in the line of fracture, and we'll need to pull that in order to set the jaw."

"And her private parts?" Tommie asked.

"Let me give her something for the pain first, and then we can talk about that outside."

After Porter had given Thalia a variety of painkillers, he took Tommie by the arm and ushered him into the hall. He closed the door behind him.

"You told me that she was raped six or seven times," Porter said. "Is that right?"

"Yes."

"Are you sure about that?"

"Why? Aren't you?"

"I don't know."

"Are you saying she's lying?" Tommie's voice rose in indignation. "You've been her doctor since we've been here, and now you're saying your patient is a liar? Did you think she was lying in the summer when she said she was pregnant?"

"No. I've got proof of that."

"You've got proof here, too. You've seen her face."

"All I'm saying is that, yes, she's clearly suffered some kind of an injury, one that might have affected her mental state. But my examination . . . well, I just want to make sure you know what you're doing if you go around accusing someone of rape."

"We've already told the police, and they already have one of the men who did it in custody."

"Do you know for a fact that he did it?"

"That's what the police said. Do you think they're lying, too?"

"Of course not. Listen, I'll make arrangements for Thalia to be admitted to Queen's Hospital and then I'll check in and see her there. I'll examine her again, and maybe I can run some other tests. I just want to be sure. How's that?"

"That's fine."

With that, Porter left, but not without doubts. Still, he was a doctor, not a police officer. It wasn't his job to investigate claims of rape and make arrests. If the police said they had one of the men who did it, well, then it must be true. At least they had one of the men who had done something.

But rape? He wasn't at all sure about that.

* * *

While Machado looked for the young men, Captain McIntosh had been busy, as well. Around dawn on Sunday morning, Deputy Sheriff William Hoopai had found other proof that someone had been to the old animal quarantine station recently. On a concrete slab near the side of the road, he saw a woman's hair clamp and five green beads that might have come from a necklace or bracelet. He immediately drove back to police headquarters and turned them over to McIntosh, who took the baubles and stuck them in his pocket. McIntosh then instructed patrolman Henry Sato to drive him in Haruya Ida's touring car to the Massie house.

Tommie Massie met McIntosh at the door of the house on Kahawai Street. He glanced dully over McIntosh's shoulder at the car by the curb, where Sato patiently waited. It looked very much like his own personal vehicle, the one he and Thalia had been driving since they had been in Honolulu, right down to the make and color.

"Lieutenant Massie, may I speak to your wife for a moment?" McIntosh asked.

"Do you have anything new to report?" Tommie replied.

"I just need to speak to Mrs. Massie briefly, if I may. This won't take long."

Thalia's voice, weak and trembling, called from inside the house. "Who is it, Tommie?"

"It's the police."

McIntosh heard shuffling sounds, as if someone were sliding her feet along the floor. Thalia appeared at her husband's side, wearing a robe wrapped tightly and tied with a sash. She was not wearing her glasses and squinted to see the captain.

"What else can I do for you, Captain?" she asked. She slurred her words and was unsteady on her feet, thanks to the drugs given to her by Porter.

McIntosh reached into his pocket and produced the hair clamp and beads. "Do you recognize these?" he asked.

She held out her hand and McIntosh dumped the items into her palm. She held them close to her face. The squint of her eyes radiated wrinkle lines across her cheeks.

"Yes," she said. "That's my barrette. And those beads are from the necklace I was wearing last night."

She handed the items back to McIntosh, who returned them to his pocket. "I'd like to ask you to step outside, if you don't mind," McIntosh said.

"Why?" Tommie asked.

McIntosh pointed over his shoulder toward the car. "I'd like for Mrs. Massie to examine the suspects' automobile."

"Is that it?" Tommie asked. He seemed more interested in the vehicle now than when he had first glanced at it.

"That's what I need to ask your wife, Lieutenant."

"Let's go, Tommie," Thalia said.

With her husband holding her arm to keep her steady, Thalia followed McIntosh to the street where Haruya Ida's touring car was parked at the curb. She leaned forward and carefully inspected the vehicle. She rubbed her hand along its lines and circled the car. Then she reached out and touched the untorn top. She swayed a bit, and Tommie clutched her arm to hold her upright.

* * *

When her assailants were finished with Thalia, they piled into the car and sped away, leaving her sprawled in the dirt. She squinted after the dark-colored, older car, speeding away as it left her behind; its torn top flapped in the night air. At first, all she saw were vague outlines and shadows.

But then the outlines and shadows seemed to sharpen. The dark color lightened and the lines of the vehicle modernized. The flapping top silenced as the rip mended itself. And then, for one fleeting second, there it was: a relatively new, tan Model A Ford touring car, almost exactly like hers and Tommie's.

* * *

She opened her eyes and looked at McIntosh. She nodded. "Yes," she said, "it was a car like that."

That, combined with Mrs. Massie's identification of Ida and her knowledge of the license plate number within one digit, cinched it in McIntosh's mind. They had the right people. From the Massie house, he instructed Sato to take him to the quarantine station on Ala Moana. It was time to see the scene of the crime for himself. After arriving, Sato pulled the car to the side of the road, leaving tire impressions in the soft dirt, and waited for further instructions.

"Just drive around a bit," McIntosh said. "I want to get the lay of the land."

Sato slowly drove across the dirt toward the quarantine station and circled around. The car dipped as it plunged into a shallow puddle of water and then evened out again. Sato continued to drive around, running back through the puddle a second time. McIntosh gazed intently out of the window, but didn't speak. Sato, too, looked for evidence, but didn't see anything but the tire tracks he was leaving.

At last McIntosh was satisfied. "Okay, let's go back to headquarters."

Sato swung the car in a wide arc and crossed over the road once more, leaving still more tracks.

Chapter Seven

The Identification

"Our first inclination is to seize the brutes and string them up on trees."

After hearing from Lieutenant Massie and Captain Pace, Captain Ward Wortman did the only logical thing a man in his position could do: he cancelled shore leaves and confined enlisted personnel to the base pending further order. Once word got around about what had happened to Thalia Massie—and it surely would, because military bases were like small towns, and gossip moved swiftly at all levels—the men would have blood in their eyes as they hit Honolulu. They had no love lost for the locals, nor the locals for them, and trouble would be sure to follow.

Wortman also let Admiral Yates Stirling know what had happened, and he told the Admiral that the police had some of the assailants already in custody. He knew of Stirling's famous temper and hoped the latter news might mollify him a bit.

Yates Stirling was the top man in all the military in the Territory of Hawaii. In his early sixties, with graying temples and strikingly blue eyes, he carried himself with rigid military bearing, his spine as unyielding as his racism, a trait he had honed while serving a tour of duty in the Philippines in the early 1900s. There, he had overseen a reign of terror on the native population that included mass killing and destruction of villages and farms.

As Wortman expected, Stirling was outraged. As he later wrote in his memoir, through the whitewashed prism of idealistic hindsight, "I was aghast. I knew Thalia Massie as a friend of my daughters, one of the younger set, demure, attractive, quiet spoken, and sweet, minding her own affairs. I knew her to be the daughter of prominent people in the Eastern States, raised in a cultured American home. God, what an awful thing to happen to this delicate girl."

"Wortman," Stirling said, "our first inclination is to seize the brutes and string them up on trees. But I suppose we should let the local authorities deal with them. We may have our own problems once word gets out to the men."

"That was what I thought as well. I've already cancelled all liberties, but that may not be enough. Rumors are swirling around the base, and some of the men may want to take things into their own hands if justice doesn't move fast enough."

"Let me see what I can do about that," Stirling said. "I need to talk to some people."

* * *

One of those people was Territorial Governor Lawrence Judd, whose ancestors had arrived in Hawaii as missionaries over a century earlier, dedicated to converting the native population to Christianity, while at the same time acquiring great wealth. In fact, Judd's grandfather, Dr. Gerrit P. Judd, had been prominent in the successful effort in 1848 by the whites from the mainland in influencing King Kamehameha III to abolish the system of feudal land ownership by the chiefs, or the *ali'i*, in favor of a system that allowed, for the first time, private ownership of real estate. Called the Great *Mahele*, it ceded over nine hundred thousand acres of Hawaiian land to the crown, nearly one-and-a-half million acres to the government, more than four million acres to the chiefs, and less than thirty thousand acres to commoners. The chiefs were then free to sell, trade, or bargain with their acreage. It wasn't long before the white missionaries had bilked the chiefs out of most of their land, purchased huge tracts from the government, and obtained long leases on crown lands, thereby controlling most of the real property in the territory to the exclusion of the natives.

Judd, a dropout from the University of Pennsylvania, had been born in Hawaii and returned there in 1909 to work for Alexander and Baldwin, one of the Big Five—the corporations that controlled the sugar industry and related businesses, thus dominating virtually all commerce and business in the islands. The other four were American Factors, C. Brewer, Castle & Cooke, and Theo. H. Davies & Co. Judd later moved to Theo H. Davies, and, after serving in the army in World War I, he was drafted by the Big Five to run for the Territorial Senate. He served in that capacity throughout the 1920s, and was selected in 1929, at the age of forty-two, to succeed Wallace Farrington as territorial governor.

Admiral Yates Stirling arrived unannounced at Iolani Palace, which housed the governor's office, on the morning of Sunday, September 13, ready to throw his considerable weight around. That weight consisted of millions of dollars injected into Hawaiian commerce by navy and army officers and enlisted personnel, not to mention an upcoming construction project at Pearl Harbor that promised additional multi-millions. Judd was in Hilo, on the Big Island, at the time, but promised to hurry back to Honolulu as soon as word reached him that the head of the military in Hawaii had come calling. When the military said "Jump," the governor said, "How high?"

* * *

Grace Fortescue, a woman of elegance and dignity, swept across the lobby of an exclusive hotel on Long Island. In her forties, she kept her figure trim and her hair, just starting to gray, swept back from her face. She had been living there alone since separating from her husband, Granville Roland Fortescue, who answered to the name "Roly." Although the couple had once been well to do, they had fallen on hard financial times recently, as well as on hard marital times. The result was for Grace to take up residence on Long Island while Roly resided at a Manhattan club.

Their marriage had been through a series of ups and downs since they tied the knot in 1910, when Grace was twenty-six, living on inherited money and celebrities in their respective family trees. Roly's cousin was Theodore Roosevelt, while Grace's father was cousin to Alexander Graham Bell. Unfortunately, celebrity relatives alone, were not enough to keep the wolves at bay. Roly's free spending and the couple's high-society lifestyle had their consequences, not the least of which was the depletion of their inherited funds. By the time they separated, the aura of wealth and prestige they maintained was merely a façade. But they still kept up appearances. After all, the only thing worse than being poor was looking poor.

One of the products of the marriage of Grace and Roly was a family consisting of three daughters: Thalia, born in 1911; Marion, in 1912; and Helene, in 1914. As part of keeping up appearances, all of the girls attended the best boarding schools, although Thalia had been somewhat rebellious as a teenager, manifesting her rebellion through heavy drinking and smoking. Her marriage in the summer of 1927, at the age of sixteen, to Naval Academy cadet Thomas Hedges Massie, offered the promise of maturity and security for Grace and Roly's oldest. It also removed one liability from the Fortescues' ledger.

Grace had not seen Thalia or Tommie since Tommie's assignment to Pearl Harbor, nor was she expecting to hear from her daughter or son-in-law that

Sunday afternoon in September as she crossed the lobby from the elevators to the front desk. She ignored the bellhops and other staff, who were beneath her station, but instead searched for the manager. He greeted her with a broad smile reserved for the wealthy—or at least those he perceived as wealthy. He was able to put the smile on and take it off as if it were a mask.

"Good morning, Mrs. Fortescue," he said.

"I was told that you had an emergency cable for me from Hawaii."

"Yes, Hawaii. I guess it's still morning there, isn't it."

She responded with a frosty silence.

He fumbled about on a ledge beneath the desk for a moment. Then he pulled up a yellow envelope from Western Union. "It's from Lieutenant Massie." As he handed it to her, he added, "I hope everything is all right."

She took the envelope from him. With a slender finger, she used her nail to tear it open. She turned away from the desk and pulled out the slip of paper that contained the message. She felt as if all the blood rushed from her face as she read.

She spun on her heels and addressed the manager. "I need you to make arrangements for me to travel to Honolulu. Immediately."

"Yes, ma'am. Is something wrong?"

"My daughter needs me."

* * *

Captain McIntosh faced a group of men in his office who would assist in the continued investigation, including, at Admiral Stirling's insistence, Navy Lieutenant Commander Richard Bates and members of the Navy's shore patrol, along with detectives Arthur Stagbar and Thomas Finnegan. Down the hall, in the assembly room, Detective Machado waited with Joe Kahahawai, Henry Chang, and David Takai.

"Do we have any word yet on this Ahakuelo?" McIntosh asked.

"Not yet," Stagbar said.

"Okay, well, I want to question these boys myself. All of them. But I want to get the fourth one in before I get started, so let me know as soon as we have him. In the meantime, we need to get identifications of these boys from Mrs. Massie. Stagbar, you and Finnegan get one of our wagons and take them out to the Massie house. Ida, too. She's already identified him, but I want her to see them all there together." Then he addressed the navy men. "Follow along behind, just in case you're needed for any reason."

A bit later, a two-vehicle procession arrived at the Massie house, just as Thalia and Tommie were preparing to leave for Queen's Hospital. While Detective Stagbar waited at the wagon with the four men, Lieutenant Commander Bates and Detective Finnegan went to the door. Bates knocked loudly.

After a moment, Tommie opened the door. His eyebrows went up in surprise at the appearance of Bates. "Commander, what are you doing here?" he asked.

Before Bates could answer, Finnegan said, "Lieutenant Massie, I'm Detective Finnegan. Captain McIntosh sent us here to speak to your wife, if we may."

"She's getting dressed. She's on medication and under doctor's orders to go straight to Queen's Hospital and check in."

"This won't take long. We just need to get her identification, and then you can go."

"She already identified the car."

"What now, Tommie?" Thalia called from the interior of the house. "Why do these people keep bothering us?"

"It's the police again."

There was a long pause then she said, "I'll talk to them."

Massie sighed and stepped aside. "This way."

He led Bates and Finnegan to a back bedroom, where Thalia sat on the edge of the bed, wearing a lightweight dress. A small suitcase rested on the floor beside her. It was the first time Finnegan had seen her, and he was taken aback by the swelling of her face. He also noted that she seemed to be unsteady in her posture, swaying as she sat, and uncertain in her speech. She slurred her words, and she had difficulty focusing on the visitors.

"Mrs. Massie, I'm Detective Finnegan. We've got some suspects that I'd like to bring in and see if you recognize any of them. What I'd like you to do is talk to them a little bit and listen to their voices." Finnegan was aware that, from prior statements, Thalia had said that she didn't see any faces, but that she could tell from their voices that they were Hawaiians. "If you do recognize any of them, don't say anything about that in front of them. You can tell me after they leave."

"Are these the ones who did it?" Thalia asked.

"They're suspects."

"You're not bringing those savages into our bedroom," Tommie said.

"Of course not," Finnegan said. "We'll do this in the living room. I'll go out and get them, but what I'd like you to do while I'm outside is to close the shades and make it as dark as possible. Like it was last night, or as close to it as you can get. You won't have anything to worry about, Mrs. Massie. We'll be right here with you the whole time."

While Finnegan summoned Stagbar and the suspects, Tommie and Bates led Thalia into the living room. She sat in a chair and grabbed her glasses from a side table. Bates closed the curtains, casting the room in dim light, though not completely dark, and they waited.

After a moment, Stagbar and Finnegan ushered in Joe, Henry, David, and Horace, and lined them up in that order, with Joe closest to the door. Thalia perched on the end of her chair, about two yards away from the line-up. She clutched her glasses in her lap, but she didn't put them on.

"Go ahead," Finnegan said.

She pointed at Joe. "What's your name?"

"Joe Kahahawai."

"Are you Hawaiian?" Thalia asked.

"Yeah."

"Do you ever go by the name Bull?"

"No. Sometimes by Joe Kalani, but never by Bull."

The detectives watched the suspects closely, looking for any telltale signs of recognition or deception. Finnegan noted that Joe had not hesitated in answering her questions and had no visible reaction to seeing her. Another interesting thing of note was that Thalia Massie also had no visible reaction to seeing him, or any of the others. He couldn't help but think that, if these men had brutally beaten and raped her the night before, she should have at least been uneasy, if not downright frightened, being this close to them.

She shifted her gaze to Henry. "What's your name?"

"Henry Chang."

"Are you Hawaiian?"

"Yes." Apparently he didn't realize the significance of being half-Chinese, with distinctly Asian features, when he answered affirmatively, but Thalia nodded her head as if making some kind of mental note.

She continued down the line. "How about you?"

"My name is David Takai. I am Japanese."

"You're sure you're not Hawaiian?"

"I am Japanese."

At last her look fell on Horace Ida, whom she had identified earlier in Captain McIntosh's office. She looked him over from head to foot. It appeared to Finnegan that she was seeing him for the first time.

Before she could ask, Horace said, "I am Horace Ida. I am Japanese, not Hawaiian."

"Where were all you boys last night?"

"We go to the dance at Waikiki Park," Joe said. "Then we went to a luau at Correa's."

"Did all of you go there?"

The suspects all answered their assent, speaking in a jumble of voices.

Thalia raised her hand, as if to silence them. When they stopped talking, she asked Henry, "Were you at Waikiki Park last night?"

"Yes."

She repeated the question with David and Horace, who both also answered in the affirmative.

Thalia stood and, for the first time, held her glasses to her eyes. Unknown to the police, she suffered from Graves' disease, which caused her eyes to bulge and significantly impaired her vision. She stepped forward, directly in front of Horace. She examined his face closely, then moved down and repeated the examination on David, then Henry, and ended with Joe. Finnegan watched her closely, and noted that she seemed to have no reluctance to be so close to any of them, nor did she flinch or exhibit any adverse reaction.

When she had completed her examination, she moved back to her chair and sat again. She asked a few more questions about their attendance at the dance the night before and where they had gone afterward, reserving most of her questions for Henry Chang. At last, she looked at Finnegan and nodded. "I'm finished."

While Stagbar led the four men out of the house, Finnegan stayed behind and waited until the front door had closed. "Well, did you recognize any of them?" he asked.

"The two Hawaiians. Chang and Kalani or Kahahawai, whatever his name is."

"How about the others?"

"I'm not sure of the Japanese boy, Ida."

That surprised Finnegan. He understood from Captain McIntosh that, just hours earlier, she had positively identified Horace Ida as one of her assailants, and that he had been the driver of the car in which she had been abducted. Now she wasn't sure, even though she had gotten close to him and stared him right in the face.

"What about the other Japanese? Takai?"

"I've never seen him before."

"You're sure?" Finnegan asked.

"I'm positive."

"But you're not sure about the other Japanese?"

"I keep telling you people that the men who attacked me were Hawaiians. Not Japanese."

"Horace Ida is Japanese."

"I told you I wasn't sure of him."

"Okay, thank you, Mrs. Massie."

As he left, Finnegan couldn't quite understand what had just happened. He took Stagbar aside out by the vehicles. "This doesn't make sense to me," he said. "We know these boys were all together last night. So if any of them was involved, that means all of them must have been."

"She seemed pretty sure," Stagbar said.

"And what about Ida? Are we sure she identified him earlier?"

"That's what the captain said. Of course, if she's so sure her attackers were all Hawaiian, why would she ever have said one of them was Ida in the first place? You don't even have to talk to him to see that he's Japanese."

"Should we go back in and talk to her again?"

"No, I don't think so. Not in her condition. Let's just take these boys back and turn them over to McIntosh. We've done our jobs."

Chapter Eight

The Alibi

"Do you know this is Bennie?"

Ben Ahakuelo lived with his mother on Frog Lane, a crowded tenement street across from the same athletic field where his friends had been picked up by Detective Machado, but he had been across town with his own barefoot football team at the time. A celebrated athlete on Oahu, in addition to being a star football player, he had even boxed for the Hawaiian team in New York at the AAU Championships.

When he arrived home that Sunday afternoon, he was surprised to find police officers waiting. Despite the fact that he was dirty from having played football, he was refused the opportunity to clean up before being taken downtown to police headquarters for questioning. He didn't know what he was being questioned for until he was ushered in, past a large number of navy personnel, to meet with Captain McIntosh.

"What am I doing here?" Ben asked.

"You're under arrest for the rape of a white woman on Ala Moana Road last night."

McIntosh might have expected Ben to register shock or dismay, but if so, that would have been because he didn't know Ben Ahakuelo. Ben had faced rape charges before, the fiasco involving the Chinese girl Rose Younge, which ended with him serving prison time along with his friend Henry Chang. At least that time, he had actually had sex with the girl, along with half a dozen other boys.

"I wasn't on Ala Moana last night," Ben said. "I was at Waikiki Park at the dance. There were all the white women there I wanted, and I danced with a lot of them."

"So you're telling me that if this particular white woman says you raped her, she'd be lying."

"Like I said, there were plenty of white women at Waikiki Park. Why would I need to rape one?"

"Then you won't have any objections if we take you over to Queen's Hospital so this woman can have a look at you?'

"I'm ready to go whenever you are."

This time McIntosh made the trip along with other officers, ready to witness for himself the identification. He had no doubt she would point the finger at this boy, like she had at Chang and Kahahawai, the other two Hawaiians. And Chang and Ahakuelo had an appetite for rape, as had been shown by the prior charges. He wasn't about to let himself get bogged down in the niceties of facts. All the facts he needed were that Ahakuelo had served time for rape before, he was in the car last night with Ida and the others, and he was Hawaiian.

McIntosh had called ahead to the hospital to let Thalia know they were bringing in "Bennie" for her to identify. But when the police arrived and ushered Ben into the hospital room, things didn't go exactly as planned.

Thalia, who had been reclining in her bed, sat up straight as Ben entered and stood at the foot. "Are you Bennie?" she asked.

"No."

Thalia was taken aback. Ben continued, "My name is Benjamin. Benjamin P. Ahakuelo. Not Bennie."

Frustrated, Thalia lay back against her pillow. She glanced at McIntosh and shook her head. McIntosh had an officer take Ben out of the room while he waited behind.

"Is he one of them?" McIntosh asked.

"I don't know. I don't think so."

"He's Hawaiian."

That seemed to give her pause, but she shook her head again. "I can't be sure. I don't think so."

* * *

Thoroughly frustrated, McIntosh returned to headquarters. He had Ben locked up, along with the other men, in isolated cells. He now had all five of the suspects in custody, and he wanted to keep them apart so that they couldn't corroborate stories and fabricate some plausible lie that they would all stick to. By evening, he was ready to start interrogating them, one at a time. Joining him for the interrogation were Deputy City and County Attorney Griffith Wight and investigator Henry Silva. After they got started, United States Attorney Sanford Wood joined the group. Four expert interrogators trying to chip away at the their stories, looking for inconsistencies and holes to support the prosecution's, and Thalia Massie's, version of events.

But when all the pieces were added together into one whole, it told the same overall tale, which was totally inconsistent with Thalia Massie's. The story went something like this:

Horace Ida, Ben Ahakuelo, and David Takai had met up earlier in the evening at a speakeasy in Honolulu. Horace and David were planning to soon leave Hawaii for the mainland and wanted to celebrate with a few beers. From the speakeasy, they went to the home of their friends, Wilhelmina and Sylvester Correa Jr., whose father was city supervisor for the city of Honolulu. In honor of his daughter Beatrice's upcoming wedding, Mr. Correa was sponsoring a luau at his house near the Kauluwela School, where some of the men had been picked up by Detective Machado, and which was close to where Ben lived.

After spending time there, the three decided to go to the dance being held at Waikiki Park. Horace dropped off Ben and David at Waikiki then returned to the Correa luau looking for others of their friends. Joe Kahahawai and Henry Chang had arrived at the luau and were also looking for more excitement, so they loaded into Haruya Ida's car, and Horace drove them all to Waikiki Park, where they joined up with David and Ben.

The dance broke up around midnight, so they all decided that they would give the luau one last shot, maybe see if any beer was left. Driving away from Waikiki along Beretania Street, they encountered more friends in an open convertible driven by Tatsumi "Tuts" Matsumoto. After a brief diversion with Tuts and his carload, they arrived at the Correa house at 12:30. Things were winding down at the luau, and there was no more beer, so they decided to call it a night. Ben Ahakuelo walked home, while Horace, Joe, and Henry were going to drop David off at his house, which was also nearby. That was where they were headed when they encountered Homer and Agnes Peeples at the intersection of King and Liliha Streets. David got out there and walked home.

After an admitted physical altercation between Joe Kahahawai and Agnes Peeples, Horace dropped off Henry and Joe, and then he went home. The next thing he knew, Detective Cluney was rousting him and taking him to police headquarters. No, they had not been on Ala Moana Road; no, they had not encountered a white woman there; and, no, they damn sure had not raped anybody.

Their individual stories fit together into a cohesive whole, with only two minor deviations. The first had to do with the route they had taken from Waikiki Park to the Correa house. Horace said he had turned off Kalakaua Avenue on King Street then doglegged on Keeaumoku Street over to Beretania before heading west again. The other three said they had continued on Kalakaua past King Street, then turned left on Beretania. This was a new shortcut that had recently been constructed, extending Kalakaua, which used to end at King, to Beretania. Not a significant difference in the stories, but a difference nonetheless. Small lies were the building blocks to bigger lies, and the interrogators were anxious to find other blocks.

One of those other blocks, the other deviation in their stories, related to the brown jacket Horace had put on upon being picked up at his home by Detective Cluney the night before. Horace had told Captain McIntosh he had been wearing it that night, but he now said that he had not been wearing it when he and his friends had been out to Waikiki Park and to the Correa luau. The others either agreed that he wasn't wearing it, or said that they simply couldn't remember. It was a minor discrepancy at best, but one that would come back to haunt Horace Ida.

* * *

"Okay, what do you think?" McIntosh asked after the last of the interviews.

"If they're telling the truth about where they were, then it doesn't fit with the timeline we're getting from Mrs. Massie," Griffith Wight said. "If they were at Sylvester Correa's house at 12:30, I don't see how they could have met up with her when she says she was grabbed on John Ena, then taken out to Ala Moana and raped. The times don't fit."

"But she's positive Chang and Kahahawai were two of the ones who did it."

"But not Takai and not Ahakuelo. And she can't make up her mind about Ida."

"Look, if they were all together, that means all of them were involved," McIntosh said.

"Or none of them."

"We've got the license plate number. That proves something," McIntosh said.

"Then we've got to break their story somehow," Wight said. "I wouldn't want to walk into court right now with no more than we've got."

"Don't you worry about that, Griffith," McIntosh said. "I'll nail that down personally. If we get positive IDs, will that satisfy you?"

"I don't know how you plan to do that, but yeah, if you can get positive identifications, then I can work with that."

* * *

Around noon on Monday morning, the five suspects were taken to the Emergency Hospital and were examined by Dr. Thomas Mossman. The exam extended to the clothing they had been wearing the night of the assault, and not just their persons. As Doctors Liu and Porter had examined Thalia for signs of trauma that would indicate violent rape, so, too, Dr. Mossman was looking for telltale signs: cuts or bruises that would indicate a physical struggle, rips or abrasions on skin or clothing, even bodily fluids such as blood or semen. His findings were negative: no signs of trauma and no evidence of seminal fluid or other bodily secretions.

The next day, it was on to Queen's Hospital for yet another line-up in front of Thalia Massie. This time, however, they would be taken in one at a time.

Griffith Wight and Captain McIntosh stood with Thalia by her bedside, while Tommie sat in a chair, as the suspects were brought in by detectives. Wight placed a chair next to the foot of the bed when Horace Ida came in. He had Horace sit in the chair with his back to Thalia, so she could view him from the back, as she had seen the driver of the car that night. Since Horace had been driving his sister's car, and his sister's car was the one used in the attack, it stood to reason that Horace had been driving it when Thalia was abducted. Horace was also wearing his brown jacket.

He sat in the chair and fidgeted. Thalia observed Horace from the back, this time with her glasses on. She reached out and felt the material of the jacket. After Horace was led out, she confirmed that Horace had been the driver that night. She remembered the jacket he had been wearing, she said. "It's the one he was wearing just now."

Then it was time to bring in Ben Ahakuelo, whom Thalia had failed to identify the day before. "We're bringing in Bennie now," Wight said.

Detective Luciano Machado escorted Ben in and had him stand at the foot of the bed. "Do you know that this is Bennie?" Wight asked.

McIntosh leaned over and whispered to Thalia. "Yes."

"Yes," she parroted. Then she addressed Ben directly, "You know you did this to me. Why don't you come clean?"

'Oh, yeah?" Ben said. "I don't know you and I don't know anything about it." He smiled when he said it, and a gold filling in a tooth caught the light from overhead.

Tommie leaped to his feet. He took a quick step forward, as if going for Ben. Ben quickly dropped into a boxer's crouch, fists poised in front. The quick movements by both men took everyone by surprise.

Before the detectives could react, Tommie abruptly retreated, fear evident on his face.

Ben straightened and dropped his hands. "Yeah, that's what I thought, *haole*."

Machado grabbed Ben by the arm and pulled him through the door.

The tension shot out of the room with Ben's departure. Tommie's face was still ashen, but McIntosh smiled at Wight. "He fits the personality type. Aggressive."

"He's one of them," Thalia said. "I recognize him by his gold tooth."

Chapter Nine

The Lawyers

"The district attorney was too deaf to conduct a trial."

One early October day, roughly three weeks after Thalia Massie claimed to have been attacked, Admiral Yates Stirling and Tommie Massie met a Matson Lines ocean liner at the pier at Honolulu Harbor after its weeklong voyage from San Francisco, surrounded by cheery throngs awaiting passengers. While muscular young natives dove into the harbor to retrieve gold coins tossed overboard by arriving passengers, attractive dark-skinned girls circulated with leis made of plumeria and other fragrant flowers, draping them around necks and bestowing kisses. But Stirling and Massie were in no mood for leis, kisses, or gold coins.

"There she is," Tommie said, pointing halfway up the gangplank.

Stirling's eyes followed Tommie's index finger and landed on Grace Fortescue, walking almost regally down the plank. Walking a half-step behind was a young woman, probably in her late teens. Her blondish hair twirled in the tropical breeze, and she bore a slight resemblance to Thalia Massie.

"Who's the girl?" Stirling asked.

"That's Thalia's kid sister, Helene," Tommie said.

Tommie greeted Grace and Helene at the base of the gangplank. Grace rebuffed his effort at a hug, but he planted a kiss lightly on her cheek, then on Helene's.

"Thank God you're here," Tommie said.

Stirling stepped forward. "Mrs. Fortescue, I'm Admiral Stirling."

Grace extended her hand, and he kissed it. "This is my daughter Helene," she said. Helene, still a step behind, nodded but made no effort to extend her hand.

"Let me start by saying how sorry I am by what has happened," Stirling said.

"What is being done about it?"

"The police have caught the men who did this. Natives. They're locked up now awaiting trial."

"Trial?" Grace seemed shocked, as if the idea of a trial had never occurred to her.

"Yes, trial. The local authorities have to at least go through the motions to satisfy the native population."

Grace pondered that for a moment and then turned to Tommie. "I want to see Thalia."

"She's at the hospital for a procedure," he said. "I'll take you there."

"In the meantime," Stirling said, "I'll see to it that your luggage is delivered to the Massie house."

* * *

Thalia sat up in her bed, while Lieutenant Commander Porter, her doctor, listened to her heartbeat. A Chinese nurse stood by with a thermometer, waiting her turn.

"Sounds fine," Porter said. He straightened up and stepped aside. "Let's get your temperature now."

Just as the nurse approached, the sound of voices filtered in from the corridor.

"Let me go see who that is," Porter said. "If that's your husband, I need to speak with him."

After he left the room, the nurse extended the thermometer toward Thalia's mouth. Thalia pursed her lips and glared at the young woman.

"Is there something the matter, ma'am?" the nurse asked.

Footsteps behind drew Thalia's attention before she could respond. "Oh, Mama," she said. "I'm so glad you're here."

She burst into tears as Grace rushed to the bed and hugged her. Tommie and Helene stood at the doorway and watched. The nurse sighed. She grabbed her chart and headed out the door, to return later to do her job. Grace turned and watched the young woman leave. After she was gone, Grace looked back at Thalia.

"Are all the nurses like that one?"

"Some are Hawaiian."

Grace blew air through her lips in a snorting sound. "I'll not have those people touching my daughter."

* * *

Porter spoke to Tommie in the corridor while Grace comforted her daughter. Tommie bore an expression on his face that suggested he was having difficulty understanding what he was being told. Porter spoke slowly, enunciating carefully, to ensure that he was at least not misheard, though he couldn't guarantee not being misunderstood.

"The uterus wasn't enlarged, and the curettage was meager at best," Porter said. Tommie still didn't seem to understand. "That means she isn't pregnant."

That part made sense to Tommie, who nodded slowly.

"Look, lieutenant," Porter said, "I don't want to tell you what to do, but are you sure you want to pursue these rape charges?"

"Don't you think I have a right to see the animals who did this to my wife locked up?"

Porter took a deep breath. "If they raped your wife, sure, I guess I would see your point."

"What do you mean 'if'?"

"Tommie, we've been through this before, but I'm just saying I don't see any evidence of multiple rape." He paused again, not sure whether to go on and provoke a fight. "I'll be happy to intercede with Admiral Stirling on your behalf. Maybe get you shipped off to another post. We can say it's for Thalia's health, and nobody will know any different. Then you can make this all go away without any questions asked, and without making her get on a witness stand and testify in front of everyone." He stopped, then added, "And be cross-examined."

Tommie's face reddened. A tic played at the corner of his eye. He was obviously struggling with his temper. "You think I haven't heard the rumors? That I beat Thalia because she was sleeping around? If I go away, it'll look like that's true. I can't do that."

He turned and stormed off.

* * *

Aggie Ahakuelo, Ben's mother, sat in her tiny house in Hell's Half Acre and dabbed at tears blurring her vision. Bennie had been in trouble before, and even though he had largely been able to escape hard consequences for his behavior, she worried that this time might be different. This time the might of the United States Navy would be brought to bear against her son. She didn't know if Bennie had done what he was accused of—he had denied it to her, but he hadn't been entirely truthful the last time, with Rose Younge—but she also knew that, with white society and the military lined up against him, it wouldn't matter; he would be powerless to defend himself.

Aggie didn't have the funds to hire any lawyer, much less a good lawyer. But she knew someone who might be able to help. She didn't like charity, but her son needed her. And so she made a phone call that she hoped would bring relief, although she knew it might well be ignored. After all, it wasn't every day that commoners picked up the phone and called royalty. But Aggie wasn't just any commoner. As a girl, she had danced in the court of Queen Lili'uokalani. And her son's plight, and the plight of his fellow Hawaiian, Joe Kahahawai, was well known, even to Abigail Kawananakoa—Princess Kawananakoa, from the line of Hawaii's kings and queens. Although the Hawaiian monarchy had long since been overthrown, and its queen at the time, Lili'uokalani, had been imprisoned, as far as the *kanaka* people were concerned, Princess Kawananakoa was royalty. As a young beauty, she had wed the nephew of Queen Kapi'olani, but she reached new heights in obesity as she neared fifty years of age. Still, once a princess, always a princess. And a fabulously wealthy princess at that.

So the princess took Aggie's call. Soon, Ben Ahakuelo would have his lawyer, one of the best the Territory of Hawaii had to offer: William H. Heen.

Heen, a native of Hawaii, had been born on Maui in 1883 to a Chinese father and a Hawaiian mother. He was educated locally at Iolani School in Honolulu and Oahu College, before going off to the mainland to continue his education. He obtained his law degree from Hastings Law School at the University of California in 1904 and then returned to his native Hawaii, where he was admitted to the Hawaii Bar in 1905. His career followed a steady upward trajectory from that point, including serving as a deputy county attorney in Honolulu and then as a deputy attorney general for the Territory of Hawaii. In 1917, he was appointed judge of the First Circuit Court—the first non-*haole* judge in Hawaii—by President Woodrow Wilson. He stepped down from the bench when he was elected city and county attorney for Honolulu in 1919, although others still often called him Judge Heen. Later, he went into private practice. It was at the age of forty-eight that Princess Kawananakoa prevailed upon him to defend Ben Ahakuelo and his Hawaiian brethren.

Heen then drafted fifty-five-year-old William Pittman to join in the defense. Unlike Heen, Pittman was a *haole* through-and-through. Born a Southerner, in Vicksburg, Mississippi, he obtained his law degree in the state of Washington and then practiced in Nevada and California before transplanting to Honolulu in 1915.

Heen and Pittman undertook the defense of all but one of the Ala Moana Boys, as they had become known, with Heen listed as counsel of record for Ben Ahakuelo and Henry Chang, and Pittman for Joe Kahahawai and Horace Ida.

The exception was David Takai, whom Thalia Massie had still not identified as one of her attackers.

David was at first represented by attorney H. E. Stafford, who urged him to testify against his friends in exchange for a deal prosecutor Griffith Wight had extended: reduced charges, with no jail sentence, and a five-thousand-dollar reward. He would then be free to return to the mainland, as had been his original plan, but flush with cash. To Stafford's chagrin, David refused. He insisted that, yes, he had been with his friends that night, but no, they had not encountered Thalia Massie. Not even the promise of money and freedom could compel him to lie about his friends.

And so Stafford did what a lot of lawyers would say was only common sense: he withdrew from representing David Takai. The court then appointed a new lawyer for David, Robert Murakami, of Japanese ancestry, although born in Hawaii. Murakami was young, having graduated from Chicago Law School only six years earlier, but he had already been thrown into the crucible of law practice and race relations in Hawaii. Just three years earlier, a Japanese teenager named Myles Fukunaga had been convicted and sentenced to death for the abduction-murder of Gill Jamieson, the ten-year-old son of a prominent *haole* businessman in Honolulu. In a trial presided over by Judge Alva Steadman, who would preside over the Ala Moana case, Fukunaga was sentenced to death by hanging, a sentence handed down on October 8, 1928, just twenty days after the crime had been committed.

A series of appeals followed, including on the grounds of insanity, a position pursued and argued by three-year lawyer Robert Murakami. The United States Supreme Court ultimately rejected all appeals, and Fukunaga was executed on November 19, 1929. It was a brutal introduction for Robert into the world of law, and the Ala Moana case would prove no different. Maybe it toughened him, though, for his future career, which eventually included appointment to a federal court judgeship. At least for the Ala Moana case, though, he would be able to ride the coattails of experienced trial lawyers like the Bills—Heen and Pittman.

* * *

The Ala Moana Boys were arraigned on October 8, with a trial date set for November 16. The prosecution asked for bail to be set at $10,000 each, but the judge set the figure at $3,500, and then ultimately dropped it to $2,000. It took a little time for their families to raise the necessary ten percent to post, but as the trial date neared, all five of the Ala Moana Boys managed to meet bail and were released. That was good news for the poverty-stricken areas of Honolulu, where they and their families and friends resided, but it was viewed as an outrage by the *haole* minority and the military.

Notwithstanding the fact that they were essentially guests in another's house, the predominantly white military personnel, many of whom were from the American South, viewed the dark-skinned islanders as a lesser race—or races, when you took into account Filipinos, Chinese, Japanese, and others who called Hawaii home. What separated the races was skin color, and many of the men believed, as did Grace Fortescue, that God intended that the white race rule over the inferior dark-skinned races. As if the racial superiority of whites wasn't evident on its face, just consider what a gang of dark-skinned brutes had done to Mrs. Massie. Who knew—maybe it would be their wives or girlfriends next if the savagery wasn't stopped.

After learning that the defendants had been released on bail, Admiral Yates Stirling arrived unannounced at Iolani Palace to meet with Territorial Governor Lawrence Judd. He was promptly ushered into Judd's office.

"Good to see you, Admiral," the bespectacled governor said. "Please, have a seat."

Stirling chose to stand instead. "I guess you know what kind of a situation we have, Governor."

"I believe I do. But things are proceeding quickly. It's been less than six weeks from the arrests, and we've gotten indictments and now a trial setting for mid-November. Two months is swift justice."

Stirling walked past Judd's desk and stared out the window. Hands behind his back, he spoke without turning around.

"We knew how to handle these animals when I was in the Philippines. We were downright ruthless."

Judd took off his wire-framed glasses and rubbed dust from the lenses with a handkerchief. "But you're talking about during wartime, Admiral. We're at peace."

Stirling spun hard on his heels, and his voice took a steel-edged tone. "Tell that to Mrs. Massie. These five animals took her off into the jungle and had their way with her. They nearly beat her to death and then they left her to die. If that's not war, I don't know what is."

"With all due respect, Admiral, we don't know for certain that these boys did it. We still haven't had a trial yet and—"

"The best thing that can happen for the Territory is that they be convicted and sentenced as soon as possible. I've got naval maneuvers coming up, and my men won't go easily to sea knowing that their loved ones will be left behind while savages roam the streets at will. They should be locked up at once and then, after the trial, the key should be thrown away."

Judd sighed heavily. "It's the law, Admiral. Bail was fixed and they all met it. We had no choice but to let them go until the trial. This is still the United States."

"Do you understand that two of them have been convicted of rape before?"

"I've seen the records. They weren't convicted of rape, only of—"

"I don't care about the legal niceties. They assaulted a young woman and they were convicted. All of them are thugs. Hoodlums. What if they escape while they're out?"

"And go where? We're on an island, Admiral."

"You're a most exasperating man, Governor. Why are you defending these brutes?"

"I'm not defending them. They're simply entitled to their day in court, just like anyone else. And if they can post bond, they are free to go until the trial, just like anyone else."

Stirling walked to a Queen Anne chair across from Judd's desk and sat. Judd waited for what he knew would be a veiled threat. It was the usual approach when the military wanted something.

"We're limiting shore leaves," Stirling said, "but we can't forbid them altogether. The men would never go for that, being cooped up all the time on base. And if they decide to take matters into their own hands, I can't stop it completely. I'm not saying I expect trouble, but one never knows."

"I trust the police to deal with whatever arises. And there's always the National Guard if matters get out of control."

Stirling leaned forward and put his elbows on Judd's desk. "I understand the locals have collected money and bought the highest-priced legal talent they could find. They want their boys acquitted even if they're guilty."

"Griffith Wight will be prosecuting. I'm perfectly comfortable with him handling this case. He's helped to spearhead the investigation, and he knows the case as well as anyone."

"He's just an assistant county attorney. And I have it on good authority that the only reason he's handling it is because the city and county attorney is too deaf to conduct a trial."

Stirling had concerns about Wight's experience. Although he had excellent credentials, including an undergraduate degree from Yale and a law degree from Stanford, Wight had spent fifteen years, combined, in the Army and working in his family's lumber business after graduating from Yale before he even started law school, and had obtained his law degree just four years earlier, in 1927. Stirling feared he wouldn't be a good match in the courtroom for the likes of William Heen and William Pittman.

Stirling stood again and began pacing. "What kind of message does it send, Governor, if we can't even send our best prosecutor into the courtroom because he's infirm? We need to find the best there is."

"I'm sure Mr. Wight will do just fine."

"He'd better."

Or what, Judd wondered.

PART TWO

TERRITORY OF HAWAII V. BEN AHAKUELO, ET AL

Chapter Ten

Thalia for the Prosecution

"I started to pray and that made him angry and he hit me very hard."

The trial began with jury selection on Monday morning, November 16, 1931, in the Judiciary Building, also known as *Ali'iolani Hale*, which translates to "House of the Heavenly Kings" or "House of the Heavenly Chiefs." It was originally intended as a royal palace for Kamehameha V, although the *haole* elite had different plans for it after the overthrow of Queen Lili'uokalani and the Hawaiian monarchy. No longer the home of royalty, it was still watched over by the statue of Kamehameha I—Kamehameha the "Great"—which stood regally in front.

The trial was to be presided over by Judge Alva Steadman. Steadman, like others participating in the trial, had an impressive pedigree. With an undergraduate degree from Stanford and a law degree from Harvard in 1922, he found himself a long way from his native South Dakota when he first alighted in Honolulu. But fate smiled on him when he married into the Cooke family, of Castle & Cooke, one of the Big Five companies that controlled commerce in the Territory. From there, his practice moved to the fast track, and he was soon appointed to the judiciary, where he made a name for himself, at least among the *haole* community, as a fair and honest judge, although his views on the racial superiority of whites were well known. So, too, were the desires of his family-by-marriage for a quick conviction in the Ala Moana case.

Jury selection took two days—not surprising given the notoriety of the case, the explosive nature of the charges, and the racial tension that permeated the courtroom just as it did the entire island. The final jury, which would not be sequestered during the trial, consisted of twelve men: two Chinese, two Japanese, one Portuguese, one "American" (which meant *haole*), and six who were mixed race of Hawaiian and *haole*. All were gainfully employed, three by Big Five corporations.

Testimony commenced on November 18, and the courtroom was crowded with *haoles* and military personnel, there to support the victim, Thalia Massie. Grace Fortescue was present, as she would be throughout the trial, but Tommie was there only for the start, before being sent to sea on maneuvers. There were also plenty of locals, including the families of the defendants, who filled the rows immediately behind them.

The first witness was the one every spectator in the crowded courtroom had come to hear.

* * *

Thalia Massie, looking demure and innocent, took the stand. After the twenty-year-old was sworn in and introduced herself, Griffith Wight cut directly to the heart of the case—the night of September 12.

"Mrs. Massie," Wight said, "where were you shortly after 11:30 p.m. the evening of September 12th?"

"I was at a dance at the Ala Wai Inn, and I left shortly after 11:30."

Just as it didn't take Wight long to jump into the middle of the facts, so, too, it didn't take Thalia long to change her facts. She had previously told the police that she left the Ala Wai at midnight, but that didn't fit with a timeline of events that established that the defendants could not have been where she said they were at the time she said. So she turned the clock back a half-hour to see if she could fix that small hole in her story.

"Why did you leave?" Wight asked.

"Because I was bored and tired of the party."

"Did you leave alone or was someone with you?"

"Alone."

From there, Wight took her down Kalakaua Avenue and over to John Ena Road, "because it was better lighted than Kalakaua Avenue," she said. It was at the point where the sidewalk ended on John Ena that trouble befell her.

"A car drove up beside me," she said, "and two men jumped out. One struck me on the side of the jaw and put his hand on my mouth, and he and the other man pulled me in the car."

"Do you know what men got out of the car?"

"Yes," said the woman who had repeatedly stated before that she couldn't recognize any of her assailants. "Chang and Kahahawai." She even pointed them out in the courtroom.

"Do you know which one hit you in the jaw?"

"Yes. It was Kahahawai."

"Did you do anything?"

"I screamed and tried to get away from them. They dragged me in the car and two held me down. My back was away down further than this . . ."—she indicated how she had been slumped down—". . . so I couldn't be seen from outside the car." Demonstrating remarkable memory that had previously eluded her, she was even able to describe exactly where the men were in the car. "Kahahawai was on the right holding me and Chang was on my left."

"After they dragged you into the car as you have described," Wight said, "what happened next?"

"I tried to talk to them but every time I did, Kahahawai hit me. I offered them money if they would let me go."

"Was the car still or in motion at that time?"

"In motion. As soon as they dragged me into the car, they started immediately. They were holding me in the back, and I begged them to let me go. Whenever I spoke, he would hit me."

"Who?"

"Kahahawai." She paused and then added, "Chang hit me, too."

"Now, Mrs. Massie, what was the condition as to light or lack of light where these men grabbed you on John Ena Road?"

In her initial reporting of events to the Clarks and Bellingers, as well as to the police who questioned her at her home the night of the attack, Thalia repeatedly insisted that it had been too dark to identify any of her abductors, other than to know that they were Hawaiians. But on the witness stand, under oath, she now said, "It was not very dark." She explained, "There were some street lamps nearby." She also said that it was Ben Ahakuelo who had taken her purse, and she recognized him. "He turned around several times and grinned, and I saw his face. I also saw that he had a gold tooth." Pressing on, she said, "Once he told Kahahawai to hit me again."

So now she had positively and unequivocally identified Henry Chang and Joe Kahahawai as the ones who grabbed and hit her, and Ben Ahakuelo as the one who sat in the front seat, on the right side, and grinned, with his gold tooth, as she was being beaten.

"Do you know who was on the left side, the driver's side?" Wight asked.

"Ida." She pointed Horace out in the courtroom and said that, on the night of September 12, she "noticed he was wearing a brown leather jacket."

At that point, Wight introduced into evidence the jacket that Horace had put on when picked up in the wee hours by Detective Cluney, and that he had worn to Queen's Hospital to be identified by Thalia Massie. The same jacket that he swore he had not been wearing earlier that night when out driving his sister's car, a fact confirmed by his friends long before anyone knew the significance of the jacket as a point of identification.

Thalia also said that she saw Horace's face when he "turned half way round" on Ala Moana. The light there wasn't as good as on John Ena, she said, but "it was light enough for me to see his coat and face when he turned."

"Could you approximate how many times you were struck while in the automobile?"

"No. I was struck in the car many times." She gestured at her face with her hands. "Across the face, here. My nose. Around the face."

Thalia estimated the speed of the car as around forty miles per hour, and then it pulled off of Ala Moana Road on the right "and drove into some trees and bushes."

To make the point that the car was being driven to the old animal quarantine station, Wight clarified. "Away from the sea?"

"Away from the sea."

"When they stopped, what happened?"

"They stopped the car and jumped out. They dragged me out of the car."

"By that you mean Chang—"

"And Kahahawai."

"After they dragged you out, did they drag you some distance?"

Thalia gestured from herself to a spot on the wall, about thirty feet from where she sat in the witness chair. "About from here to where the courtroom ends."

Wight paused. He had gotten to the critical point in her testimony, and he wanted to milk the moment. He glanced at his notes then back at Thalia. "When they dragged you to that spot, what did they do?"

"Chang assaulted me."

"When you say assaulted, you mean he had sexual intercourse with you?"

"Yes."

Every eye in the courtroom shifted to Henry Chang, squeezed in with the other men behind their lawyers.

"How do you know it was Chang?" Wight asked.

"Because he was holding me in the car and he dragged me over there. He helped the others drag me over there. He never let go of me."

"Did you consent to this act?"

It may have seemed like a stupid question, but it was necessary to establish one of the elements of rape—lack of consent. Thalia nevertheless acted as if she thought it was a stupid question, or at least as if the answer was obvious.

"Certainly not," she said, her voice full of indignation. "I tried to get away but I couldn't. I couldn't imagine what was happening. He just hit me. The others were holding me, holding my arms."

"And when Chang completed this act, what happened next?"

"Then one of the others did it. I don't know which one."

"When you say 'did it,' do you mean have sexual intercourse with you?"

"Yes."

"Now, what happened after that?"

"After that Kahahawai assaulted me."

"By that you mean have sexual intercourse with you?"

"Yes."

So after having started two months earlier with a story of merely having been beaten by unknown Hawaiian assailants, then moving to having been raped by unknown Hawaiian assailants, Thalia now was not only able to identify her attackers, she was also able to partially recall the order in which she had been raped—identifying at least who had been numbers one and three. But Wight needed to drive home the identification, since he knew that the defense would attack her earlier failures to recognize her attackers.

"How do you know it was Kahahawai?" he asked, referring to rapist number three.

"Because he had been sitting beside me in the car, and I recognized his face. He had a short-sleeved shirt on. He knocked me in the jaw. I started to pray and that made him angry, and he hit me very hard. I cried out, 'You've knocked my teeth out,' and he told me to shut up. I asked him please not to hit me anymore."

His own voice now filled with indignation, Wight appealed to the God-fearing jury and audience members. "He hit you when you started to pray?"

"Yes," Thalia said.

"You say your jaw was broken?"

"Yes."

"Was that the hardest blow struck?"

"Yes." And so, with a flourish of melodrama, the brutality of the attack was tied to Thalia's entreaties to God. How could anyone not be outraged?

"During the short time you were in these woods with these men, do you know how many times you were assaulted?"

"From four to six times. I think Chang assaulted me twice because he was standing near me and he said he wanted to go again. The others said all right and a little later he assaulted me."

"Mrs. Massie, do you know any other individual besides these two men who assaulted you?" Presumably he meant other than Chang and Kahahawai, because she had already said there was a third, who came second in time, but she couldn't say who he was. But now she knew.

"Ida," she said. "I felt his coat against my arm." The coat she felt when Horace had been paraded into her hospital room; the coat he had likely not even been wearing the night of September 12.

"What was your physical condition when this was going on, as to strength?"

"They hit me so much that I was sort of dazed."

"Had you any strength left?"

"Not then. I had struggled as hard as I could."

"Did you or did you not hear any remarks, any language from these defendants?"

"They said a lot of filthy things to me."

"You mean obscene things?"

"Yes. They called each other by name."

"What names were they?"

While in her original statements, Thalia had claimed that she heard only the name "Bull," she now had more recall on this point as well. "I heard the name Bull used, and I heard the name Joe. I heard another name, it might have been Billy or Bennie, and I heard the name Shorty. Then I heard one of them say 'hurry up, we have to go back out Kalihi way.'"

Once the assault was over, she said, "One helped me to sit up. He pointed and said, 'The road's over there,' then they all ran off and got away, and I turned around and saw the car—the back of the car was towards me—and I saw Ida get in the front seat of the car." When prompted by Wight, she also added that she "noticed" the license plate number. "I thought the number was 58–805"—the number she had given McIntosh after previously denying, three times, ever having seen the number.

Wight led Thalia through being picked up by the Bellingers and the Clarks, the clothes she had been wearing, including the barrette and the beads that had been found, as well as the items in her pocketbook that had been recovered by police. This led to another bit of testimony that added to the drama of the affair—never mind that it failed to match reality.

Thalia said that after she got home, "I took off my clothes and took a douche. The douche was unsuccessful, though. A couple of weeks later I found I was pregnant."

It seemed as if the air had been sucked out of the courtroom. Observers held their collective breaths. This was new news, indeed. It was also inconsistent with what Lieutenant Commander Porter had told Tommie Massie.

"What did you do about that?" Wight asked.

"I went down to the Kapiolani Maternity Home and had an operation performed by a doctor."

"You are a married woman. How do you account for the fact that your husband was not responsible for your condition?" Or, he might have asked, any one of half-a-dozen other Navy men?

"Because I had my period shortly before the twelfth."

"How much before, do you think?"

"Well, I stopped about two days before, and my husband and I had not had intimate relations between that time nor have we since."

And there you had the prosecution's case: the defendants grabbed Thalia Massie off the street, raped her, and left her dazed, bleeding, and pregnant. She had positively identified several of her attackers and the vehicle they had been driving. What could be left but for the jury to convict?

* * *

The defense, however, had a different story, at least in one respect. Thalia Massie may very well have been grabbed off the street and driven to Ala Moana Road, and she may have been beaten and raped and impregnated, but if so, the defendants had absolutely nothing to do with it. In fact, there were witnesses who would testify positively that the Boys were clear across town at the time of the assault and couldn't possibly have been involved.

William Heen started his cross-examination by placing Thalia at the Ala Wai Inn, arriving there about 9:00 or 9:30. "Was any liquor served at any time?"

"Yes."

"Did you and your friends have any liquor before going to the Ala Wai Inn?"

"Yes. We each had one drink."

"You got liquor there?"

"Someone gave me a drink when there—I drank half of it."

The police detectives had reported that, when they questioned Thalia at her house, she appeared to have been drinking, although she did not appear drunk. Given the time lapse between her presence at the Ala Wai Inn and being questioned at home several hours later, it didn't make sense that she had had no more than a drink and a half, unless she had been drinking at home prior to the detectives' arrival. But the testimony of other witnesses would later suggest that she had been at least a little tipsy at the time she left the Ala Wai.

"About what time was it that you left the Ala Wai Inn?" Heen asked, mindful that her prior statements to the police indicated she had left at midnight.

"It was about 11:35," Thalia said.

That not only didn't match Thalia's earlier statements to police, but also it didn't match the testimony that Heen knew would be given by other witnesses. She had been prepped well by the prosecution, and it appeared to Heen that she was attempting to allow more time for the rape to have occurred. He would make that clear to the jury later. He also knew that this particular lie really didn't matter from a timing standpoint, but he wanted the jury to see that she was lying.

He glanced at the jury to see if they had any reaction. There was none. Their faces remained expressionless, though surely, he thought, they could see the utter convenience of now trying to change the time that she left.

"And your purpose for leaving the Inn was because you were bored and tired?"

"Yes. I always leave parties if I am bored or tired."

Heen paused and looked through his notes. "You walked right out, did you, on the sidewalk?"

"Yes."

"You turned and walked towards Diamond Head way?"

"Yes."

"And you were alone all that time?"

"Yes."

"Then you turned down John Ena Road?"

"Yes."

"As you passed those stores on John Ena Road, did you notice whether they were open?"

"No, I didn't pay much attention to my surroundings."

"Did you notice whether there were any cars driving on Ena Road at that time?"

"I didn't notice any."

"Did you notice whether or not there was a dance going on at the Waikiki dance hall?"

"At that time I didn't know the exact location of Waikiki Park, and I didn't know it had an entrance on John Ena Road."

"So you walked right on down to near this junction of Ena Road and the road that goes to the Fort?"

This was a reference to Fort DeRussey, a place she knew and had been before. Heen wanted the jurors to see how unlikely it was that she could be familiar with the Fort but claim to be unfamiliar with other obvious landmarks, like Waikiki Park, where a dance was going on at the time she claimed to have walked the route she described.

"Yes."

Before Heen could ask his next question, Judge Steadman interrupted. "I think it's about time that we recess for lunch. Let's be back in our places at two o'clock."

* * *

During the break, the lawyers huddled with their clients to discuss the morning's testimony. They weren't too concerned about Thalia's statement that she had left the Ala Wai Inn at 11:30, because the boys had rock solid alibis up until at least shortly after midnight. They also knew that Eustace Bellinger and his friends had picked up Thalia on Ala Moana Road at about 12:50 a.m., and Thalia told them that the attack had ended only minutes before. Both Bellinger and George Clark Sr. would so testify. Whatever had happened to Thalia Massie, if anything, had not occurred between 11:30 and midnight.

They also intended to present witnesses to alibi the Boys for the period beginning about midnight and continuing to the time of the confrontation with Agnes Peeples at 12:35, and others who would place Thalia Massie on John Ena Road between 12:10 and 12:15. They had no intention of contending that Thalia Massie had not been attacked, but they were confident that the facts would establish that their clients couldn't possibly have been involved. It would sure help, though, if they could poke holes in Thalia's identifications of four of the five.

And Robert Murakami remained befuddled how his client, David Takai, whom Thalia had never accused of anything, was even still in the case.

When court resumed at 2:00 p.m., try as he might, Heen was unable to shake the witness from her identifications of her assailants—even though those identifications conveniently came to Thalia hours and even days after the assault, following an initial period of adamantly claiming that her attackers had all been

Hawaiians, but that it had been too dark to actually see their faces. The lawyers' sources for this information were confidential, but the white minority in Hawaii believed, correctly as it turned out, that police officers had provided Thalia's initial statements to the defense without the knowledge or consent of the prosecution.

The United States Supreme Court would not decide the case of *Brady v. Maryland* until 1963, a decision that required prosecutors in criminal cases to provide exculpatory evidence to the defense. But in 1931, prosecutors had the luxury of concealing that kind of evidence, even though it might clearly support a defendant's claim of innocence, or at least allow the defense attorneys to impeach prosecution witnesses. And so a number of the investigating detectives, who believed that the Ala Moana Boys were being railroaded, had decided to level the playing field.

Heen took Thalia back through the abduction, which she recounted just as she had while answering Griffith Wight's questions. "And you say Kahahawai got behind you and struck you?" Heen asked.

"Yes."

"With his closed fist?"

"Yes."

"Where did he hit you that time?"

"Here," she said, pointing at her jaw.

"He struck hard, did he?"

"Yes."

"Did it stun you at that time?" In other words, did it impair your ability to accurately remember exactly what happened and who your attackers were?

"Well, I was startled very much and surprised. It was all so unexplainable and sudden."

"Besides being startled, were you afraid at that time?"

"Yes. I tried to get away from them."

"Were you nervous?" Heen asked.

"I was frightened."

"Frightened and nervous?"

"Well, what do you mean by nervous?"

"Did what happened there at that time unnerve you?"

"No, it frightened me."

"I ask you again, did the blows stun you?"

"Not to any appreciable extent."

Frustrated, Heen changed subjects. Despite Thalia's stubborn protestations that she was able to retain her senses, he hoped the questions at least raised doubts in the jurors' minds as to the newfound clarity of her memories of the attack. She pegged Joe Kahahawai as wearing blue trousers and a blue short-sleeved polo shirt, although how anyone could have distinguished blue trousers from black at night was a mystery. She put Henry Chang in dark trousers and a white long-sleeved shirt, with the sleeves rolled up and unbuttoned at the collar. Like Joe, she dressed Ben Ahakuelo in blue trousers and a blue shirt and had Horace Ida in dark trousers and wearing a brown leather coat. Although she never identified David Takai as one of her attackers, she did place a fifth assailant in the car, although she claimed that she couldn't see him or what he was wearing.

She also claimed, again, to have seen Horace Ida's face. Heen asked, "Ever lived in the Orient?"

"No."

"And at that time you saw what little you did see of Ida's face, did you recognize him as Japanese?"

"Yes. Well, I didn't exactly. I knew he wasn't Hawaiian."

Heen was stunned. The detectives had made him aware that, in her initial reports, Thalia had adamantly insisted that all of her attackers were Hawaiian, yet now she was claiming that she knew all along that at least one of them wasn't. For someone who had no recollections of the attack at the time, her recovered, and altered, memory was quite remarkable. Heen hoped the jury would see it for what it was: words put in her mouth by the prosecution.

Heen moved back to the details of the attack, again trying to either shake her story or find newly invented details that he could impeach. He also returned to laying the groundwork for the timeline that would be the centerpiece of the defense.

"About how long did it take you to go from the Ala Wai Inn to the point where you were picked up by these boys?"

"I was walking quite slowly. I suppose five or ten minutes."

So if she left at 11:30, it was about 11:35 or 11:40 when she was picked up. During that time, the alibis of all the defendants were golden. If she left at midnight, then she was picked up at 12:05 or 12:10 a.m. Heen would address that with other witnesses later.

Continuing with the timeline, Heen asked, "Do you know how long it took the boys to take you from the spot where they picked you up to the place where they stopped?"

"It couldn't have taken more than two or three minutes."

"About how long, do you remember, did it take—in this place where the trees were and where you were assaulted?"

"I don't know. I was so dazed after a while and I expect I lost all track of time."

Aha, Heen thought. Earlier she had denied being stunned, yet now she volunteered that she was dazed. "You were quite dazed from the start, weren't you? After they dragged you to this spot?"

Apparently realizing her error, Thalia answered, "No."

"What names did you hear called?"

"I heard the name Bull used a lot, and I also heard the name Joe and another name which might have been Billy or Bennie and the name Shorty."

"You said, I think, that Kahahawai, at the time he assaulted you, struck you once more in the jaw."

"Yes."

"That stunned you, didn't it?"

"No. It hurt very badly and I thought he had knocked all my teeth out, and I said, 'Look out, you have knocked one of my teeth out' and I begged him not to hit me."

"Did you scream when he struck you on the jaw?"

"Well, I had been crying out."

"At the time he struck the hardest blow, were you attempting to scream?"

"No. I started to pray and it made him angry, so he hit me."

Still unable to shake her testimony on the details, Heen reverted to the timeline again. "About how long were you in this spot altogether?"

"Well, perhaps it was twenty minutes."

Heen looked at the jury again. Surely they were calculating times. Five or ten minutes after she left the Ala Wai, she was abducted, driven for another two or three minutes, then dragged into the trees and assaulted for twenty minutes. She had testified that each one of her five assailants had raped her, and that Henry Chang had raped her twice. That was six times—was twenty minutes enough to account for six rapes?

The jury would also hear that she had been picked up by the Bellingers and the Clarks at 12:50, and she told them that the assault had ended only a few minutes prior. Logic and Thalia's own testimony dictated that the total elapsed time from abduction to rescue was thirty to thirty-five minutes at a bare minimum. Working backwards from the time Thalia was rescued, the abduction and assault had to have occurred between 12:10 or 12:15 a.m. and 12:45 a.m.

But Horace Ida had been driving his sister's car in a near collision with Homer and Agnes Peeples, a good ten minutes or more drive away from the abandoned quarantine station, at about 12:35 a.m., a time when the assault would have to have still been in progress.

"Do you recall saying to the police officers on this night when you returned to your home you thought these boys who assaulted you were Hawaiian?" Heen asked.

"I remember telling the people who brought me home that. I don't remember what I said to the police."

"Do you remember saying on that same occasion something to this effect— that you didn't hear any names called except the name Bull?"

"No, that wasn't so."

"Do you remember making a statement to this effect, on that same occasion to someone, that you were unable to identify any of the boys because it was dark?"

"No, I don't remember making any such statement."

"Do you remember making a statement to this effect on that same occasion that you thought you could identify these boys if you heard their voices?"

"I don't remember what I said. A whole lot of them ran in and out. There was so much confusion, and I wasn't in a condition to answer questions at that time."

As Thalia's previously crystal clear memory on direct examination now grew dimmer and dimmer, Heen continued to hammer her with rapid-fire questions. "Do you remember stating, upon being questioned, that you couldn't identify the car, that you weren't sure what kind of car it was?"

"I didn't think about the car. Mr. McIntosh asked about it."

"Have you seen this car since that night?"

"Yes."

"It was pointed out to you later?"

"Yes. The next day they brought the car up."

"Now, I ask you whether or not you remember making a statement to this effect on that night when the police officers arrived there that you thought it was a Ford or Dodge touring car? An old car?"

"I don't remember saying anything as to the age of the car."

"Do you remember making a statement that it was an old touring car to the officers?"

"I don't remember what they said or what I said to them."

Heen paused and glanced at the jurors again. And, once again, they were inscrutable. But surely he was scoring points. Surely they could see that she was lying.

"Do you remember saying to these officers before you saw Mr. McIntosh that the top in the back of this car was loose?"

"No."

"Now, do you recall upon being asked whether you knew the number of the car and you said no?"

"Nobody asked me until Mr. McIntosh did. I didn't think of the number until Mr. McIntosh asked me."

And until she heard it on police radios and was told it by others, Heen thought. He would make that clear with police officers. But now was a good time to stop, with Thalia's lies and vague memory fresh on the minds of the jurors, hopefully overshadowing her previous precise memories that were at odds with what the officers would say.

Chapter Eleven

The Prosecution Continues

"I was instructed to keep that under cover."

After Thalia Massie testified, the prosecution called Navy Lieutenant Commander John Porter, who testified to the injuries Thalia had received. He also testified that "She was suffering pain and I gave her several opiates and sent her to the hospital, where she was kept under opiates for several days, and I would say her condition was highly nervous, and being under opiates, she probably didn't know just exactly what she was doing at the time."

It was unclear whether the prosecution appreciated the effect of that testimony, but William Heen drove it home on cross-examination. He got Porter to testify that, after sending Thalia to the hospital, he next saw her around seven or eight o'clock that night.

"Did it appear at that time that she had taken her opiates according to the orders given by you?" Heen asked

"Yes, sir."

"Did you continue your order that Mrs. Massie be given opiates every four hours?"

"As needed."

"And you said you had given her these opiates on account of her condition," Heen said, "and that as you said on your direct examination, being under opiates she did not know exactly what she was doing at that time?"

"From the time I saw her, from her nervous condition and so forth, she appeared dazed, sir, for four or five days."

"And she appeared to you, as you stated on your direct examination, that she didn't know what she was doing?"

"Well, she didn't know what she was doing for the first four or five days, with the shock and so forth, and with the pain and with the opiates. I really don't believe she knew exactly what she was doing. I don't. I still stick to it."

Heen quit at that point, leaving unasked the question that he would later ask the jury to ponder: If she didn't know what she was doing during those four to five days, didn't that also mean that she didn't know what she was doing when she identified the defendants as her attackers?

* * *

Other prosecution witnesses included George Clark, who testified about picking Thalia up on Ala Moana Road at 12:50 a.m., and Agnes Peeples, who testified about the altercation at King and Liliha Streets at 12:35.

Police detective John Cluney then told how he had arrived at the Ida house by tracking down the owner of the vehicle with license plate number 58–895, and then spoke to Horace. "I asked him if he operated the car," Cluney said, "and he said no, he loaned it to a Hawaiian boy, and I asked if he knew him, and he said he didn't know his name, and I said 'Who was in the car?' and he said 'Four other boys' but he didn't know them."

At that point, unprompted by any question, Cluney said, "So I got to the police headquarters and going to the detective department, going into the assembly room, where the detectives sit down, a big room, in the office up there. Ida said he admitted that one of the boys in his car struck Mrs. Peeples, but as far as the striking of this white woman, he said he didn't know anything about it."

Wight dropped his hands to his side and stepped back. He raised his eyebrows, as well as his voice—a nice calculated show of shock for the jury. "At that time, had you mentioned to him that a white woman had been struck?"

"I had not."

Wight turned and looked at the jury. He searched their faces to see if they were asking themselves the question he wanted them to ask, and drawing what he believed to be the obvious conclusion: If Ida wasn't involved in an attack on a white woman, how did he know to volunteer that he hadn't been involved in such an attack? There was only one answer: he had been there for the assault on Thalia Massie.

"He admitted he struck a Hawaiian woman in the car on Liliha Street, on King Street," Cluney said, "but he denied at the time hitting any white woman."

With that, Wight passed the witness. It was a cardinal rule of litigation practice: quit on a high note. And boy, what a high note, Wight thought. It also left Heen and the defense attorneys a bit flustered. This was the first they had heard of this, and they weren't sure how to deal with it.

"What time did you get to Ida's place?" Heen asked Cluney.

"It was just a few minutes before three o'clock."

"Did you make a record of that?"

"I believe I have a report on file in the office."

"Where is that report?"

"I haven't got it with me."

Heen addressed Judge Steadman. "I would like to have that report brought here."

"I have no objection to Mr. Cluney getting it," Wight said.

With that, Judge Steadman excused Cluney to fetch his report, allowing Heen to postpone his cross-examination until he had a chance to review it. The prosecution then called Officer Claude Benton to testify about the inspection he and Officer Percy Bond made of the scene at the old quarantine station and the discovery of tire tracks.

"We noticed this particular track in the road leading into that road some fifty feet off the entrance and there was a mud puddle there," Benton said. "In the very center of this puddle, there was a little water, but in the edges the mud was quite thick, these particular tracks running astraddle of the main puddle, leaving the tire tracks very plainly there."

Benton identified the tire treads he found as three Goodrich Silvertown cords and one Goodyear All-Weather, with the Goodyear on the left rear. He said he had first noticed the tire tracks early on that Sunday morning, after Thalia Massie had been brought to the station and he and Officer Bond had been sent to the site to look around.

Wight asked about Haruya Ida's car, which Benton and Officer Lau drove to the quarantine station, with Horace Ida in tow, so they could compare tire treads. Benton testified that they brought the car up there "the following morning," and Wight asked, "That morning, the Sunday morning?"

"Yes, later in the morning."

According to Benton, he parked the Ida car about one foot away from the other tracks for comparison purposes. "As far as we could tell," Benton said, "they were identical, the same as the first tracks we had seen there before."

"Do you know what kind of tires this car had, this number 58–895?"

"It was equipped with three Silvertown cords and one Goodyear All-Weather."

"Where was the Goodyear All-Weather tire on this car number 58–895?"

"Left rear tire."

Wight paused to let that sink in then went for the clincher. "You say the marks of this car, left by car 58–895, and the former marks you had seen on the ground, were identical?"

"Identically the same."

To remind the jury that Horace Ida had been with the officers at the time, Wight asked, "Did Ida say anything when you made this examination?"

"He denied that he had been in there."

"Did he deny that they were the same marks?"

"He did not deny that, sir."

Wight paused again and looked to Judge Steadman. "Your Honor, I should like to take this jury out to show them this location."

Heen stood. "Yes, we would like to go out there, if the Court please, but when we go out there, we would like to go out to Waikiki Park and to John Ena at the same time and make that all one job."

After some arguing about whether the visit would be for anything other than viewing the site, court was recessed and the jury taken to the quarantine station on Ala Moana Road, to the spot on John Ena Road where Thalia Massie claimed to have been abducted, and to Waikiki Park. When they returned to the courtroom, Bill Heen began his cross-examination of Officer Benton. He took the witness through his first visit to the quarantine station, which occurred about three o'clock the morning of September 13, the night McIntosh had sent him to do a preliminary search in the dark, the night he discovered the cigarette packages, ginger ale bottle, barrette, and a ladies' pocket mirror.

"Now, you said you examined the tire tracks that early morning when you went down there, and you had your flashlight?" Heen asked.

"Yes, sir; I did."

"And you found those various makes of tire tracks, did you?"

"Yes, sir; I did."

"Three of the same kind; that is Silvertown and one Goodyear?"

"Yes."

"And you made a close examination of that, did you?"

"I did."

Heen paused and studied his notes. He wanted the jury to ponder what Benton had said: that in the middle of the night, in dark conditions and using only a flashlight, he had been able to discern details of four tires in brown mud. He flipped through the pages of Benton's report from that night, which had been given to him by the prosecution. Unlike reports of officers and detectives like Harbottle and Furtado, whose stories were not favorable to the prosecution, Griffith Wight had no problem turning over documents helpful to his case—or at least that he thought were helpful to his case.

"Did you make any report of your examination down there," Heen asked.

"I reported to Chief McIntosh my findings. At the detectives' office he notified me that car number so-and-so had been picked up."

Heen raised Benton's report in the air. "Did you make another report outside of this one?"

"No, sir."

"I wish to offer this into evidence," Heen said to the judge.

"No objection," Wight said, pleased to have Benton's report in evidence.

"Received and marked as Defendant's Exhibit two," Steadman announced.

Heen then read the entirety of the report into the record, which he felt was more notable for what was not in it than what was in it. After he finished reading, he looked sternly at Benton. "Now, Mr. Benton, if you thought at the time you discovered these tire marks on those premises on Ala Moana Road that they were important evidence, why didn't you include that in your written statement?"

Benton sat silently. Heen felt as if he could almost see the wheels turning in Benton's head as he struggled to manufacture an answer. Why, indeed, would a police officer sent to examine what might well have been a crime scene, and who discovered important evidence at that scene, not include it in his written report?

"I simply reported my findings to Chief McIntosh," Benton said at last. "And I take orders from him. If he would dispatch me to that effect, then I would."

"He told you not to put that in this report?"

Benton paused again. "He didn't tell me not to put it in the report."

"Then why did you leave it out?"

"Because I merely reported my findings to him. Then this automobile came up. Upon investigation of these particular tracks and the tires that was on this particular car, it was followed through by other detectives."

Now it was Heen's turn to pause, to let the jury digest what they had heard. Benton thought it was important evidence at the time, important enough to examine the tracks with a flashlight to learn what kind of tires they were, but not important enough to include in his report. It just didn't make sense. What did make sense was that Benton had not paid any attention to any tire tracks at the scene that first night, if, in fact, there were any tire tracks there at all.

After Heen passed the witness, Wight tried as best he could to salvage the mess Benton had made.

"When you made this report out," Wight said, "had you at that time taken out car number 58–895 and compared the tracks or had you made this report before that?"

"I made that report before that."

"When did you realize the great significance of those tracks?"

"After I made my report."

"You mean after you took the car out and compared the tracks?"

"No, sir. I was ignorant of the fact that this supposed car was used in this Ala Moana case."

Wight asked a few more questions, but the damage had been done. Everyone in the courtroom was thinking the same thing: surely Benton knew that, at some point, *some* car would be located that had been involved. After all, Thalia Massie said she had been dragged into a car with a torn roof. Whether it was the Ida car or not, tire treads would be important evidence if any car was located. And Benton had already said he knew, at the time, that it was important evidence. If he had really examined tracks in the mud in the dark of the night, surely he would have at least made a note of that.

If tracks had really been there.

* * *

When Detective John Cluney resumed the stand to be cross-examined by Bill Heen, he sat stiffly on the front edge of the witness chair, his back straight, chin up. Everyone knew that the guts of Heen's cross-examination would deal with the near-lethal thrust Cluney had delivered: Horace Ida knew about the white woman being attacked before anyone even brought it up.

Heen wasn't entirely sure how to deal with that. Had he been told prior to trial that Horace had disclaimed to Cluney any knowledge of a white woman, Heen would have had time to do more investigation. He might even have learned that the dispatcher, Cecil Rickard, had mentioned it to Horace. As it was, he now had to deal with the statement after it had been sprung on him by surprise, and his options were limited. One of the first things you learned in law school was not to ask a question if you didn't already know the answer, so he knew he had to tread lightly around the issue. But lightly or not, he had no choice—he had to deal with it somehow, to discredit it as best he could. Maybe the best approach was the same strategy he had followed with Benton, who had failed to include supposedly important information in his report. Why was he just now hearing about this prosecution-friendly evidence at trial? Was this another case of invented testimony not included in a police report?

The problem was that Heen didn't know what was in the police reports since they had not been provided to him by the prosecution. Although Cluney had been dispatched to fetch his report and bring it back, he now confessed sheepishly that he didn't write his own report, but merely made notes on the report of another officer, so he had nothing of his own to turn over. Cluney had made a statement, Wight said, but it was a statement made to Wight "in my preparation for this trial," so it was privileged and he didn't have to give it to the defense.

Heen studied his notes as he stood at the lectern for a silent moment, still figuring out the best approach. He opened slowly and carefully, taking Cluney back through picking up Horace and bringing him to Captain McIntosh at the police station.

"Before you took him in there, you had no talk at all with Ida?" Heen asked.

"I did. I had a talk with Ida."

Heen took a deep breath then plunged ahead. "What did you ask him?"

"I told him it looks pretty tough. I believe that is all I did say."

"What were you alluding to?"

"I was referring to Mrs. Peeples and this assault case."

"What did Ida say to you?"

"He says 'I'll admit'—he says 'one of the boys struck this Hawaiian woman but I don't know anything about the white woman.'"

"Did you tell him he was suspected of having assaulted a white woman?"

"I did not."

"He just said that voluntarily?"

"Yes."

Heen paused. It was time to ask a question he didn't know the answer to. So Heen worded his question in such a way as to lay a trap for the unwary Cluney.

"Did you put that down in your written report?" Heen asked.

"I did not," Cluney said. Not, "I didn't prepare a written report," but simply "I did not." The clear implication, which apparently neither Cluney nor Wight picked up on, was that Cluney didn't just put comments on another officer's report but did, in fact, make a written report of his own.

"Didn't you think it was important at that time, that that evidence was important at that time?"

"I knew it was important evidence."

"And you didn't put it into your report?"

"I did not." Again, no protest that he had not prepared a report. Then he added a kicker. "I was instructed to keep that under cover."

Heen stepped back, eyebrows raised in surprise. Not only was it apparent that the prosecution had lied about Cluney writing a report, it now appeared that someone on the prosecution team had deliberately concealed evidence. Ordinarily it wouldn't have made sense for the prosecution to conceal evidence that supported its case, unless it could be discredited upon further investigation. But when concealment foreclosed any investigation, and the evidence then could be used to blindside the defense at trial, it made perfect sense. Dirty pool, at its worst.

"Who instructed you to keep that under cover?" Heen was barely able to conceal the anger in his tone as he spoke.

"I had a conversation with Mr. Wight."

Every eye in the courtroom, including those of Judge Steadman and the jury, turned toward Griffith Wight at the prosecution table. Wight kept his head down and wrote furiously on his notepad, as if unaware that a spotlight had just been turned on his unethical behavior.

"Did Mr. Wight tell you why you should keep that under cover?"

"He said it was good stuff."

I'll just bet, Heen thought. "To hide?"

"I don't know what his intentions were," Cluney said. But everyone else did.

Heen shifted gears for a few more questions, then circled back to the non-report. Time to remind the jury of Griffith Wight's dirty tricks. "What time did you make that report that you signed and which they refuse to produce at this time?"

Wight stopped writing on his notepad and sprang to his feet. "I object to that remark. It is absolutely unfair. They asked me to produce my evidence so that they could rebut it. I think it is unfair. I request that the jury be instructed to disregard it."

All that Heen could think of was that great line from Shakespeare's *Hamlet:* "The lady doth protest too much, methinks." But he kept silent. Let the jury infer whatever it wanted to. And regardless of what instruction the judge might give, they would remember the remark, the context, and the conduct of Griffith Wight.

"The jury has heard the court rule," Steadman said, "that there is no duty on your part to produce that report and I assume, of course, that the jury will understand the law on the subject and will not draw any improper conclusions or deductions from the questions."

But Heen decided to drive the spear in a little deeper. "Did you tell Mr. McIntosh, before you went home that morning of the thirteenth, before you went home about five o'clock, about what Ida had said to you before Ida went into his office?"

"I did not. They were investigating that case. I left."

"You knew at that time, didn't you—you just stated that they were investigating this assault case and the Peeples case."

"Yes, sir."

"And you knew at that time that this car was suspected of being involved in this assault on Ala Moana Road?"

"Yes."

"And you knew at that time that that was very important evidence when Ida told you that he didn't assault this white woman. You knew that?"

"Yes."

"Knowing that, why didn't you report that that evening to Mr. McIntosh while they were making this investigation?"

Cluney squirmed in the witness chair. Heen could tell that he knew there was no good answer.

"While Mr. McIntosh made the investigation, I left," Cluney said, dodging the question. "I was to leave at four o'clock but I left at five."

A petulant tone was starting to infiltrate Cluney's answers now, and Heen knew he had him. "You knew at that time that they were investigating this assault case?"

"Yes."

"And you knew that Mrs. Massie was there?"

"Yes."

Heen stepped back, arms held out, palms up, in an almost pleading gesture. "Why didn't you, having good evidence involving Ida, why didn't you do it at that time?"

"I didn't do it, that's all."

Chapter Twelve

The Prosecution Rests

"... the prosecution has utterly failed to prove its case."

After putting on witnesses to describe the various line-ups and Thalia Massie's identifications of the Ala Moana Boys, on November 23 the prosecution called its last witness, Captain John McIntosh. McIntosh carried a small notebook with him as he sat in the witness chair. After having him identify himself as captain of detectives, and having been on duty the night of September 12 and 13 as a special investigator, Wight asked, "Upon that date, did you see a man by the name of Ida?"

"I did." McIntosh pointed Horace out as "the man with the brown suit—brown coat and green shirt."

Heen interrupted. "May I inquire if this is your last witness?"

"I believe so," Wight said.

"At this time, we would like to have Mrs. Massie recalled for further cross-examination on account of discovering certain evidence after she left the stand, and we have to lay a foundation for that evidence."

"They have the right to recall her as their own witness," Wight said.

"No," Heen responded. "It is further cross-examination. I am addressing this to the discretion of the court."

Judge Steadman pondered the request for a moment. Although Thalia Massie had already testified, and the defense had the right to call her to the stand as part of its case, if there was newly discovered evidence that might impeach the prosecution's evidence, it was more equitable to present it to the jury now, while the prosecution's case was still fresh in their minds. He also knew that it might support motions that the defense would assert once the prosecution had rested—motions he would surely deny, but it would eliminate a point of error on appeal if he permitted the testimony now as cross-examination rather than later.

"I think it would be proper," the judge said.

Seeing where the judge was heading, Wight played the sympathy card. "That poor woman went through two days' examination. I think she went through a merciless cross-examination."

Yes, Heen thought but didn't say, *and she lied her way through every minute of it.*

"Is there just one point you wish to take up with Mrs. Massie?" Judge Steadman asked Heen.

"Yes, we have what we consider impeaching testimony, and we have to lay the foundation for it, and this evidence was discovered by us yesterday morning."

Judge Steadman nodded. "You will have Mrs. Massie recalled."

With that, Wight moved back to his examination of McIntosh. After setting the stage, he handed Horace Ida's brown jacket to McIntosh and introduced it into evidence as Prosecution's Exhibit B.

"Did you or didn't you have any discussion relative to that coat with Ida in connection with the night of September twelfth or morning of September thirteenth?"

"I did."

"What did he say about the coat?"

"I asked him if he had worn that coat Saturday night and he said he had not."

Wight moved on, but there would be more discussion of that jacket to come later. Turning to other physical evidence, he asked, "Did you happen to examine any part of the person of Joe Kahahawai?"

"Yes. One of his hands, the right hand, I believe."

"What did you notice on that hand?"

"There was a scab on the right knuckle of that hand, and it had been recently split across the scab."

"Did it show anything?"

"It showed blood."

Wight looked at the jury, to emphasize what they had just heard: Joe Kahahawai, the prize fighter, the man who had punched Thalia Massie on the jaw, had blood on his punching hand that night.

"Did he say anything about that mark?"

"I asked him how he had come by that cut, and he said he was a boxer and had been punching the bag at the National Guard Armory."

"Did he say anything about the cut in the scab?"

"I asked him how the cut came to be in that state, and he gave no excuse for it."

"Who was present when you discovered that scab?"

"You were present yourself, and I believe Mr. Silva of your office was present."

Wight paused again to let the jury take note of his own involvement in the investigation right from the start. What he hoped they took from that was that his questions represented far superior knowledge than did the cross-examination efforts of defense counsel. He had been present, not they. He knew what he was talking about, not they.

"Do you know who discovered that cut in his hand?"

"Officer Furtado, I believe. No, I wouldn't be sure. I don't know."

Disappointed that McIntosh had not given him his due, Wight pressed. "You would not know if it was I or not?"

"No, I don't know."

Without rising, William Pittman said, "We will give you credit for it, Mr. Wight."

Pittman had said it in a flat, even tone, but Wight was unsure if it was intended as humor or sarcasm. He hesitated then said, "Thanks."

Embarrassed, Wight shifted gears again. After establishing when Thalia Massie came to McIntosh's office, he asked, "To the best of your memory, what did she say that night?"

Heen came to his feet. "Did you make notes?" he asked.

"I have the original notes made here at the time," McIntosh said. He held up the small notebook he had carried with him to the stand.

Because there was no requirement that the police provide exculpatory evidence, or any kind of evidence, for that matter, to the defense, neither Heen nor Pittman and Murakami had seen McIntosh's notes before trial. But if McIntosh had used them to refresh his recollection for purposes of testifying, then the defense could demand to see them.

"In shorthand?" Heen asked.

"No, in longhand."

"Did you go through that—" he pointed at the notebook—"this morning to refresh your recollection?"

"Not this morning, no."

But the answer wasn't a flat-out no. It suggested that McIntosh had reviewed them, but simply at an earlier time. "A few days ago?" Heen asked, hopeful.

"I did."

"May I look at that please?"

McIntosh looked at Griffith Wight, then at Judge Steadman, who nodded. A court bailiff approached the witness stand, took the notebook from McIntosh, and carried it to Heen. He and Pittman thumbed through it as Wight resumed his questioning.

"To the best of your memory, what did she say that night?"

McIntosh recounted the entire horrific story as it had been told to him by Thalia, starting with the visit to the Ala Wai Inn and ending with the attack, in which she said she was raped "five or six times." He described her appearance by stating that "one eye was partially closed, her mouth was swollen and cut, and there were ironwood pine needles in her hair, and her hair was hanging down."

According to McIntosh, and in contradiction to Thalia's testimony, "She said along about midnight she left the Inn to go for a walk in the fresh air." In the course of the recitation, he acknowledged that, when he asked Thalia what nationality her attackers were, "She said she should say Hawaiians," and that, when asked if she would know them on sight, she said "she wasn't sure." But, he testified, although she said she caught only a fleeting glimpse of the license plate as the car left, "She said as far as her memory could serve her, she thought the number was 58–805."

In quick order, McIntosh testified as to the items that had been found at the quarantine station, which belonged to Mrs. Massie, including the green beads and the hair barrette. He also testified about his interviews with the defendants and the different routes they said they had taken that night while heading to a luau at the Correa house. Wight's purpose here was to show inconsistencies in their stories that, he believed, meant they were lying.

After Wight passed the witness, Heen began his cross-examination, and he wasn't about to let the inconsistencies in Thalia's testimony go unchallenged. "On your direct examination you stated that she told you it was about midnight when she left the Ala Wai Inn to take a walk for fresh air."

"That is what she told me in her statement—'around about midnight' I think are the words she used."

Opening the notebook containing McIntosh's notes, Heen said, "Now it appears in your written statement that you took at that time, on page four of this book, you have this, 'Around 12:30 or 1 a.m. I decided to go for a walk and some air.'"

Not at all what Thalia Massie testified to a couple of months later. McIntosh shrugged. "If that is there, that is what she said."

Griffith Wight leaned across from the prosecution table to look at the notebook. Heen slid it over so that Wight could see what he was referring to.

"Between 12:30 and 1:00 a.m.?" Heen asked.

"I don't dispute that. If that is there, that is what she said."

Heen held the notebook open, with the open pages facing McIntosh. "I want you to see it. Probably you might disbelieve my statement?"

"No, I don't disbelieve. That statement is as she made it."

Heen nodded. He didn't bother to glance at the jury to see their reactions. They couldn't have missed the fact that she moved her departure time up an hour for her testimony, and that even in her statement to McIntosh, she had given two times: midnight and 12:30 to 1:00.

"And she told you at that time, did she, that she thought there were only four men in the car?"

"I think she said at least four."

"Do you remember whether or not she told you 'There were two in the backseat; they were Hawaiians'?" He paused and held the notebook for Wight to see the page he read from. "I am reading this with Mr. Wight checking me."

"Yes."

"There were two in the backseat, they were Hawaiians. Do you remember her saying that?"

"Yes."

"On your direct examination, you said she was assaulted five or six times. I think that is correct, isn't it, Mr. Wight?" He turned toward the prosecution table as he asked the question.

"Yes," Wight said, apparently forgetting that he wasn't the witness and wasn't required to answer any of Heen's questions.

Turning back to McIntosh, Heen said, "It appears in this written statement made by you at the time she said she 'was assaulted six or seven times.' This is correct, is it, as against your statement on direct?"

"That statement is absolutely correct." A tone of defensiveness crept into McIntosh's voice. It didn't matter what Mrs. Massie might have said on the stand; he was damned if he would allow his own credibility to be questioned, as if he had dishonestly written the statement he took that night from her.

"Did she tell you what nationality these men were in that car that picked her up?" Heen asked.

"I think she said 'I should say they were Hawaiians.'"

Heen looked at the notebook. "It says here, 'What nationality were they?' Answer: 'Hawaiian.'" He paused and let that soak in. Then he pressed his advantage. "If she said that, then you are mistaken, are you not, when you say she stated 'I should say they were Hawaiians'?" He stared at McIntosh, to make sure he understood. There was a big difference between a positive and absolute assertion that they were Hawaiians and a qualifier such as "I suppose I should say."

McIntosh hesitated, trying to remember exactly what was actually said and what was in his notes. "I think I repeated that question. I think later on you will find she said, 'I should say they were Hawaiians.'"

But what she actually had said later in her statement to McIntosh, in response to the question of nationality, was "Hawaiians, I would say."

Heen was finding McIntosh's notes of his interview of Thalia Massie to be a gold mine, full of nuggets to impeach Thalia's courtroom testimony. During her direct examination by Wight, she claimed to have heard her attackers use names like Bull, Joe, Bennie, and Shorty. But that was not what her statement to the police on the night of the attack said.

After McIntosh acknowledged that she referenced "common" names like Joe and Bull, Heen asked, "Did she say she heard the name Shorty?"

"I don't think so."

"If she had, you would have put that in your written statement?"

"Certainly."

"And, not appearing in this statement, she didn't mention the name Shorty?"

"She couldn't have."

"Did she tell you at that time she heard the name Bennie or Billy mentioned?"

"I don't think so. I think she just mentioned two names, Bull and Joe."

Having exposed that lie, Heen moved on to the car. "Did you show her the Ida car, 58–895?"

"I did."

"Was she unable to point out anything in that car?"

"She wasn't able to identify the car."

"You made a thorough examination of that car?"

"I did."

"Did you find any beads in that car?"

"I did not."

"Did you find any blood spots in that car?"

"I did not."

"Did you look for fingerprints?"

"I did."

"Did you find any fingerprints that compared with the fingerprints of Mrs. Massie?"

"There was nothing on the car that could be used for purpose of comparison." When pressed, McIntosh clarified, "There was a conglomeration of fingerprints on the car, and they couldn't be used for comparison."

Moving on from the physical evidence, none of which pointed a guilty finger at the defendants, Heen attacked the so-called "line-up" in which only Horace Ida was brought before Thalia. The one in which McIntosh strongly suggested to Thalia that Ida was one of her attackers before she even had a chance to study his appearance. Heen got McIntosh to establish that Horace wore a brown leather jacket that night at the police station. Then he asked, "Did you tell Mrs. Massie to look at Ida?"

"I did not."

What McIntosh had actually done was to tell Horace to look at Thalia: "Now look at your beautiful work."

"Did you observe Mrs. Massie looking at Ida?" Heen asked.

"Ida wasn't in the office when she was with me." Apparently he had forgotten that he had Detective Cluney bring Horace in after he had taken her statement.

"Don't you know that Mrs. Massie went up to Ida and said to Ida, 'Where are the other boys?'"

"No, no."

Heen was incredulous. He raised his voice. "You didn't hear that?"

"She did not."

"Mrs. Massie did not tell you at any time that morning that Ida was one of the boys?"

"She did not."

Heen knew that McIntosh was not telling the whole truth, but he had no way to prove it. It was Horace Ida's word against McIntosh's. A defendant in a rape case against a respected police detective.

After getting McIntosh to concede that Horace Ida refused to implicate himself for anything other than the Peeples altercation, Heen asked, "On the night or early morning of September 13, 1931, after Cluney brought Ida to your office, did Cluney at any time before he went off duty that morning tell you that Ida had said to him words to this effect: That 'we admit one of the boys assaulted Mrs. Peeples, but we deny having assaulted this white lady?'"

"I don't remember Cluney ever telling me anything like that. Not to me."

Heen glanced at Griffith Wight, whose head was buried in his notes. "And you were Mr. Cluney's superior officer at that time?"

"I was."

"And not Mr. Wight?" Wight's head popped up. He wore a look on his face that suggested he had no idea where Heen was going with this line of questioning.

"Haven't you heard prior to the taking of the stand here that Mr. Cluney had the information to the effect that Ida had told him that they did not assault this white woman without being asked about it?"

Wight stood. "Objected to as immaterial and hearsay."

"Objection overruled," Judge Steadman said without hesitation. He appeared intrigued by the line of questioning.

"I did hear that," McIntosh said. "And I tried to think if Cluney ever did say that to me at any time, and I have no recollection of his ever having said it. Not to me."

Heen then led McIntosh through other physical evidence, including the clothing that had been worn by Thalia Massie and also by the defendants. As for Thalia's dress, there was no evidence of semen on it, which seemed unlikely if she had been raped as often as she claimed. There was always, *always* a telltale trace of semen in gang rape unless the attackers wore prophylactics.

"In connection with this investigation made by you, did you send Mr. Finnegan with these boys to the Emergency Hospital to be examined as to their private parts, as to whether or not there might be traces of semen on their private parts?" Heen asked.

"I did."

"Did you get a negative report about that?"

"Negative."

"And your instructions were in connection with that, were that the underwear which the boys were wearing at that time should also be examined to determine whether or not they showed traces of semen?"

"I think that was included in my instructions."

"You only think so, or don't you know?"

"I know there was one pair of trousers or underdrawers returned to me from the Emergency Hospital that were negative, and I don't know whom they belonged to."

Heen pressed the attack, finally drawing an admission from McIntosh that the underwear that the men had been wearing the night of the assault had all been examined for semen, and "nothing adverse" had been found. Again, highly unbelievable if there had been a gang rape.

Heen moved on to the second "line-up"—the one at the Massie home that included all of them except Ben Ahakuelo, after which McIntosh conducted his own interrogations of them.

"You repeatedly questioned these boys and accused them of being involved in that assault, didn't you? Heen asked.

"I did."

"And they consistently denied their guilt, didn't they?"

"They did."

Returning to Horace Ida's brown jacket, Heen set the scene of Thalia's identification of him on the day the men were all brought to the hospital. "He was made to stand at the foot of the bed, which was then occupied by Mrs. Massie?"

"Yes."

"And made to turn halfway around?"

"He sat in a chair at the foot of Mrs. Massie's bed with his back turned towards her, with his jacket on, and he turned his profile around."

"After that, what did she do?"

"She felt the jacket. He was brought forward so she could feel of the texture of the coat, and I remember she pulled back as though the thing was repulsive to her, and after that he was taken out."

"Did she say anything to him?"

"I remember she said to the boys, 'Look at your handiwork. Aren't you proud of it?' And she said to Ben, and he denied he had assaulted her, and she said, 'You know you did,' and he said, 'Oh, yeah!' and they denied it."

Heen pressed for more details. "What did Mrs. Massie say to Ben at that time?"

"She told him very, very forcibly that he was one who had assaulted her, and he said, 'Oh, yeah!' and he said, 'I don't know you. I don't know anything about it.' He said it with a leer and a sneer."

"Did you tell Bennie to open his mouth in there at that time?"

"I did not."

"Did he open his mouth in there at that time at the request of Mrs. Massie?"

"I don't remember."

"Did Mrs. Massie at that time tell you that she was able to identify Bennie because of a gold filling in his tooth?"

"Not at that time. Not that I remember."

Heen looked at the jury. Surely they remembered Thalia's testimony about seeing the gold tooth and being able to identify Ben Ahakuelo because of it.

"Did she, Mrs. Massie, tell you at the time you talked to her early Sunday morning that she would be able to identify one of the boys because she had seen this boy with a gold tooth, or, rather, a gold filling in the tooth?"

"She did not."

"And are you certain, Mr. McIntosh, that at that time on Tuesday when Ben was taken into that room, he did not at any time open his mouth so that Mrs. Massie could look at the gold filling?"

"Not while I was in the room. But I was out of it once or twice, I know."

The last part of McIntosh's answer presented at least a plausible explanation for why McIntosh might not have known about a gold tooth as a marker of identification, but it smacked of nonsense. There had been other detectives in the room at the time, and surely one of them would have mentioned such an important detail as that to him. No, it was pretty clear, at least as far as Heen was concerned, that the gold tooth was merely a convenient fabrication, maybe even made up by Thalia Massie on the spot in the courtroom, the first time she actually noticed the filling—which likely had not occurred until after the trial had started. Or she had actually said it at the hospital, but was lying when she said she recognized Ben by the tooth?

After Heen finished his questioning, Wight made a token effort at rehabilitating the witness, though much of the damage had already been done. He knew that his best strategy was to get McIntosh off the stand as quickly as possible, but only after first planting plausible explanations for his implosion.

"Now you stated, Mr. McIntosh, that Ida's underwear or a certain part of Ida's underwear, or, rather, a pair of underdrawers of Ida's was sent to the hospital." Wight pretty much stammered out the question, himself shaken by Heen's cross-examination. "Do you know whether or not that was the underwear he had worn on the night in question?"

"We sent to his house, and as far as I recollect, Mr. Wight, he said that was the pair of underwear he wore that night."

"He *said* so," Wight said, "but was there any other proof that this was the same pair of drawers that he had worn that night?"

McIntosh brightened as he saw the opening that Wight had presented him. "I had no proof that it was."

"Was it the underwear that he went down to the police station in that day?"

"I don't know whether he had it actually on that day or not."

"Could it have been on him, though, at the time he was at the police station?"

Heen sat silently, although he could have objected to the speculative nature of the question. It was too much fun, however, watching Wight fixate on Horace Ida's underwear.

"No," McIntosh said. "He said, if I remember, I think—I would not be sure, which officer it was, but somebody went to his house and got the underwear."

"Was that a clean suit of underwear or a soiled suit of underwear?"

"No, it had been soiled."

But not, Heen thought, *with semen.*

Wight then tried to bolster testimony about the car, but the most he could get out of McIntosh was that, while Thalia could not identify Haruya Ida's car, she did say that "it was a car like that."

After a bit more questioning on more sanitary topics than Horace Ida's underwear, Captain John McIntosh finally left the stand some time after 2:00 p.m.

* * *

Anticipation was high in the courtroom when Thalia Massie resumed testifying. Everyone, including the judge and the jury, wondered just what the "impeaching" testimony was that William Heen intended to elicit from her. Thalia fidgeted as she took her seat. Her gaze drifted from the prosecution table to her mother, sitting on the front row. Grace, who faithfully attended every day of trial to support her daughter, and who was still living at the Massie house while Tommie was at sea on maneuvers, nodded and smiled. They both wondered, as did the rest of the courtroom, what lay in store.

After reminding everyone that Thalia had been taken to the Emergency Hospital in the early morning hours of Sunday, September 13, 1931, Heen asked, "Now I will ask you whether or not while you were at the Emergency Hospital you had a conversation with one Miss Fawcett, who was nurse in attendance at that time?"

"Yes, I spoke to the nurse."

"Do you remember saying to Miss Fawcett at that time that you did not recognize the persons who assaulted you?"

"I don't remember. The only thing I remember saying to her was that the men who assaulted me seemed to be experienced in that sort of crime."

Yet another new detail from Thalia.

"Did you tell her at that time that these men who assaulted you were Hawaiians?"

"I don't know."

"Do you recall Miss Fawcett saying to you at that time that some of them might, that they might have been Filipinos, or some of them might have been Filipinos?"

"I don't remember anything she said to me except she told me not to get upset."

Thalia squirmed in the chair, seemingly unable to sit still. Grace continued to make eye contact whenever Thalia looked her way, willing her daughter to be strong. It was quickly becoming apparent from the tenor of the questioning that the defense was going to produce witnesses to testify that, on the night of the assault, in the early stages, Thalia had consistently told the same story, and that the story she told then was at odds with what she now testified to under oath.

Heen continued with barely a breath for air. "Did you not at that time say there were no Filipinos among these men who assaulted you, because you knew the difference between them and Hawaiians?"

"I never heard the term 'Filipinos' used in any connection with this case."

"Did Miss Fawcett at that time ask you if you knew the car number and you stated at that time that you did not?"

Thalia shook her head emphatically. "I don't remember anyone asking me the car number until Mr. McIntosh did."

Heen switched gears to Dr. David Liu, who had examined Thalia that night. "Do you recall telling Dr. Liu that there were five or six men who assaulted you and you couldn't identify them?"

"No."

"Do you remember if Dr. Liu asked you if you had been able to see the number of the car these men had who assaulted you?"

"No."

"Did you at any time tell Dr. Liu that you had seen the number of the car?"

"I don't remember telling Dr. Liu anything."

When Thalia left the witness stand for the second, and final, time, Heen was sure he had set her up for the liar that he knew she was. He couldn't wait to put his own witnesses on the stand.

At that point, Griffith Wight announced, "I don't intend to put on any more witnesses. The prosecution rests."

Before moving to the defense case, the lawyers made motions based on the prosecution's case. William Pittman went first.

"In order to protect the record on behalf of the defendants, I shall now renew our motion that the Government be called upon and compelled to elect which one they rely on as having actually committed the rape and which ones they hold as accessories, and if Your Honor overrule it, I will make an exception upon the same grounds formerly stated at the opening of the trial."

In other words, if not all of the defendants committed rape, then tell us which ones did and which ones didn't; don't hold all of them responsible for the same crime if at least some of them can be treated as accessories instead of the primary culprits. It was a long shot, and Pittman knew it. He didn't have to wait long for a ruling.

"The motion is denied and the exception will be noted," Judge Steadman said.

Then Robert Murakami rose to his feet, to offer a motion on behalf of David Takai, who even now had never been named by Thalia Massie as either a rapist or an accessory, nor had she placed him by name in the car or at the animal quarantine station. The prosecution continued to abide against Takai based solely upon statements from the other defendants that Takai had been with them that night. That meant, the logic followed, he must also have been present at, and guilty of, the rape.

"On behalf of the defendant David Takai, I move for a directed verdict on the grounds the prosecution has utterly failed to prove its case against the defendant Takai beyond a reasonable doubt, and assuming all the evidence is true and assuming the jury does believe every bit of it, that there is not sufficient evidence in a case of rape, which crime requires corroboration. Inasmuch as the prosecuting witness herself has denied, and in her statement in open court, and elsewhere, that she is able to identity this defendant, and that the court would have to, if there was a verdict against defendant Takai, grant a motion by defendant Takai to set aside the judgment. So that at this time we move for a directed verdict on behalf of the defendant David Takai."

And with that stream-of-consciousness statement, Murakami fell silent. What he was saying to the judge was that, notwithstanding the prosecution's belief, based upon out-of-court statements, that he had been in the car that night, there was no "*in court*" evidence of that fact. If there was no evidence that placed him at the scene, there wasn't anything for the jury to decide about him, so he should be declared not guilty based on lack of evidence.

Judge Steadman made short shrift of the logic. "The motion is denied."

And now it was time for the defense.

Chapter Thirteen
The Timeline
"A white man was following her."

Based upon the timeline established by the defense attorneys during their cross-examination of the prosecution's witnesses, there were gaps during which an assault could have taken place. Although Thalia had originally told the police that she left the Ala Wai Inn around midnight, she had now testified that it was about twenty-five to thirty minutes earlier. That meant the assault could have happened anywhere between 11:35, the time she said she left, and 12:50, the time she was picked up by the Clarks and the Bellingers.

Realistically, though, the time starting with 11:35 was not helpful to the prosecution, as she also had said that the assault ended shortly before she was picked up on Ala Moana Road. Taking into account her testimony that the whole thing lasted about twenty minutes, and given that the confrontation between Joe Kahahawai and Agnes Peeples had occurred between 12:35 and 12:40, and given how long it would have taken for Horace Ida to drive from Ala Moana Road to King and Liliha Streets for his near-miss with the Peeples, the only time in which the assault could possibly have happened would have been between about midnight and 12:25 or 12:30. If it had been another twenty minutes or so before Thalia was picked up by the Clarks and Bellingers, she could be forgiven for saying the assault had just ended. Surely she would have been in a daze.

Right off the bat, the defense attorneys worked on plugging that gap between midnight and 12:30. "Your Honor," Heen said, "we call Tutsumi Matsumoto to the stand."

Matsumoto, who went by the nickname "Tuts," was a diminutive Japanese man in his mid-twenties. He had known Ben Ahakuelo since 1924, although he didn't know the other defendants before that fateful September night. Tuts was obviously nervous as he approached the witness stand and sat. He glanced at Ben, but immediately diverted his attention to Bill Heen, who stood ready to question him. Heen established that Tuts and his friends Bob Vierra, George Silva, Matilda Silva, and Alice Alves had been at the dance at Waikiki Park the night of the assault on Thalia Massie.

Tuts testified that he remained at the dance until it closed at midnight, and shortly after that he went to his car, along with Bob Vierra and George Silva. The two girls had left with someone else, but were replaced by two others who waited by Tuts's 1926 Ford: Sybil Davis, whom they knew, and Margaret Kanae, a Hawaiian friend of Sybil. One of the girls spotted Ben Ahakuelo outside the park as they left, Tuts said, but he didn't see him as they were loading up in the car. After leaving the park on John Ena Road, Tuts turned away from the ocean and went to Kalakaua Avenue then turned left toward downtown Honolulu. He followed the Kalakaua extension to Beretania Street and then turned again toward downtown.

What happened next, as Tuts described it, could have been a scene right out of the movie *American Graffiti*, but Hawaiian style.

* * *

Traffic clogged as Tuts drove on Beretania, moving at a speed of about twenty-five miles an hour, and neared the congested area around the Honolulu Academy of Arts and Thomas Square Park. Sybil looked back over her shoulder at the young men seated behind her. There was no rumble seat, so Vierra and Silva sat on the convertible top, which had been put down, facing the back. She started to say something, when she spotted a familiar face in the car directly behind them.

"Bennie and them is following us."

Tuts looked in his sideview mirror. A beige, newer model Ford touring car nudged forward, its nose just abreast of the rear fender of the older Ford. Ben Ahakuelo sat in the passenger seat, but Tuts didn't recognize the Japanese man who was driving.

Just as they passed Lincoln School, Bob Vierra suddenly jumped from his perch in the back. He landed nimbly on the running board on the passenger side of the touring car, grabbed hold of the windshield frame, and held on.

Ben laughed. "Bruddah, you *pupule*. You kill yourself."

"Tuts drives like a turtle, real slow."

"Where you going?"

"We going over to Judd Street. Where you going?"

"To Correas. They having a luau. We were there before; maybe they got some beer left. You go wit' us?"

"Nah, we go on to Judd Street."

A voice from the backseat of the touring car asked, "You got a match?"

"What fo' you need match?" Bob couldn't see who had spoken and was afraid to lose his concentration while holding on to the side of the windshield frame.

"Light my cigarette."

"Sorry. Don't gotta match."

Tuts slowed his car as he approached Fort Street. A large crowd had gathered on the sidewalks and spilled into the street. "Bobby," Tuts called, "get back on the car. Might be an accident up here."

Bob looked ahead then back at Ben. "Gotta go, brah. See you later."

The touring car slowed to match the speed of Tuts's car. Timing his leap, Bob jumped back onto the older car. The driver of the Ford slowed to allow Tuts to clear his nose, then turned onto Fort Street as Tuts continued forward.

* * *

Tuts's story matched with the story the Boys told the police when they had first been picked up. Given the time the dance ended and the time it would have taken to drive to this part of Beretania, moving at twenty-five miles per hour, would have put the interaction at 12:15 to 12:20 a.m. After later reading about the events on Ala Moana Road, Tuts went down to the police station and gave a statement of the night's events.

To head off cross-examination that might suggest that Tuts had been influenced by his old friend Ben Ahakuelo to fabricate this story, Heen asked, "As you can remember now, between the time you last saw Ben Ahakuelo at Waikiki Park on the night of September 12th, 1931, and the time you made your statement to the police, had you seen Ben Ahakuelo at all?"

"No, not between. I saw him at the police station that day, the day they took us down there. They were in this other room."

"Did you talk to him at all before you made your statement to the police?"

"No, sir."

On cross-examination, the best Griffith Wight could do was to hammer Tuts on his time estimate as to when he had left Waikiki Park, which Tuts originally told the police had been about 12:20, but he now said was closer to midnight. It was a futile effort to impeach the testimony that established that Ben Ahakuelo had been at the dance, and that he had been on Beretania Street, near Thomas Square a bit later. Because the Peeples altercation had happened at 12:35, it was clear that Tuts's testimony of leaving Waikiki Park shortly after midnight was more accurate than his prior statement that it was twenty minutes later.

The others who had been in the car with Tuts backed his story in all details. Bob Vierra said he saw Ben Ahakuelo when he left the park, which he said was about fifteen minutes after the dance ended. Sybil Davis put the departure time closer to midnight. A multitude of other witnesses placed Ben Ahakuelo and other of the defendants in Waikiki Park prior to the end of the dance, and just outside of the park as the dance ended. Later witnesses placed the Ala Moana Boys at the home of Honolulu City Supervisor S. P. Correa at 12:30, where the luau was winding down, after also having been there earlier, around 10:30 or so.

The window in which Thalia Massie could have been abducted and raped by the Ala Moana Boys had been nearly closed shut.

* * *

Another link in the timeline would be to trace Thalia Massie's movements, starting with the time she left the Ala Wai Inn and continuing until the time she claimed she was abducted. For this portion of the timeline, the attorneys relied upon the testimony of three people: Alice Aramaki and Mr. and Mrs. George Goeas. George Goeas testified on the afternoon of November 24, while his wife testified the next day, and she was immediately followed on the stand by Alice Aramaki. George Goeas worked in the insurance department for the Dillingham Company, while Alice Aramaki operated a barbershop on John Ena Road. The Goeases and Alice did not know each other, nor did they speak to each other prior to the trial, but their testimony was nevertheless remarkably similar.

* * *

It was shortly after midnight, and the dance had just ended at Waikiki Park. George Goeas and his wife exited the side entrance on John Ena Road and headed toward their car parked across the road from the entrance. It had been a good night, full of fun and dancing, and a little drinking, perhaps, but a great night out on the town. After the dance, they planned to stop at one of their favorite places to eat, a saimin wagon in an empty lot just beyond a huddle of stores on John Ena Road. They crossed the road to their car and skirted around the front to the driver's side. George held the door for his wife, who got in and scooted across the seat.

As George got in behind his wife, he noticed a young woman on the sidewalk, no more than three or four yards away. A white woman. Coming from the direction of Kalakaua Avenue and heading *makai*, or toward the ocean. She wore a green dress and had a strange way of walking, with her head down and hanging to her right, and shuffling her feet. About a yard behind her, a white man, wearing dark pants and a light shirt, walked slightly to her right. George heard her speak as the couple passed by. Or, rather, mumble. It appeared as if she might be speaking back over her shoulder at the man following her, but George couldn't understand what she said. As best he could tell, the two people were together, but maybe they'd had an argument. Or maybe there had been too much to drink for one or both of them.

He paid the couple no further mind as they passed by. He slid into the driver's seat, started the car, and headed toward the saimin stand on John Ena.

* * *

Alice Aramaki, a barber, lived and worked on John Ena Road. Very convenient not to have to go far to get to work or to get home at the end of a long day. Her shop was right next to a store called Kimoto's, run by her sister. On the *makai* side, next to the store, was John Ena Auto Stand, and in the vacant lot just beyond the row of businesses was a saimin stand at the corner of John Ena and Hobron Lane.

Alice closed her barbershop at midnight, as usual on Saturdays. She often got late customers either finally getting around to haircuts before Sunday, or coming or going from Waikiki Park. Sometimes even military men, some of whom lived close to Fort DeRussey. She closed up just as the music ended at Waikiki Park and watched as people straggled out of the exits, got into their cars parked on John Ena, and gradually left.

She turned off the lights and locked the door, then walked next door, where her sister was still working. Kimoto's didn't close until 12:30 on Saturday nights, hoping to gain some traffic from patrons leaving the dance. Alice went inside the store, which was open in front. She stood next to the ice box and watched people leave the park. A warm breeze filtered inside. In the near distance, she could hear the surf at the beach.

About ten minutes or so after she had closed up her barbershop, she saw a white woman pass by on the sidewalk. The woman wore a long green dress, and her head hung down. She walked slowly, but didn't appear to stagger. In her peripheral vision, Alice saw another figure close behind. As she watched, a white man came into view, maybe five or six feet behind the woman. The man wore dark trousers—she couldn't tell if they were navy or black—and a white shirt. He walked faster than the woman, as if trying to catch up to her.

Then they passed from her view. Had Alice stepped outside, she could have seen where they were going, but she had no interest or reason for doing so.

* * *

George Goeas and his wife sat in their car at the saimin stand and waited on the noodles they had ordered. He had driven the car onto the vacant lot and parked at an angle, facing the sidewalk. After a moment or two, the same woman and man they had seen earlier across from the park moved into view. The woman still walked a little in front, her head still hanging down and to the right. The man still seemed to be following on her right side.

As the couple passed the Goeases' car, the man crossed to the woman's left and cut quickly in front of her. After a while, they moved out of view.

* * *

Although none of these witnesses could positively identify the woman in the green dress as Thalia Massie, it meshed with facts that had been developed. More importantly, as far as the defense was concerned, it placed Thalia Massie on John Ena Road at about 12:10 or 12:15 a.m., and may well have been the last time anyone had seen her until she was picked up at 12:50 a.m. by the Clarks and the Bellingers. The only possible time during which the rape could have occurred was between those two times.

The way the defense lawyers saw it, there was only one logical conclusion that could be drawn: it would have been impossible for the defendants to abduct Thalia Massie between 12:10 and 12:15, take her to Ala Moana Road and rape her five or six times, then drive alongside Tuts Matsumoto on Beretania Street at 12:20, appear at the Correa luau at 12:30, and finally nearly collide with Agnes and Homer Peeples between 12:35 and 12:40.

Chapter Fourteen

Tying Up Loose Ends for the Defense

"She said, 'I am positive they were Hawaiians because of the way they spoke.'"

During direct examination, Griffith Wight had used deft wording in his questions to make it appear to the jury that Officer Claude Benton, who matched tire tracks at the crime scene to Horace's car, had taken the Ida car there on Sunday morning, prior to McIntosh being driven there in that same car by Officer Sato. The defense put Benton back on the stand to clear up any confusion as to when he had actually been at the site.

"You said that the next morning after you first examined the tire tracks on these premises, the old animal quarantine station off Ala Moana Road, you went down there again to make comparison of the tire marks with the tires that were on the car that Ida had?" Heen asked.

"I did."

"When you said the next morning, do you mean the same Sunday morning or Monday morning?"

"It was the following morning. If this case had taken place early Sunday morning, this was Monday morning that we went."

The significance of the day became clear when, as part of the defense case, Heen later put Officer Samuel Lau, an identification officer with the Honolulu Police Department, on the stand.

"Were you on duty on the fourteenth of September, 1931?" Heen asked.

"I was."

"I will ask you whether you went down to the old animal quarantine station on Ala Moana sometime that day?"

"I did."

"About what time was that, to the best of your recollection?"

"Sometime in the morning, about ten o'clock."

"And with whom did you go?"

"With Officer Claude Benton and Horace Ida."

* * *

While Horace Ida waited in the backseat, Samuel Lau grabbed his camera and a box of white powder from the trunk of the car and then got out and joined Benton, who was already looking around. The powder was to sprinkle in any tire tracks they found to make them stand out better when he took photographs. Benton walked around for a few minutes, a frown on his face, then finally stopped beside a track in the mud and stared at it.

"Is that what you were looking for?" Lau asked.

"There've been so many cars going in and out of here since yesterday, they've wiped out everything from the other night."

"But what about this track? It looks pretty clear."

"I don't know. Maybe. It sorta looks like the tread on Ida's car. But I don't know."

"You know Captain McIntosh was up here yesterday in Ida's car, don't you?"

Benton looked up. "He what?"

"He had Sato drive him up here yesterday in Ida's car."

Lau and Benton stared at the track. "You think that might have been done yesterday by the captain?" Lau asked.

"How can I know for sure?" Benton paused then added, "But I guess it's possible."

"Well, then if it's all the same to you, I'm not going to photograph that track. We'd never be able to prove when it was made or who made it."

* * *

After telling his story, Lau waited patiently for Heen's next question. "At that time did you have any talk with Horace Ida?" Heen asked.

"I did."

"What was said at that time?"

"Officer Benton and I went into a huddle and after, we decided not to photograph the particular tire mark. We thought we would tell Ida that tire mark was found early Sunday morning, in an attempt to get him to confess. Ida didn't deny that mark was made by his car, but he did deny being there."

Heen studied his notes for a moment then looked back at Lau. "Do you recall Ida saying at that time, 'There are a lot of other cars with the same kind of marks'?"

Lau nodded. "He said that."

When Heen passed the witness, Wight went after him aggressively. "Wasn't it your duty to take photographs in a case of this nature?"

"I went down there with every intention to take photographs. Officer Benton and I agreed it would be of no value to take them."

"Didn't you say at the time, 'What is the use of taking pictures? I believe Ida.'?"

"I didn't say that. After the defendant Ida had denied being there, I said, 'Well, I will take your word for it.'"

Wight lifted his eyebrows in astonishment. A sarcastic whine crept into his tone. "You will take the defendant's word rather than the whole prosecution's case?"

But Lau would not back down. "I said, 'I will take your word for it' when he denied. We were trying to get him to confess, trying to make him believe that was his track."

Wight bore in. "Would you take a defendant's word in such a serious crime as this, is that your idea of being a proper police officer or detective?"

"Not necessarily. I don't say that."

"Is it not your duty to help all you can in every way?"

"I did in every way."

Wight shifted gears slightly and came at Lau from a different angle. "Didn't you go to see Benton last Friday night?"

"I did."

"Did he ask you to go to see him?"

"No."

"At that time, what did you say to him?"

"I told Benton that Judge Heen had called me up and wanted a report from me as to what took place when I went with him at eight o'clock on Sunday morning. I told Benton, 'I didn't go to work with you at eight o'clock Sunday morning.' That's the reason I called."

Wight put his best look of skepticism on his face. Here was a witness, a police officer, who had been contacted by defense counsel, William Heen, and who was then calling another police officer to change his testimony.

"Anything else?" Wight asked.

"I said, 'Isn't it a fact the reason I didn't photograph those marks was because there was a doubt in your mind and my mind as to whether those marks were made Saturday night or whether they were made when Captain McIntosh drove the car there?' He said he didn't recall."

Wight put a note of steel in his voice. "Isn't the reason you went and talked to Benton was to try to get him to stand in line?"

"I did not."

There had been rumors floating around Honolulu that a number of police officers who had been involved in the investigation didn't believe in the guilt of the Ala Moana Boys. They believed that the Boys were being scapegoated as a sacrifice to the *haole* elite and the United States military. Heen knew it to be more than just rumors. In fact, the defense intended to call as witnesses a number of police officers who secretly offered to testify on behalf of the defendants.

"Isn't it a fact," Wight said, "that ever since the first day of arrest, you said that these men were not guilty and you bucked this case?"

"I didn't buck it."

∗ ∗ ∗

Other officers who testified got the same treatment that Wight had given Lau, but they, too, held their ground. Detective George Nakea testified about his interview of Thalia Massie, along with Detective Bettencourt, in the early morning hours of Sunday, September 13. He confirmed that Thalia said that she couldn't recognize the car or her assailants, other than believing that all of them were Hawaiians.

Officer George Harbottle offered essentially the same testimony. He said that Officer Furtado asked Thalia, "How were the boys going at the time they assaulted her, and she said they picked her up in an automobile, two men jumped off the car, and when he asked her what kind of a car it was and she said it was a Ford car with a back flapping. She said she could not identify the car because she was thrown in the car and every once in a while she got a glimpse of it. The car was an open car, she said, and the top was flapping as if it was torn.

"He asked her what kind of a car it was, and she said it was either a Ford or a Dodge, she didn't know what kind it was. And then he questioned her further, and he said if she really could identify the boys, and she stated that she could not. And he asked her if she could tell them by their voices, and she said yes, that is the only way she could identify them is by the voices."

The best Wight could do with Harbottle was to point out portions of his testimony that had been omitted from his written report, but in the end, he made the same attack as he had made on Lau. "Did you go to Mr. Heen's office and make a statement?"

"I did go there to make a statement," Harbottle said. "I got a call from him, he wanted to see me. I didn't know what it was all about."

"You didn't know what he wanted to see you about?"

"No."

"You didn't know he was a defense counsel in this case?"

"I didn't know."

"You never read the papers, or haven't in the last couple of months?"

"I hardly ever read the papers."

"You can read?" Wight asked, in his most derisive voice.

Harbottle's answer contained iron. "Yes, I can. I do."

William Simerson, the traffic officer who had gone to the Massie home along with merchant patrolman William Gomes, reiterated what the other officers had said. By now, the cumulative effect had to have been staggering.

"Did you hear her say anything about being able to identify the persons who assaulted her?" Heen asked, referring to Furtado's questioning of Thalia Massie.

"She said she could not," Simerson said.

"Did she say anything as to whether or not she was able to identify the car which the men had who assaulted her?"

"The only thing I could remember is she said that it was some kind of an old touring car, whether it was a Ford or a Dodge."

"Did she, Mrs. Massie, say anything about the nationality of the men who assaulted her?"

"Yes, she said she was positive that they were Hawaiian boys."

On cross-examination, Wight could do no more than use sarcasm, as he had done when he asked Harbottle if he could read, and attack Simerson's loyalty to the police department.

"Now what were her words when she said or described what nationality these boys were?" Wight asked.

"She said they were Hawaiians."

"That is exactly her words?"

"Well, I could not say exactly word for word, but sounded something like that."

"What were the words, word for word?"

"I cannot remember."

"As near as you can remember?"

"Something like that," Simerson said, harkening back to his prior answer. "She said they were Hawaiians."

"She did not use the word 'she,' did she?" Wight asked, making sure this officer hated lawyers as much as most police officers did.

"She did not use the word 'she.' She said, 'I am positive they were Hawaiians because of the way they spoke.'"

Wight moved away from literalness and sarcasm to the question of bias on the part of Simerson. Referring to the time that Thalia Massie was brought to the police station early on the morning of September 13 to be interviewed by Captain McIntosh, Wight asked, "You were up at the police station afterwards when Mrs. Massie was being questioned by Mr. McIntosh?"

"Yes."

"You were there when she walked out with her husband?"

"I must have been. I didn't see her walk out, but I was there."

"Didn't you see Mr. and Mrs. Massie walking out, and you and Bettencourt and a few others laughed at them?"

Simerson looked as if he had just been slapped. "I laughed at them?"

"Laughed at them, yes."

"I did not," he said, his voice rich with indignation.

"Did you hear others laugh at them?"

"No."

"Haven't you consistently made statements that these men are innocent?"

"No."

"And have taken that attitude consistently all the time?"

"No."

"Didn't we have to call you up to have you quit making statements around that they were innocent men, and to get you to back up the police force. Didn't we have to do that with you?"

"About making statements?"

"Didn't we have to, didn't you have to be called up and unofficially complained about, about making statements adverse to this case, as a police officer?"

"Yes."

"Did you make any statements to any newspaper or reporters?"

"No."

When Wight finished, Heen rose to mop up any possible mess left by Wight's cross. "When was the first time any of us saw you about this case?"

"Last night," Simerson said.

"Mr. Simerson, has Mr. Wight or anybody in the police department been telling you not to say anything about this case?"

"No, Mr. Wight has not said nothing to me about it."

"Nobody at all?"

"No, sir."

"Now, who was it who told you to back up the police department?"

"Nobody told me to back up the police department. They told me not to shoot my mouth around about this case."

"Who told you that?"

"Some of my brother officers down there."

"Were you called on the carpet for it?"

"No, no."

"Well, have you been shooting off your mouth about the case?"

Simerson drew himself up in the witness chair. "I have not.

The last police officer to testify was Cecil Rickard, the dispatcher. Based on notes he had made at the time, he testified as to the times he made radio calls about the Ida car, including at least a couple during the time Thalia Massie had been examined by Dr. Liu at the Emergency Hospital, while radio reports were audible in patrol cars outside the louvered windows.

"How many times did you send out this car number 58–895 that night?" Heen asked.

"When I sent out the car number first, we sent out three calls, the first call, and again I sent it out again, three times, about six times altogether. One call is three times, repeating the number three times; the second call repeating the number three times."

"How did you call that number the first time, using the words that you used at that time?"

"'Car Number 58–895,' and I called it out as a Chevrolet touring the first time I called it."

"Did you say 'look for that car'?"

"I told them to look for that car. I told them this: 'Radio patrol cars one and two, please pick up car number 58–895 as a young woman has been assaulted on the corner of King and Liliha Streets about five minutes ago' and I repeated the whole thing over to them again three times."

* * *

Dr. David Liu, who examined Thalia Massie at the Emergency Hospital, backed up what the officers who had testified for the defense said. "She told me she didn't know who they were," he said. "She told me they were rather dark." He also added that "she didn't seem to show any emotion outside of crying," and that he noticed "alcoholic breath."

Nurse Agnes Fawcett, who had some conversation with Thalia at the hospital while Dr. Liu was out of the examining room, offered even more detail. "I know I went back into the room after the examination was over, and I said to her, 'What nationality were they?' and she said, 'Hawaiian,' and I said, 'Are you sure they were not Filipinos or some other nationality?' and she said, 'Oh, no. I know the difference.'"

"What else did they say there at that time as to whether or not she was able to recognize the men?" Heen asked.

"No, she told me she couldn't recognize them."

"Are you positive of that, Miss Fawcett?"

"Yes."

Then, to head off any claim that the defense lawyers had tampered with her testimony, Heen asked, "This is the first time you have seen me?"

"Yes, to my knowledge."

"You have never seen any of the lawyers on this side of the case, have you?"

"I don't recognize any of them."

"When was the first time I talked to you?"

She considered him for a moment then said, "I don't even know your name now."

* * *

There was still the matter of the brown jacket that Thalia Massie said Horace Ida had worn the night of the attack. Although Horace had worn it to the police station when he had been picked up by Detective Cluney, he denied wearing it when he and his friends had been out on the town earlier. But when he was brought to Queen's Hospital to be identified by Thalia Massie, and was told to wear the same thing he had worn the night before, he put the brown jacket back on, a choice that had come back to haunt him. A simple misunderstanding, he told his lawyers. When he was told to wear what he had worn the night before, he thought they meant what he had worn to the police station, not what he had worn when cruising the streets of Honolulu.

"Your Honor, we call Haruya Ida to the stand," said Bill Pittman.

Haruya was noticeably nervous as she took the stand, and it appeared as if she had been crying. Pittman spoke gently and quickly moved to the night of September 12. Haruya testified that she had loaned her car to Horace, who left the house around 7:30 p.m. Haruya then departed to attend a wedding, arriving back at 12:45 a.m. Horace came home shortly after she did.

"Did you notice how Ida was dressed when he came in that night about 12:45?"

"Yes."

"How?"

"He was wearing a white shirt and black pants."

"Did he have a coat of any kind or character on or in his hand when he came in?"

"No, he had nothing in his hand."

"You were there when Ida left about 7:30?"

"Yes."

"How was he dressed when he left the house?"

"He had a white shirt and black pants."

"The same as when he came back that night?"

"Yes."

"Did he have any coat on?"

"No."

"Did he have any coat in his hand?"

"No, nothing."

Pittman moved forward to Detective Cluney's arrival at the Ida house at three o'clock. "Did you see Ida go out with the policeman?"

"Yes."

"Do you know whether or not at the time Ida went out with the policeman he had any coat on?"

"He put the jacket on."

After Pittman finished his questioning, Griffith Wight started his cross-examination. "Earlier in the evening when your brother left with your car at about 7:30, did you follow him out to the car to see if he had that leather coat in the car?" In other words, just because you didn't see him wear or carry it out of the house, that doesn't mean he didn't have it with him that night.

"I did not," Haruya answered.

"You don't know whether he had it with him that night?"

"No, he didn't have it."

"How do you know?"

"Because when he went out, I saw him."

"How do you know he didn't have it in the car?"

"Because when he went out with that detective, he had it."

Chapter Fifteen

The Defendants Speak

"Were you afraid she was going to choke you to death?

In criminal law, it is always risky for a defense attorney to put his client on the stand. Although the Fifth Amendment to the Constitution affords citizens the right not to incriminate themselves, and simply to remain silent, it is also true that juries usually want to hear from the accused. Getting on the stand and testifying opens up the witness to cross-examination and, particularly with a guilty client, can often cause more problems than it solves. But when a defense lawyer is absolutely convinced of a client's innocence, the decision to put that client on the stand is a bit easier to make. That belief bolsters another belief—that if the client is innocent, he cannot be tripped up on cross-examination. Of course, one does not always lead to the other.

After deep consideration, Bill Heen, Bill Pittman, and Robert Murakami decided to put some of the Ala Moana Boys on the stand. For Murakami, the decision to put on David Takai was influenced by the fact that, even after the prosecution rested its case, Thalia Massie had *still not identified him as being one of her assailants.* As for which of the others to put on the stand, they decided that the jury would want to hear from Horace Ida, the driver, and Joe Kahahawai, the man who had struck Agnes Peeples.

Shortly before noon on Wednesday morning, November 25, Bill Heen called Joe Kahahawai to the witness stand. Wearing a white shirt and dark pants, Joe focused his attention on his lawyer and tried to ignore the hostile faces making up more than half the crowded courtroom. Although Joe was a big, strapping fellow, with broad shoulders and powerful arms, he seemed small and frail under the glares of the white faces in white uniforms.

After establishing that Joe had attended school at Saint Louis College—not a university, but instead a Catholic high school, to which he had been awarded a scholarship for his football prowess—Heen asked, "And during all the time that you attended Saint Louis College, were you ever called Bull?"

"No."

"After you attended school, up to the present time, were you ever called Bull by anybody?"

"No, sir."

"Was that your nickname at any time at all?"

"No."

Heen carefully led Joe through the events of the evening of September 12, from the luau at the Correa house to Waikiki Park, where he and his friends remained until the end of the dance. Leaving at about midnight, they returned to the Correa house, where the luau was winding down. From the Correa house, Ben Ahakuelo, who lived close by, walked home, and then Joe, Horace, and Henry left to take David Takai to his house near King and Liliha Streets.

Things took a turn as they approached the intersection at King and Liliha. "As we were about to turn into King Street," Joe said, "there was a car who came up from Kalihi way and they came—well, I don't know how fast they went, but they almost hit our car at the rear of that car."

He said the other car "stopped about ten or fifteen yards up from our car, about in the middle of the street, but in the beginning she curse at us."

"Who?"

Joe's voice started to rise as he recounted the story. "I don't know who it was. Maybe it was a lady or a man, I don't know. So we proceeded our car next to theirs and then I jumped off, and as soon as I jumped off, I came up to that car, and I told them, 'What the hell is the matter with you?' That is what I told them. And so the lady, well, she came out and she tried to choke my neck, so I tried to shove her off, and then I started to talk to the man in the car, and then I saw he had a crank. Well, I would not be a fool to stick my head in the car and then let him hit me on the head, so I drew back."

"Go on."

"And the lady, well, she came back again and she grabbed my neck. Well, since she choked my neck, well, I didn't pay attention to it—well, I didn't mind it, see, but after that she started to choke my throat. Well, from there I slapped her and as soon as I slapped her, I saw that she fell down near to the running board of the car."

It wasn't until the next day, Joe said, when Detective Machado picked him up at the football field, that he knew anything about an assault on a white woman.

"Did you grab any white woman while you were riding on Ida's car and pull that woman into the car?" Heen asked.

"I did not."

"Did you beat up any woman, assault any woman, punch her or hit her that night?"

"No, except one."

"Any white woman?"

"No, it was a Hawaiian woman. I slapped her in the face."

Knowing that, on cross-examination, the prosecution would focus on Joe's hands, hoping to imply that Joe had used his fists that night on more than just Agnes Peeples, Heen tried to head that off. "Did you have a scab on your hand, on one of your hands?" he asked.

"Yes."

"At the time you were arrested?"

"Yes, sir."

After identifying the location as being between the fourth and last fingers on his right hand, Heen asked, "Did anybody discover a little crack in that scab?"

"Yes."

"Who?"

"Mr. Wight."

"Did he say anything about it to you at that time?"

"Yes, he told me how did I get it, and I told him. I told him I went down to the Guard and hit a punching bag down there."

"The National Guard, you mean?"

"Yes."

"Are you a member of the National Guard?"

"Yes."

Continuing with the tactic of bringing out, yourself, evidence that is harmful to your case or your client, so as to defuse it, Heen asked, "Have you been convicted of any offense?"

"Yes." Joe looked down, as if embarrassed.

"What?"

"Assault and battery."

"Once, or more than once?"

"Once."

* * *

Wight wasted no time before going on the attack. "Didn't you, on the twentieth of September, 1930, commit robbery in the first degree . . ."

Heen stood. "If the Court please, I—"

"Wait a minute, until I have finished my question," Wight said. Then he continued, ". . . against one Hayako Fukinado?"

"I object to that, if the Court please, as not proper cross-examination," Heen said. "Under the statute, he can only ask him about a conviction, and counsel knows that. I submit, if the Court please, that that question was asked solely for the purpose of creating prejudice in the mind of the jury."

The lawyers argued briefly about the law of prior bad acts. Heen's argument was that, for purposes of impeaching a witness, you could only introduce evidence of a conviction, not a charge. In response, Wight argued that he was not introducing evidence to impeach, but that he was simply cross-examining a witness who had already, at Heen's questioning, testified that he had been convicted of assault and battery. Judge Steadman agreed with Wight.

"The statute touches only whether you could introduce evidence—you could not introduce evidence of any other offense except where there has been a conviction, but I don't understand that cross-examination is thus limited. The objection is overruled."

A ridiculous ruling, Heen thought. Under that rationale, you could always get in evidence of a prior charge, even without a conviction, under the guise of cross-examination.

Judge Steadman instructed the court reporter to read the question again. When she was finished, Joe simply said, "I did not rob."

Having made no headway, Wight moved on. Referring to when he had questioned Joe at police headquarters, Wight asked, "Do you remember my asking you this, and was this your answer? My question was this: 'Does somebody call you Bull on account of your being a fighter?' and you answered 'I don't know why they call me Bull.' Do you remember saying that?"

"Yes, I did."

Heen pondered whether this was something he needed to clear up on redirect examination. Joe had not said that anyone actually called him Bull, but merely that, if they did, he didn't know why. He would play it by ear as to whether to revisit that later.

Wight painstakingly took Joe back through the events of September 12, before arriving at the Peeples confrontation. "Now when you hit her, how did you hit her?" he asked.

"I slapped her," Joe said.

"And she said you did it with a clenched fist."

"I did not."

"Did you slap her lightly or hard?"

Joe pursed his lips and looked at the ceiling, then back at Wight. "Well, maybe it was hard for her. I don't know."

Wight switched into the same sarcastic mode he had employed with police officers whose testimony was not quite to his liking—asking if Harbottle could read or if Thalia Massie had used the word "she" when talking to Simerson. "You knocked her down, didn't you?"

"Yes."

"Were you afraid she was going to choke you to death?"

"No. How would you like it if a lady choked you?"

"Were you afraid she was going to choke you to death?"

"No."

"Couldn't you have pushed her away gently and stopped her? You are strong enough, aren't you?"

"Sure."

Moving on, Wight covered the manner in which the defendants had been dressed that night, focusing particularly on Horace Ida. "How was Ida dressed that night?"

"Well, he had a white silk shirt and a kind of black and white striped pants."

"Did he have a leather coat on when you left the dance hall?"

"He did not."

"Do you remember when you were questioned on Sunday the 12th of September and again on Monday the 13th of September by me, with Mrs. Hannah Matthews, the stenographer of the police station, taking down short-hand notes, that you were asked, 'After twelve o'clock when you left the dance hall, how was Shorty dressed?,' and you said that he had a leather coat on, or wore that until he dropped off at Correas? Do you remember saying that?"

"That is what *you* put in there," Joe said, referring to the written statement he had been provided to sign.

"Not what I put in there," Wight said, but he realized he might have lost the advantage on this line of questioning, now that his own ethical conduct had been called into question. Given the questions about his collusion with Detective Cluney to conceal information about the statement of Horace Ida protesting a lack of knowledge about an attack on a white woman, it was better to simply move on. He pressed briefly, but was able only to get Joe to state that he didn't remember making any such statement.

On redirect examination, Heen again turned to the issue of Horace's brown jacket and the written statement Joe had signed for Griffith Wight. "Now you said that Ida did not have any jacket on while you were testifying here this afternoon, that he had a white silk shirt and dark trousers with white stripes. Now which is the truth, did he have a jacket on that night after you left the park or that he didn't have?"

"He didn't have."

"How did you happen to say to Mr. Wight that he did have?"

"Well, he put it in the statement, and then after I signed the statement, I scratched it out."

Heen looked at the document that Wight was holding. Addressing Wight, he said, "Let me look at the statement to see if it is scratched out."

In a voice barely audible, Wight said, "It is scratched out."

Heen bent and squinted at the page. "That is exactly what he said," Wight protested, "and he admitted saying it, too. I intend to call the stenographer in to testify to it."

Heen held out his hand. With a great show of reluctance, Wight gave the statement to him.

"If the Court please," Heen said, "I offer this in evidence."

"No objection," Wight said.

Heen came around the counsel table and approached Joe on the stand. He handed the document to Joe, who lowered his head and studied it. Heen stood next to Joe and looked at the paper in his hand.

"Is that your signature?" Heen asked.

"Yes."

"And you put those corrections there? First the answer was 'He had a leather coat on'?"

"Yes, sir."

Heen continued reading. "'He wore that until he dropped off at Correa's.' That is scratched out. You scratched that out and said he had no leather coat on, but wore a white silk shirt and a kind of white pants until he dropped off at Correa's?"

"Yes."

When given the opportunity for re-cross, it was damage control time for Griffith Wight, whose ethics were again under attack. "Do you remember, Joe," he said, "when I asked you whether he had a leather coat on that night and you said—do you remember me asking you, 'After twelve o'clock, when you left the dance hall, how was Shorty dressed?' and you said he had a leather coat on and he wore that until he dropped off at Correa's. That is what you said in before the stenographer, isn't it?"

"Yes."

"Then it was two or three hours later that you came in and changed this thing, wasn't it, and signed this thing and changed it, is that the truth?"

"I don't remember."

"It was a long time afterwards, wasn't it?"

"I don't know. I don't remember."

"You remember you came back after and signed it?"

"Yes."

"It was after you had been in the room that the other boys were, the big assembly room."

"Yes."

Satisfied that he had planted the thought that Joe's decision to scratch out language on the statement had come after discussion with the other defendants, Wight sat down. Heen approached the lectern again. He had two very simple questions.

"When they were in the big room, did they keep you separate?"

"Yes, they did."

"Did you talk to Ida at all about his shirt or jacket?"

"No."

*　*　*

Late in the day on November 25, David Takai—the lone "unidentified" defendant—took the stand. Although Robert Murakami had been appointed as his attorney, the lawyers agreed that Bill Heen, who had been pulling the laboring oar for the defense, would conduct the examination.

Heen started by asking the twenty-two-year-old, "Have you ever been called Bull?"

"No."

David then corroborated the story about leaving the dance at around midnight and heading back to the Correa house, where they had been earlier, and the interaction with Tuts Matsumoto's car. He also testified about the confrontation with the Peeples car at King and Liliha and that he walked home from there because he lived close by. He was shocked at being picked up the next day by Detective Machado, and felt uncomfortable when he and the others, besides Ben Ahakuelo, were taken to the Massie house in Manoa and lined up in front of Thalia, where she was permitted to question them.

"She asked me 'are you Hawaiian?'" David said. "I told her no, I was Japanese."

"Did she ask your name?"

"Yes, she did."

"And did she identify you at that time?"

"No."

After a few more questions about the line-up, Heen asked, "Did you admit to anybody at all, any officers of any kind, that you assaulted Mrs. Massie?"

"No."

"Did you assault Mrs. Massie at any time?"

"No."

* * *

The trial broke at the end of the day on November 25 and, after a one-day respite, resumed on Friday morning, the 27th, with David Takai still on the stand. An interesting bit of legal wrangling started off the day. After consulting privately with Griffith Wight, Bill Heen addressed the judge.

"In order to obviate the necessity of calling Mr. Wight to the stand, if the Court please, I will call on him to stipulate." By that, Heen was asking Wight to agree that the court could accept certain facts as true without the necessity of having to prove them.

Wight stood. "I will stipulate, Your Honor, I went to Mr. Stafford, who was formerly this man's, this defendant's attorney, and I told him that inasmuch as Mrs. Massie had not identified this defendant, if he would turn State's evidence against the other defendants, I would either *nolle prosse* the case against this defendant, or move for a suspended sentence for this defendant." By *nolle prose*, Wight meant that, had Takai agreed to testify against the others, Wight have dropped the case against him.

With that stipulation in place, Heen asked David, "Did you have a talk with Mr. Stafford along the line stated by Mr. Wight just now?"

"Yes."

Wight stood a moment too late to stop the answer. "I will object to that as immaterial."

"There is nothing before the court," Judge Steadman said. "He has answered 'yes.'"

"I move to strike the answer," Wight said.

Heen said, "We submit that what he told him under these circumstances is evidence tending to show innocence on the part of this defendant."

"What the witness told who?" Steadman asked.

"What the witness told Mr. Stafford. In other words, it is a consistent denial of his guilt and the guilt of these defendants. It is just the opposite of an admission."

What Heen hoped the jury would understand was that, notwithstanding a promise of dismissed charges or a suspended sentence, David Takai was still unwilling to implicate the other defendants. He had nothing to lose, and everything to gain, by implicating them, so why would anyone other than an innocent man subject himself to the risk of a criminal trial?

"Do you propose as the next question to ask the witness what he told Mr. Stafford?" Steadman asked.

"Yes."

The judge shook his head. "That clearly would not be admissible. I have no objection to letting the answer stand. I will let that answer stand, that that was communicated to the witness."

"Did you at any time agree to turn State's evidence?" Heen asked David.

"No."

Wight stood again, but again too late. "I object to this question, and I move the answer be stricken and the jury warned to disregard the answer." But, as Heen had heard it said before about striking answers that have already been heard by the jury, "You can't throw a skunk in the jury box and then tell it not to stink."

"Did you have any other further questions you intend to ask along this line?" Steadman asked Heen.

"I was going to ask 'Why?'"

"If you wish to stop here, I will agree to leave that answer in, if you will stipulate you will stop that line of examination," Wight said.

Of course, the jury could already infer the "why" based upon the stipulation Wight had stated earlier and David's answer to that last question. Heen had already won the battle on this point regardless of how the judge ruled on Wight's objection, so he passed the witness to his opponent.

There was virtually nothing Wight could do on cross-examination other than try to prove that the defendants had at least a little time in which to coordinate their stories, and to take potshots at testimony of the encounter with Tuts Matsumoto. Referring to the stenographer who took David's statement at the police station, Wight asked, "Why didn't you put in that written statement the fact that you saw Matsumoto's car?"

"I told you this and she was taking down the thing, but I don't know why she did not have the thing in there."

Wight pressed but, as with Joe Kahahawai's testimony about his including the brown jacket in Joe's statement that Joe scratched out, he walked into the same trap. "Why didn't you put in the fact that you saw Matsumoto's car in the written statement?" he asked a second time.

"I told you this matter, and you told her not to take it down."

Wight raised his voice, as if he was surprised. "I told her not to take it down?"

"I don't know, maybe somebody else."

"You heard this remark?"

"Yes."

"What else did you hear somebody say not to take down?"

"I don't know, but you folks—somebody told the woman, 'Don't take this, that is all right.'"

With nothing more to go on, and not even Thalia Massie willing to say that David Takai was one of her assailants, Wight sat down.

* * *

Horace Ida was the last of the Ala Moana Boys to testify, called to the stand by Bill Heen late morning on Friday, November 27. Horace, like the other Boys, was visibly nervous as he took the stand. A trickle of sweat slid down the side of his face when he raised his hand and swore to tell the truth. The irony of the oath was not lost on Heen. Horace had told a couple of lies in the early morning hours at the police station that had come back to haunt him. He would try to clear those up for the jury, but everyone would wonder why Horace had lied in the first place unless he had something to hide.

The first lie had to do with the brown jacket that Thalia Massie used to pin culpability on Horace. "At the time you left your home that day, or evening, on Saturday, September 12, 1931, what kind of clothes did you have on?" Heen asked.

"I had a white shirt and gray pants with black stripes."

"Did you have a jacket on?"

"No."

"Did you take a leather jacket out with you that night?"

"No, sir."

Moving forward to when Detective Cluney picked up Horace at his house at three o'clock, Heen asked, "At that time did you put on that leather jacket?"

"Yes, sir."

"And that is the first time you put on that leather jacket that night?"

"Yes, sir."

That would suffice for now, so Heen moved on to other topics, eventually landing on the car Horace had been driving that night.

"That is your sister's car, number 58–895?"

"Yes."

"Was there anything the matter with the top that night of September 12th?"

"No."

"Was it loose or flapping?"

"No."

When Heen moved to the altercation with Agnes Peeples, Horace said, "There was a car coming from Kalihi way at a fast rate of speed, and I proceeded to go down King Street, and I was ahead of this car coming down King Street. He was going to hit me so I stepped on my gas. It was on second gear. When they passed me, they cussed me."

"And some altercation happened there?"

"Yes, this woman came out cussing at us, and Joe Kahahawai went out first and then I went out from the car, and this woman came up to him and started to push him towards our car, and he tried to push the woman away, but the woman came for him and so he slap the woman down."

"When you got to the police station, did you make any statement to Cluney, John Cluney, the detective, to the effect that you boys admitted assaulting Mrs. Peeples but had nothing to do with this white woman, that you didn't assault any white woman?"

"I did not."

"Did you know anything at all about this assault case at that time?"

"I did not."

Now it was time to confront the charges head on. Heen paused dramatically, studied his notes as if searching for something, and looked up at Horace again. He asked his next questions rapid-fire.

"Did you go down Ala Moana Road at all on Saturday night?"

"No."

"Or early Sunday morning?"

"No."

"Or any time at all on Saturday?"

"No, sir."

"Did you assault any white woman at all down Ala Moana Road?"

"No."

"Did you grab any woman or take part in having a woman seized on John Ena Road and pulled into your car?"

"I did not."

"Did you commit rape on any white woman on that Saturday night or Sunday morning before you were arrested?"

"No."

"Did you help any boys to commit rape on any white woman on Ala Moana Road that night?"

"No, sir."

And now to address another of Horace's lies to the police. "When Mr. McIntosh spoke to you about this, what you did Saturday night, you told him about not knowing these Hawaiian boys?"

"Yes."

"That you had loaned your car to some of these boys and didn't know their names."

"Yes."

"You also told him you had this leather jacket on that night?"

"Yes."

"Why did you tell them these things, that you didn't know these boys and that you had a leather jacket on?"

"I tried to shield the boys."

"With reference to what?"

"Save them from trouble."

"Trouble of what?"

"This Peeples case."

"This trouble that happened on Liliha and King Streets that night?"

"Yes."

It wasn't a perfect explanation, but it was a plausible one. If Horace hadn't been present at King and Liliha, and didn't know the last names of the men he loaned the car to, then he couldn't finger them. And if he said he was wearing a brown jacket when he wasn't, then it would be harder for Agnes or Homer Peeples to point a finger at him. On the other hand, Heen knew that there was another inference that could be drawn. If you'd lie about a minor altercation, you would surely lie about a major crime. Maybe it was time to focus on the prosecution's misdeeds and the police mishandling of the investigation.

Heen asked about the visit to the quarantine station on Monday morning with Officers Benton and Lau, who drove there with Horace in tow. Horace testified that they drove alongside a tire track already in the mud, then Benton and Lau, with Lau holding his camera, huddled together before questioning him. He had no way of knowing that Captain McIntosh had been to that exact spot the previous day in Haruya's car, prior to going to the Massie house.

"What did they say to you?" Heen asked.

"They told me, 'That tire mark is the same as yours,' and I didn't say nothing. And I said, 'It couldn't be, because I didn't come here that night and there are plenty of cars in Honolulu that have the same kind of mark.' He said, 'Maybe you are right.' Officer Lau said that, and 'I will take your word for it,' and he didn't take the picture."

As Heen moved from subject to subject, he kept returning to that brown leather jacket. Thalia Massie had been sure of the jacket, but then again, she had also been sure that it had been too dark the night of the attack to recognize her assailants or to see the license number of the car. Exposure to that car number by listening to police radios sparked a remarkable resurgence of memory for her. Maybe, Heen thought, her identification of the jacket had also been sparked by something.

Horace had already acknowledged that he wore the jacket to the police station after he had been picked up by Detective Cluney, and so he was still wearing it later when he was first brought in front of Thalia Massie.

"Did Mrs. Massie mention anything about the leather coat at that time in McIntosh's office?"

"No."

The next time Thalia saw Horace was the day all of the Boys but Ben Ahakuelo had been brought to her house. "At that time, did you have your leather jacket on?" Heen asked.

"Yes."

And did she look at you at that time in her house?"

"She was sitting on a couch and she had her glasses. I don't know where she had her glasses, but she picked the glasses up and looked to me like that." He pantomimed holding glasses to his face and squinting, as Thalia had done that day.

Then the men had been brought to Thalia's hospital room one at a time a day later. "What did they do to you when you went into her room?" Heen asked.

"They made me sit at the foot of the bed, first with my back facing her and then they made me turn around, back view and front view and side view, and they made me go near her to feel my jacket."

"You still had that same leather jacket?"

"Yes."

"What did she say?"

"She said, 'That's the fellow.'"

"What did you say?"

" 'No.' I said, 'I don't know you. Couldn't be me, because I never saw you before in my life. That's the third time I have seen you.'"

"The first time was where?"

"At the station."

"And the second time?"

"At her home."

"And that was the third time at the hospital?"

"Yes."

Just as with the car license plate number, Thalia had repetitive encounters with Horace Ida and his brown leather jacket and, miraculously, she could now identify him by that very jacket.

On cross-examination, Griffith Wight bore in on the jacket and Horace's statement the night he had first been brought in that he had the jacket with him.

"Didn't you first say you didn't have the coat, then didn't you say you did have the coat in the car but didn't wear it?"

"No."

"You didn't tell me that?"

"I told you I had the coat on."

Moving along, Wight got to a version of the traditional lawyer's question: *Were you lying then or are you lying now?*

"This morning, in response to Judge Heen's questions, you admitted you told us you did have it, is that correct?" Wight asked.

"Yes."

"Now, did you have it with you or didn't you?"

"I didn't."

"Why did you tell us you did?"

"That was referring to the Peeples case."

"What did that have to do with the Peeples case?"

"Maybe she would have identified me."

A few moments later, Wight stepped into the same prosecutorial miscon-duct trap he had stepped into before regarding tampering with witness state-ments. On a line of questioning about the interaction with Tuts Matsumoto, he asked, "It is not in your statement at all. Did you mention that fact?"

"Yes, I did."

"You volunteered it?"

"Yes."

"I didn't ask you if you followed any car. You volunteered that, didn't you? In other words, you very prominently mentioned the fact you were following another car, without being asked."

"I don't know whether you asked me or not, but I said about Matsumoto's car."

"Can you explain why it is not in your statement?"

"Maybe you didn't put it down."

Realizing his mistake, Wight shifted gears again. Heen wondered if Wight was making a mental note not to ask about any other omissions from witness statements. It was already becoming quite clear—or so he hoped—that the prosecution had engaged in a pattern of misconduct, from concealing evidence to falsifying statements, and maybe even fabricating evidence, such as the tire tracks. If this case came down to nothing more than credibility, he believed the defense held the edge, notwithstanding Horace's lies.

Wight returned to one of those lies. "Why did you tell a lie about not having used your Ford car that night?"

"I told lies about the Peeples case."

"Why did you keep telling that after you knew about the Massie case?"

"I didn't tell you that."

Heen knew that Horace was telling the truth about that. By the time he learned about the Massie case, he had already been picked up by Detective Cluney and admitted, as had his sisters, that he had been driving the car that night.

"Had you hit Mrs. Peeples?" Wight asked.

"No, sir."

"Did Takai hit Mrs. Peeples?"

"No."

"Did Chang hit Mrs. Peeples?"

"No."

"Why were you worrying about protecting them?"

"They were all with me that night."

Unable to shake Horace's story, Wight finished his questioning and sat down.

Chapter Sixteen

Rebuttal

"... two men held this arm and she tried to get away from these men."

After the defense had rested, the prosecution made one last effort in rebuttal, offering a surprise witness, Eugenio Batungbacal, a thirty-five-year-old Filipino, who worked as a barber at Fort Shafter. According to Detective John Jardine's later memoir, he had run into a friend at the Green Mill restaurant on Bethel Street, who said that he'd been driving around the night of the attack with some friends, and that they had seen several men force a young woman into a car on John Ena Road.

That man was Batungbacal, who took the stand on November 27, near the end of the day. Bill Heen objected vigorously to his testimony on the basis that, if he was merely going to corroborate Thalia Massie's story, then he should have been put on the stand as part of the prosecution's case-in-chief, and not as rebuttal. The judge overruled Heen, and Batungbacal was allowed to testify.

According to Batungbacal's story, which he delivered in fractured English with the help of a Filipino interpreter, he had been on John Ena Road with some friends in his Studebaker sedan, and they stopped at a saimin stand near Waikiki Park. He estimated the time as between 11:30 and midnight, noting that the music was still playing. As they left the saimin stand, "I see about four or five men with one girl. Two men holding the woman with hands and one is following. They look like force the woman to bring it to the car."

"What was the color of these men's faces?" Wight asked.

"I don't know."

"Were there any *haoles* there?"

"Well, I don't think so, no."

"What were their nationalities, do you know?"

"I think Japanese and Hawaiian. Look like to me one Japanese and one Hawaiian. The rest I don't know."

Without asking for any more detail, Wight passed the witness to Heen, who bore down on the specifics. As a practical matter for the defense, Batungbacal had already offered up a time for the abduction that did not fit with the time-line. According to his testimony, the abduction took place before midnight, which might have been in keeping with Thalia Massie's new testimony that she had left the Ala Wai at 11:35, not midnight, but it didn't account for the testimony of numerous witnesses who placed the Ala Moana Boys at Waikiki Park until the music ended at around midnight. It also didn't match the testimony of George Goeas and Alice Aramaki, who saw a woman in a green dress being followed by a white man down John Ena Road at around 12:10 or 12:15 a.m.

Still, it was most curious testimony, and Heen sought to implode it. He recounted Batungbacal's estimate of the time based on two of his friends going into Waikiki Park around 11:30 and returning to the car fifteen minutes later. When his friends got back in the car, they drove off.

"And then you saw a woman walking down?" Heen asked.

"Yes."

"In a green dress?"

"I don't know what the green dress—or what color—but I see a woman, that's all. I don't know the color of the dress."

"Was it a long dress?"

"Long dress."

"Way down to the ankle?"

"Yes, way down."

"How far away from you when you saw this woman walking?"

"Well, about, I think, about fifty feet away, and I am still going. My car is still going."

Heen then asked him to describe the men he saw with her. "I saw the girl walking with the men the first time. I thought they go together. Just go with a party. The girl is just like drunk, you know. I don't think that the men were—we don't pay any attention."

"You said she walked as if she was drunk?"

"She looked as if she was drunk because two men held this arm and she tried to get away from these men. That is what make me believe she is drunk."

Heen pressed forward to get details of the car these men forced the women into, but was in for a surprise. "And in front of them was a car standing?" he asked.

"No."

"There was no car at all?"

"There was no car at all."

The witness had told Griffith Wight that the men forced this woman into a car, but now he was saying there was no car. Heen took Batungbacal step by step again through what he had seen, even asking him to demonstrate how the woman was walking. Then he came back to the missing car. The witness threw him another curve.

"How far were you from this woman and those men when you saw the men holding the woman?"

"Well, I told you my car was about fifty feet from the woman and men, you know, and I still keep on going, and when I saw them I think it is about twenty or fifteen feet, I think."

"You didn't see any car there?"

"No. Behind plenty. Behind, not in front." He paused then amended his answer, "One touring car that looked like they forced the woman to bring to that car parking over there."

"Where was that car now? How far down?"

"The car is, I think, if I make no mistake, about one hundred feet or more."

"This woman was a white woman that you saw?" Heen asked.

"I don't know if she is white or not."

"Don't you know she was white?"

"I don't know because she is not facing to me."

By the time Heen was finished, no one really knew what Eugenio Batungbacal had or had not seen. Heen was satisfied, though, because about the only clear point of the testimony was that, whatever Batungbacal witnessed, it happened before midnight. If this had been the actual abduction of Thalia Massie, his clients were solidly accounted for.

* * *

Batungbacal's friends, who had been in the car with him that night, couldn't offer much more detail. Roger Liu, co-partner with Charles Chang in a fruit and vegetable business, altered the timeline, though, testifying that the dance was over when James Low and Chang returned to their car. "I asked Mr. James Low," Liu said, "and he said the dance is over, and I saw some people kept coming out."

Wight questioned him about what he saw after leaving the park and driving down John Ena Road. "On your way down, did you see anything on the side of the road?"

"Yes, I saw a woman together with a bunch of boys."

"What was the nationality of those boys?"

"I am not sure but it looked like Oriental boys to me."

"All Orientals or not?"

"I am not sure of that."

"What was the woman, what was she?"

"I believe she was white."

"Do you know or do you believe it?"

"I believe it."

"What was the color of her hair?"

"Blonde."

"What kind of dress did she have on?"

"Well, I am not sure. In the dark, it looked like blue to me."

Wight got Liu to agree that the dress the woman wore that night was "something like" Thalia Massie's green dress, which had been admitted into evidence as Prosecution's Exhibit C.

"What were the boys and the woman—what were they doing?" Wight asked.

"I saw two boys was holding her arm. I believe at that time they were trying to push her in the car."

"What made you believe that?"

"I saw the lady was moving around, struggling."

"What kind of a car was this kind of car you saw there?"

"I am not sure of that. Either a Chevrolet or a Ford."

"What kind of body?"

"Touring."

On cross-examination, Heen established that Liu and his friends had told this story to the police, and had been questioned several times by Griffith Wight, even giving Wight a written statement. "Now in that written statement, did you say that you saw a woman with a green dress?" Heen asked.

"Said it looked like blue to me."

"And did you say in that written statement that these boys looked like Orientals?"

"Yes, sir."

"Are you sure of that?"

"Looked like Orientals to me."

Going through the logistics, Heen used Liu to establish that the car he was riding in was going between ten and fifteen miles an hour when he first saw the woman, at a distance in excess of thirty-five feet. Liu also admitted that the woman's back was to him when the men tried to force her into a car, but "I didn't saw them get in the car." Heen also got him to admit that he didn't notice many details about the car or the men, and that the episode he witnessed occurred "about one or two minutes" after the dance at Waikiki Park ended—a time when the Ala Moana Boys were positively seen by numerous witnesses in the parking lot outside the park.

"When you saw that these men were trying to get this woman into the car and she was struggling, did you become excited?" Heen asked.

"Well, no, I did not."

"You thought it was not strange?"

"I thought they were just a bunch of friends."

"You thought they were a bunch of friends, and you thought she was drunk, didn't you?"

"That she was moving her arms and struggling."

"And you thought she was drunk, didn't you?"

"I am not sure of that."

"And this is the reason why you did not try to help this woman, because you thought they were friends?"

After an objection by Griffith Wight, which was overruled, Liu said, "I did not pay attention much to that."

No, Heen thought, *I'm sure you didn't. So why,* he wondered, *are you here now offering testimony to support a theory that a white woman was abducted by a group of Oriental, or at least dark-skinned, men?*

"You said you have been in this wholesale fruit and vegetable business for about four years?" Heen asked.

"Three or four."

"And you do a lot of business with the Navy?"

"Yes, we do."

When Griffith Wight took over the questioning again, he tried to defuse the hint of pressure from the Navy tainting Liu's testimony. "Have any naval people come to you and talked to you about what you should say in this case?"

"Not one."

"Weren't you up in Chun Hoon's store the other night with Judge Heen?"

"Yes, sir."

Wight turned and looked at Heen, as if to say, "Take that."

"He called you up there?" Wight asked.

"Yes."

With a self-satisfied smirk, Wight sat down again.

"When I called you up there," Heen said to Liu, "I asked you to tell me what happened down there, and you refused?"

"Yes, sir, I did."

It was Heen's turn to look at his opponent, staring at Wight as he asked his next question. "You refused because Mr. Wight told you, you said, 'Mr. Wight told me not to tell; he told me not to tell anybody.'"

"Yes. He and Mr. Stagbar told me." *That's Detective Stagbar,* Heen thought.

"At that time, I told you I wanted nothing but the truth?" Heen asked.

"Yes, sir."

By the time Roger Liu left the stand, what was left of Griffith Wight's ethics was in tatters.

Charlie Chang and James Low, who had been with Eugenio Batungbacal and Roger Liu that night, also testified, but could provide no additional credible details. On Monday, November 30, the final rebuttal witnesses testified, and then court ended for the day, to resume with closing arguments the following morning.

Chapter Seventeen

Sending the Case to the Jury

"The most damnable thing in the history of the Territory . . ."

Griffith Wight stood before the jury at just past 8:30 on the morning of December 1 to begin his closing argument. The weapons he had at his disposal were the tortured testimony of Thalia Massie, the lies of Horace Ida, the tire tracks that matched Haruya Ida's car and that had probably been created by Captain John McIntosh, and emotion. Facts were his enemy, as was the clock.

His first appeal was to emotion. "This is one of the worst cases we have ever had in the history of Hawaii." Directing the jury to that history, he invoked the Law of the Splintered Paddle, which hearkened back to King Kamehameha, whose life had been spared as a young man when he was part of a military operation on the Big Island of Hawaii. When his party attacked a group of fishermen on a beach, Kamehameha caught his leg in a reef. While he was stranded, one of the men struck him in the head with a paddle that splintered. Had it not splintered, the blow might well have been fatal. But rather than finishing off Kamehameha, the fisherman allowed him to go, an act of kindness that stayed in the king's memory. When that man was later caught and brought before Kamehameha, the king let him go, noting that he had simply been protecting his family. In so doing, Kamehameha proclaimed *"Mamalahoe"*—the Law of the Splintered Paddle, which provided that, as Wight stated it, "Women, little children, and the infirm might have safety on the highways."

And it was Thalia Massie, he thundered, who deserved that safety, that protection from "lust-sodden beasts." The defendants were not men, they were not boys. "They are more like devils." Continuing to play on the jurors' emotions, he proclaimed that they must accept Thalia's testimony "unless you want to brand this girl as an unmitigated liar."

Turning at last to the one thing he had that might actually have carried any weight, he addressed Horace Ida and his lie about the brown jacket. "Ida told so many stories that you can't believe any of them."

Ignoring completely the timeline that showed it would have been impossible for the Ala Moana Boys to have been where Thalia said they had been at the time she said they had been there, he concluded, in a bit of foreshadowing, "Be men! Put yourselves in the place of the husband of the twenty-year-old girl to whom this has happened. You would want to go down and shoot the men."

With that final emotional plea, he sat down.

When the defense lawyers spoke, they trod lightly on what had happened to Thalia Massie. Unwilling to brand her a liar when she said an attack had occurred, they instead focused, not on whether an attack had happened, but rather on the impossibility that their clients could have been the assailants.

Robert Murakami, the attorney for David Takai, spoke first, agreeing with Wight that a terrible crime had occurred. "We cannot be swayed by our passion and prejudice against the crime itself. It is probably true that Mrs. Massie was assaulted, either by a gang of boys or by a man. We have shown beyond a reasonable doubt that these were not the men who committed the crime."

Murakami then walked through the timeline that had been established by the evidence.

11:30 p.m.: Last time Thalia seen at Ala Wai Inn.

11:30–11:35 p.m.: Time Thalia testified that she left Ala Wai Inn.

12:00 a.m.: Time Thalia first told police she left Ala Wai Inn.

11:30–12:10 a.m.: Witnesses place Ala Moana Boys in or outside of Waikiki Park.

12:10–12:15 a.m: Witnesses place Thalia on John Ena Road.

12:15–12:20 a.m.: Witnesses place Ala Moana Boys driving along Beretania Street.

12:30 a.m.: Witnesses place Ala Moana Boys at Correa home.

12:35–12:40 a.m.: Confrontation between Ala Moana Boys and Peeples.

12:50 a.m.: Thalia picked up on Ala Moana Road.

It didn't matter whether Thalia Massie had left the Ala Wai Inn at 11:35 or midnight, because either way, the timeline didn't work. He pointed out that Mrs. Massie and the defendants had both been seen shortly after midnight, Mrs. Massie at about 12:10 or 12:15 on John Ena Road, and the defendants shortly after midnight leaving Waikiki Park. Regardless of what anyone thought about the testimony of Tuts Matsumoto and those in the car with him, or of the people from the Correa luau, the Boys were positively placed at King and Liliha Streets, involved in an altercation with Agnes Peeples, at 12:35—a good twelve-minute drive from Waikiki Park. That meant that the assault, if it had been perpetrated by the defendants, had to have occurred in its entirety between 12:10 at the earliest, and 12:23 at the latest. That allowed thirteen minutes, at most, to abduct Thalia, drive her to the old animal quarantine station on Ala Moana Road, drag her from the car, and rape her five or six times—six, if you believed Thalia's testimony that Henry Chang went twice.

"Is that humanly possible?" Murakami asked.

Following Robert Murakami, who spoke for slightly more than thirty minutes, as had Griffith Wight, William Pittman strode to the lectern. Speaking with his southern accent, Pittman hammered not only on the mishandling of the investigation by the police, but also the mishandling of evidence and cover-up by the prosecution. The latter was a pointed attack at the conduct of Griffith Wight, who had been implicated at virtually every stage of ethical misconduct.

"This is a frame-up!" he shouted at the jury. "The most damnable thing in the history of the Territory is the fact that the prosecutor and police withheld from the defense the information they had. It was just as much their duty to shield innocent men as to find the guilty ones."

His voice rising to fever pitch, the jurors hanging on every word, he bellowed, "You cannot, if you are honest and upright men, convict these men, but you must, on your manhood, be brave and fearless and acquit them, and do it promptly. If you convict them, you have got to have no conscience, you have got to have no soul, you have got to be cowardly."

The last lawyer to argue was the one who had handled the lion's share of questioning for the defense, Bill Heen. He stood and paced before the jury, speaking without notes. "I do not intend to leave a stone unturned in my endeavor to prevent five innocent boys from being railroaded to jail."

He then launched an attack on the prosecution's case, point by point—not only on evidence that was introduced, but also on evidence that was not. "Where is the man who followed Mrs. Massie down John Ena Road? There can be no question but what that white man who was following the woman that night could have explained what happened there. The police were diligent in the case but that man had not been produced. Why wasn't he found?"

He paused and watched the jury, his eyes roaming from man to man, as if expecting an answer. "Where did Mrs. Massie get her liquor, if she was sober when she left the Ala Wai Inn and drunk when she got to John Ena Road? That is a mystery that should be explained."

Firing rhetorical question after rhetorical question, he even addressed the contradiction as to when she had left the Ala Wai. "She did not pass the stores on John Ena Road until after midnight. Her whereabouts from 11:30 p.m. to 12:10 a.m. is another mystery the prosecution has not explained."

* * *

While Heen argued, Detective John Jardine slipped out of the courtroom. He took a pack of cigarettes from his coat pocket and lit up. He inhaled deeply, then blew smoke out through his nostrils. As much as he hated to admit it, Heen was raising good questions, planting doubts in the minds of the jurors. Thalia Massie, the victim and star witness, had gaps in her testimony that Griffith Wight had not been able to plug, and now Heen was digging away at the edges of those gaps, widening them. It looked to him as if Heen had the prosecution on the ropes. And that meant the credibility of his own police department was being eroded.

Thalia's account of the assault had been hazy, at best, the night of the attack. Of course, given the shock and trauma of that night, who could blame her? What really hurt, though, was that the more she remembered with the passage of time, the more ammunition she gave the defense lawyers to chip away at her credibility. Now her hazy account from two months ago seemed to be etched with clarity, as her memory had grown stronger with each passing week. That didn't make sense.

And the testimony about a white woman in a green dress being followed on John Ena Road was particularly troubling—if, of course, that had actually been Thalia Massie. But the jury might believe it was. And they might conclude, as Heen was leading them, that the man who had been following her was actually the person who had beaten her, and that she had concocted the story of being abducted by Hawaiians to appease her husband and divert attention from the white man. The white man who might have been her lover.

As he smoked, he heard the courtroom door open. He turned and nodded at a man who exited and approached him. "I know who the woman in the green dress is," the man said.

* * *

At five o'clock that afternoon, following a two-hour break while Judge Steadman met with the lawyers, the jury reassembled in the jury box. "Something has come up," the judge said, "that is wholly unexpected. We may have some further evidence, but we do not know that yet."

After explaining that it was very unusual to break up closing argument and bring in new evidence, he told them he would not sequester them overnight, and that they could go to their homes "with the particular request that you do not read the newspapers, that you do not discuss this case, or permit anyone else to discuss it in your presence. A high obligation rests upon you, and I trust you to fulfill it faithfully."

On the morning of Wednesday, December 2, Griffith Wight called George McClellan to the stand. After establishing that McClellan worked for the Army Air Corps at Luke Field, on Ford Island, Wight established that he and his wife at been at the dance at Waikiki Park the night of September 12, and that they left immediately after it ended. From the park, they walked to a saimin stand on John Ena Road, near Kalakaua, and after finishing, they walked toward the ocean on John Ena, toward the direction of a second saimin stand, which they passed on their way to their home on nearby Kalia Road.

"How was your wife dressed?" Wight asked.

"Green evening dress."

The dress was introduced into evidence and marked as Prosecution's Exhibit M.

"What did you wear?"

"These pants, a blue sweater, and a white shirt."

"Those trousers that you have on?" Wight asked, pointing at McClellan's dark pants.

"Yes."

After McClellan left the witness stand, Wight addressed Judge Steadman. "I move that we now adjourn to go to Tripler General Hospital in automobiles so that the wife of Mr. McClellan may be interviewed."

Court was adjourned and the jurors piled into cars that had been provided, and testimony resumed in the hospital room of Mrs. McClellan, with jurors, judge, lawyers, bailiff, and court reporter crowded inside. George McClellan stood beside his wife, who sat in a wheelchair next to her hospital bed. Three rebuttal witnesses remained outside in the waiting area, summoned there at the request of Bill Heen.

After the witness was sworn in, she confirmed her husband's story and identified her green dress in response to questions from Griffith Wight.

"You know what time you left that saimin stand?" Wight asked.

"Ten after twelve."

"How do you know that?"

"I looked at the clock when we stood up to leave."

"How did you walk away from the place?"

"I started off, and my husband stopped a minute to pay the bill, and then he followed."

"During the rest of the trip, where was he?"

"Mainly in back of me. Near the corner, he started to walk alongside of me, and we kept on together."

"What corner was that?"

"The corner going down Ala Moana Road?"

"The corner that leads down to Fort DeRussey?"

"Yes."

Wight looked at Heen, who had a troubled look on his face. Wight smiled. "Up to that time, he was walking behind you?"

"Most of the time."

"Had you had any trouble, you and your husband, that night?"

"We had a little quarrel that night."

"Anything of any moment?"

"No."

"How did you carry your head?" Wight lifted his chin, and said, "Like that?" Then he lowered his chin and looked toward the floor. "Or like this?"

"I usually have a habit of hanging my head when I walk, looking down when I walk."

And just like that, Griffith Wight had a plausible explanation for the woman in green walking down John Ena Road at 12:10—and it wasn't Thalia Massie.

When Wight finished, he passed the witness to Bill Heen, who said, "No questions." He then addressed the court bailiff. "Mr. Bailiff, will you call Mr. and Mrs. Goeas in here, please, and Miss Aramaki."

The bailiff left, and returned a moment later with the Goeases and Alice Aramaki, who had been waiting in the hallway. They entered the room nervously, as if unsure why they were there.

Heen pointed at Mrs. McClellan in the wheelchair, and said, "Will you look at her, please, Mr. and Mrs. Goeas and Miss Aramaki?"

All three turned their attention toward the woman in the bed. After a long moment of silence, Heen said, "That is all."

* * *

Back at the courtroom, Heen called George Goeas to the stand.

"Just a little while ago at the Tripler General Hospital at Fort Shafter, do you recall being brought into a room there to look at a lady who was sitting in a wheelchair?" Heen asked.

"Yes."

"Have you seen that lady before?"

"Seen her many times."

"With whom?"

"Seen her with her husband."

"Do you know her husband's name?"

"McClellan."

"How long have you known this man McClellan?"

"I have seen him about, oh, about two years now. Seen him at the football games."

Goeas went on to explain that he was not personally acquainted with McClellan, but had often seen him keeping score, keeping time, and officiating at barefoot football games. He also saw him officiating at boxing matches, and had seen him on occasion, with his wife, at dances at Waikiki Park.

"And if you had seen Mr. and Mrs. McClellan come down the street that night while you were driving off on your automobile toward the saimin stand, while you were there at the saimin stand, would you have recognized Mr. and Mrs. McClellan?"

"Yes."

"This man and woman whom you saw walking down John Ena Road on the night of September twelfth this year, or early Sunday morning September thirteenth this year, was that couple Mr. and Mrs. McClellan?"

"They were not."

Mrs. Goeas agreed with her husband that the couple she saw walking on John Ena Road that night had not been the McClellans. Alice Aramaki, who did not know who the McClellans were, followed Mrs. Goeas to the stand.

Heen said, "Now, you already told us that on the night or early the morning of Sunday, September thirteenth of this year you saw a lady and a man pass by your store while you were standing in front of your store. Now, that lady that you saw walking down John Ena Road at that time, how does she compare in size with this lady you saw this morning in the wheelchair?"

"Different."

"She was a larger one, this lady you saw this morning or the lady you saw Sunday morning?"

"The one I seen down John Ena Road."

"Was larger?"

"Yes."

Heen looked at the judge. "No more questions."

* * *

The case went to the jury at a little before nine o'clock that Wednesday night, a rather unorthodox time to submit a case to a jury. Then again, this had been a rather unorthodox case from the start.

Throngs crowded the lawn outside the courthouse, most expecting a fast verdict of guilty to be rendered by the jury, but at midnight, Judge Steadman dismissed the jurors, who were transported to the Hotel Blaisdell for the night. They started again fresh the next morning. At ten o'clock that second night, a message was sent to the judge: we are hopelessly deadlocked. But Judge Steadman refused to declare a mistrial, and they resumed their deliberations again Friday morning.

Although the judge had ordered all ballots be destroyed, a rumor began to circulate as noon drew nigh on Friday that, after multiple ballots, the vote now stood at eleven to one for conviction. Around noon, the jury rebuffed the efforts of the bailiff to take them to lunch. Moments later, the lawyers, who were waiting in the courtroom, as well as the throng who had gathered in the rotunda downstairs, had their attention drawn to noises coming from the jury room. Raised voices and sounds of furniture being dragged across the floor.

The bailiff burst into Judge Steadman's chambers. The judge looked up sharply, upset at the sudden intrusion.

"Judge, we've got a problem in the jury room."

Without further prompting, Steadman leapt to his feet. "Bring me Wight and Heen."

While the bailiff went to fetch the lawyers, Steadman waited nervously. A minute later, Wight and Heen appeared at his door.

"Sounds like there are some mighty mad folks in there," Heen said.

"Follow me," Judge Steadman replied.

He led the two lawyers and his bailiff down the hallway to the jury room. There were still shouts and yells, as well as clapping hands and scraping and scuffling sounds from inside.

"Unlock it," Steadman said.

The bailiff inserted a key in the lock, turned it, and pushed the door open. The judge and lawyers were stunned by the sight they saw. Chairs had been pulled away from the table, making a clearing on one side. While most of the jurors had their coats off, two of them had also removed their shirts. About ten or fifteen feet apart, they circled each other, fists raised, like prizefighters in a ring. All the jurors turned and looked at the judge standing in the doorway. Steadman couldn't see any bruises or blood on the two men in their undershirts, but apparently the opening bell had simply not yet been rung.

"What in blazes is going on here?" the judge demanded.

Each of the pugilists pointed at other. "He called me a bastard," one of them said.

Before the other could respond, the judge said in a calm voice, "Put your shirts back on and sit down."

As the men shirted up, the other jurors pulled chairs back to the table and sat down. When the two combatants had joined them, they all looked expectantly at Judge Steadman, as if awaiting a lecture.

Steadman stood at the end of the table, flanked by Heen and Wight. "Gentlemen," he said, still in a calm voice, "I understand that in a long and difficult case like this, patience can sometimes go out the window and feelings can get rubbed raw. That's just normal human reaction. But you have a duty here that goes beyond whatever your personal feelings might be about the case, about the parties, or even about each other. The whole world is watching Hawaii right now, and you have an obligation to keep your emotions in check and to calmly weigh the evidence."

He paused and looked around the room, making eye contact with each juror. "Am I understood?"

Nods and mumbled *yes, sir*s met his question.

"All right, then," he said, "I think it would be a good idea if you have lunch now. Sometimes hunger is as big a culprit as anything when tempers flare."

It wasn't until many hours later, and still no word from the jury that a verdict had been reached, that Bill Heen advised the judge, "I'd like to make a motion on the record."

"Proceed."

"Your Honor, we move that you declare a mistrial. The jury has already been out for days and now it has reached the point, after a prolonged session engaged in deliberating upon its verdict, it has reached a point where at least two jurors have shown by their actions that they were about to resort to physical force. That suggests to me that at least some of the jurors are no longer relying on the process of reasoning in determining their verdict in this case. On behalf of all of the defendants, I move that, in light of the facts stated, the jury be called in from the jury room and discharged, and that a mistrial be entered."

"Motion opposed," Griffith Wight said.

"Motion overruled," Steadman said immediately. "The commotion transpired in the presence of Mr. Heen without objection from him and nothing more has happened now, twenty-two hours later. Since that time, the jury has asked for evidence, indicating to the court that it is still considering evidence and, moreover, since the jury has not indicated to the court it's unable to agree, and there's no reason to believe that the altercation has not been smoothed out, the motion is denied." He paused for a moment then added, "I believe it was a momentary flare-up occasioned by a word."

* * *

On Sunday, December 6, Judge Steadman assembled the lawyers and their clients in the courtroom at ten o'clock at night. Also assembled in the packed court were members of the press, a few locals, and a large group of military officers and enlisted men, painting over half the spectator seats white. At the very front, behind the prosecution table, sat Grace Fortescue and her daughters, Helene and Thalia, alongside Admiral Yates Stirling. Conspicuously absent was Tommie Massie, who was still at sea on maneuvers. Sitting behind the defense table were the Ala Moana Boys, with their families in the rows directly behind them. All eyes were on the jurors as they filed into the jury box and took their seats.

"Ladies and gentlemen," Judge Steadman said, "it has now been ninety-seven hours since the jury began its deliberations. Last night, I delivered to them what is called an *Allen* charge, which is an instruction to put aside differences and, if jurors can do so in good conscience, to reach common ground. I have now been informed by the members of the jury that they are unable to do so and that they are hopelessly deadlocked. Based upon that, I have no choice but to declare a mistrial."

The courtroom suddenly erupted in chaos. Unable to contain themselves, Ben and Horace rushed to the jury box and began shaking hands with jurors, most of whom appeared bemused at the gesture. The other defendants exchanged handshakes with their lawyers and hugs with their families.

Grace sprang to her feet and bellowed at the judge over the babble of voices. "Your Honor, you must at least keep these animals in jail until they can be tried again. It's your duty."

"Mrs. Fortescue, the law only allows me to deny bail for capital offenses," Steadman said. He had to raise his voice to be heard. "The previously set bail terms still apply."

"You mean you'll just turn them loose?" Beside Grace, Thalia began to wail.

"Madam, I have no choice."

Grace clutched Thalia in her arms. Led by Admiral Stirling and several sturdy sailors, the Fortescue women struggled their way out of the courtroom.

PART THREE

A DEATH IN THE ISLANDS

Chapter Eighteen
Somewhere Over the Pali
"The Shame of Honolulu"

If a tie in football is like kissing your sister, then imaginations can run wild on a metaphor for a hung jury, especially after ninety-seven hours. The boiling racial unrest that percolated beneath the surface now threatened to erupt like the volcanoes that had given birth to the Hawaiian Islands themselves. The native population exulted in the non-conviction as a temporary victory of justice—at least until a retrial could be held—while the white minority used the verdict as an excuse to fan the flames and coax the lava of hatred to the surface. As Admiral Stirling informed the members of the press, while standing outside the courts building with Thalia and Grace, "If anyone has any doubts what this verdict is about, he only has to look at the makeup of the jury. Seven jurors of Hawaiian or Oriental extraction, five whites. If you were to ask the jurors their votes, I'd stake my admiralship that you would find seven not-guilties and five guilties." The actual final vote, as it turned out, was six to six. Facts be damned!

"What will the Navy do?" a reporter asked.

Stirling pursed his lips, a look of outrage on his face, as if the answer was obvious. "The Navy will do whatever it has to do to protect its men and their wives. If that means canceling all shore leaves, perhaps even canceling war games scheduled in the upcoming months—well, the merchants will just have to live without those customers."

The unspoken boycott of local businesses, with the financial losses it would create, hung heavy in the air. For some in the audience, the threat seemed real. To others, it was the petulant adult version of "I'm going to take my ball and go home."

"Is that really necessary in order to protect Navy wives?" another reporter asked. Left unspoken was the question, "Don't your men have guns?"

"It's necessary to protect these animals that have been set loose," Stirling said.

The reporter who asked the question seemed taken aback. Was Stirling really concerned about the Ala Moana Boys? "How so?" the reporter asked.

"Should our military personnel feel the need to take justice into their own hands—well, there's not much I can do about that."

There it was: yes, they do have guns. And who was a mere admiral to stop their use? It was as if he had just given authorization to the entire Navy for that very thing. Years later, in his memoir, Stirling wrote: "The trial in my opinion and many others was a stupid miscarriage of justice which could have been avoided if the Territorial Government had shown more inclination to sympathize with my insistence upon the necessity of a conviction."

On Saturday, December 12, the *Honolulu Times*, a tabloid newspaper, hit the streets with a banner headline: "The Shame of Honolulu." This was a play on Lincoln Steffens' scathing collection of muckraking articles on municipal corruption, *The Shame of the Cities*, published in 1904. Setting a match to the fuse, the paper's founder, Edward Irwin, ran a front-page editorial that spoke of *kanakas* run amuck, seeking *haole* women upon whom to prey. The issue also included pages of past stories from all of Honolulu's newspapers that recounted reports and rumors of crimes committed by natives, bearing sensationalistic headlines of Irwin's own creation. "Lock up your wives and daughters," it implied, "or the dark-skinned bogeyman will get 'em."

In addition to its normal circulation in Honolulu, Irwin printed up extra copies of the paper, which he strategically delivered to naval posts on the island, including Pearl Harbor. Distributed free of charge, he placed a stamp on the edition that said, "Compliments of a Navy Man on Duty." He might as well have cried "fire" in a crowded theater.

And it had its desired effect. Thoroughly outraged by the paper's innuendo and half-truths, and whipped into a mass frenzy, hundreds of Navy men roamed the streets of the city, armed and on the prowl for the savages who threatened their white women. They had been released from their barracks before word could reach them that Admiral Stirling had canceled all shore leave, although it was an open question as to whether the admiral had been deliberately belated in issuing the order. Roving packs of military vigilantes sought out natives to assault, delivering their own brand of justice. By the end of the day, the police were called out to respond to at least eight riot calls, all involving brawls between military personnel and non-*haoles*. Concerned for the safety of the Ala Moana Boys, the Honolulu police sent radio cars to guard them, but all of them were absent from their homes.

Shortly before 10 p.m. that night, Horace Ida stood with a group of friends outside a speakeasy on Kukui Street, enjoying his freedom and the good-natured ribbing of his buddies. He was vaguely aware of the violence that was sweeping through the city, but found it hard to believe there was truly a realistic threat to his well-being. Then again, he had never dreamed he would be hauled before a jury to answer to rape charges, either. His mother and sisters begged him not to go out that evening, but denial and poor judgment led him to that street corner while the entire United States Navy was hell-bent on taking revenge on him and the four other defendants.

Hawaiianized Christmas music floated out from inside the speakeasy, in sharp contrast to the tension on the streets. One of Horace's buddies held up the *Honolulu Times*, its "Shame of Honolulu" headline screaming in Horace's face. "Listen to this, Shorty," he said. Reading in halting English, he continued. "This says that 'women routinely run the risk of being assaulted and foully raped by gangs of lust-mad youths—foul, slimy creatures crawling through the streets and attacking the innocent and the defenseless.'"

He smiled as he read it, but there was no smile on Horace's face. Another of his buddies said, "Hey, Shorty, you a slimy creature, eh, brah? You keep away from my girl, yeah?"

"But we didn't do this thing," Horace said. He was aware as he spoke of a whining tone in his voice, but there was nothing he could do about it. "We weren't even there where it happened."

"That's not what the newspapers say," his prime tormentor replied.

"It's lying."

"Newspapers don't lie."

"They lying now."

"Shorty is a slimy creature."

A deep voice came from the street behind them. "There's one of 'em."

Horace turned at the squeal of brakes. A dark-colored roadster skidded to a stop alongside the sidewalk. Three other cars stopped abruptly behind the first. Horace's heartbeat ticked up a notch. Five men in Navy whites spilled out of the lead car, at least one carrying a revolver. The leader of the vigilante group. The one they called Primo.

Horace's heartbeat went into overdrive, but his feet felt frozen to the pavement. At the sight of the weapon, Horace's friends scattered. He turned to follow, but his feet wouldn't obey. A hand gripped his arm just above the elbow. A spasm of electric shock raced through his body as the sailor's fingers squeezed a nerve. He looked down and saw the tattoo of a dagger on the forearm of the sailor who held him. A gun barrel jammed into his side. Horace glanced down and saw Primo's hand grip the butt of the gun.

A second hand grabbed his other arm. His knees turned to jelly, his feet still locked in place. Two sailors, whom he would later learn were named Lord and Jones, kept him upright, while Primo dug the revolver deeper into his side.

"Come on, mutt," Primo said. "Let's go talk a bit."

Jones, Lord, and Primo dragged Horace to the lead vehicle. Primo removed the gun from his side and opened the door. Jones and Lord forced him into the front seat, then Jones got in beside him. Primo went to the driver's side and got in, one hand on the steering wheel and one on the gun pointed at Horace's side. Others jumped into the backseat, while still others piled into the trailing vehicles. Horace thought back to the trial and Thalia Massie's testimony. She said she had been grabbed and forced into a car with men who meant to do her harm. Men she said included him. And Joe. And Bennie. And Henry. But not David. Never David.

True story or not, Horace felt a hint of sympathy for her. He was now in the same spot she claimed to be in. Would he get away with his life, like she had with hers? Would he see his mother and sisters again? And his friends?

A tear spilled from his eyelid and streaked down his cheek.

The procession of cars headed through the streets of Honolulu, to the outskirts of town, and then onto the road that headed northeast to Nu'uanu Pali. Located along the windward *pali*, or cliffs, of the Ko'olau Mountains, it commanded a majestic view of the Nu'uanu Valley from nearly a thousand feet high, looking north toward the northeast coast of Oahu. It was on the Pali that one of the fiercest battles had been fought in Kamehameha I's effort to unify the Hawaiian Islands, and where one of his most famous victories had been won. By 1795, he had been able to unify the Big Island of Hawaii, with its many chiefs, and turned his sights toward the islands to the west. In February, he assembled an army of more than ten thousand men and set sail in a flotilla of war canoes for Oahu. Invading the island, his army drove Chief Kalanikupule of Oahu and his warriors to the precipice of Nu'uanu Pali. Then over the edge, sending hundreds to their deaths.

Horace was no student of history, but he knew of the battle and what had happened on the Pali. In the hands of a much smaller army, but equally as hostile, he knew he was probably destined to meet the same fate as Kalanikupule's army. Why else would they bring him up here? There were plenty of isolated locations at which to merely administer a beating. The only thing that made sense way up here was the drop. The thousand-foot drop.

The roadster pulled to a stop near the edge of the cliff. There were other cars parked nearby, most likely young lovers on the make, as the Pali was a popular "lover's lane." Through his tears, Horace saw faint lights of homes in the darkness. Too distant to offer rescue, no matter how loud he might yell.

"Why you doing this?" he asked. His voice caught, choked with fear.

An elbow slammed into his cheek. He squeezed his eyes shut at the impact. He felt as if his teeth rattled inside his head.

"Just tell us you did it," a voice growled.

"But we didn't."

Another elbow smashed the back of his head. "Maybe a thousand-foot drop'll refresh your memory," Primo said. "We know you did it."

"We didn't."

Horace was crying now, desperate. He knew that these men, an unofficial jury not made up of his peers, had already found him guilty, had passed sentence, and were now going to mete out his punishment. He had been brought up here so they could beat a confession out of him, but that thought offered no comfort. He was reasonably sure that, if he confessed, they would summarily impose a sentence of death, whether it was a false confession or not. The result would be a headfirst fall into the thousand-foot drop. But if he denied it, he might very well be beaten to death as they tried to pound a confession out of him. His lifeless body would then likely be tossed over the edge, to rot with the bones of the warriors from long ago.

His options were nonexistent. All he had going for him was the faint hope that, somehow, some way, the truth would spare his life. That maybe he could convince them of his innocence and they would let him go, although much worse for the beating he would suffer. He could heal from a beating, but there was finality to death.

A sailor grabbed his arm. Others, from the trailing cars, stood alongside the roadster. One opened the door and pointed to the edge. "Drag him over here."

"I don't know," Jones said. "There's an awful lot of people up here."

The sailors seemed to have noticed, for the first time, the other vehicles at the lover's lane.

"No one knows who we are," another said.

"That's not the point," Primo said. "We need privacy for what we need to do. And we don't need any Good Samaritans getting involved."

"I know where there's a field," a beefy sailor said in a coarse growl. "Other side of the cliff and down below. Won't nobody be there."

"Let's do it," Primo said.

The procession pulled away. Horace didn't know whether to be grateful or not. The prospect of being thrown over the cliff was not welcome, though at least death would be quick, as it had been for Chief Kalanikupule's men. But being beaten to death in a cane field—who knew how long that might take? If he was lucky, he would pass out early.

* * *

The procession of bloodthirsty sailors descended the far side of the mountains, away from Honolulu, before arriving at a flat area that was part of a dairy farm. As promised, there were no vehicles with young lovers and fogged windshields. Just grass, moon, and wind. The cars halted and the men spilled out. Primo grabbed Horace by his elbow and dragged him from the front seat. Horace struggled for footing, but two more hands grabbed hold and pulled harder. His heels dragged the ground. Someone slammed him onto his back. The sailors formed a loose circle around him, like wolves encircling a crippled lamb.

"Get up," Primo said.

Horace rolled over and then got to his knees. Then to his feet.

"Take your shirt off."

Horace unbuttoned his shirt. Over the sounds of the breeze came swishing noises and faint clanks of metal. Belts were being removed. Tears clouded his vision, but he faintly made out images: belts wrapped around fists, belts twirling like lariats, belts cracking like bullwhips. Moonlight glinted off buckles.

Tears spilled from Horace's eyes and rolled down his cheeks. He struggled to catch his breath. A sob escaped as he sucked in air.

"All right, mutt," Lord said. "Just tell us the truth and nothing will happen. But if you lie to us—"

A belt buckle snapped through the air and slammed into Horace's back. The buckle split skin. Horace screamed.

"I told the truth. We didn't do this thing."

Another belt snapped. More tearing flesh as the buckle bit deep. He had never felt pain so intense. It was as if his hide were being flayed by a dull knife.

A belt-wrapped fist crashed into his jaw. He dropped to the ground and curled into the fetal position. He sobbed as he cried for mercy, his words barely discernible. "I swear, we didn't do it. Please, no. Let me go."

Then it seemed as if a dam had burst. Fists swinging, belts snapping, boots kicking. The sailors crowded around the crumpled figure of Horace Ida lying on the ground, like hogs at a feeding trough. There were occasional demands—"Admit it; you did it"—and constant sob-choked denials—"I swear; we didn't do it." He writhed on the ground, trying to protect his head and face, only to leave his torso all the more exposed. Then, when he wrapped his arms around himself to protect his ribs, the sailors switched the target to his head. It was a losing proposition for Horace, yet he persisted in his denials. Soon his words were wholly unintelligible. They were just sobs and cries.

At last, exasperated by Horace's stubbornness, one of the sailors brought the butt of a gun down on his head.

And Horace's writhing and struggling stopped. His body stilled and, for all appearances, his breathing stopped.

"Get him out of sight," Primo said.

Several sailors grabbed Horace by his hands and feet. They dragged him to bushes that lined the side of the road. With little effort, they flung his body into the bushes, as if loading bales of hay onto a wagon. Or tossing out the garbage.

Then the sailors got into their cars and silently disappeared into the night.

* * *

Moonlight illuminated a figure lying curled on the ground next to a clump of bushes. The only sounds were those of the wind rustling leaves and a soft whimpering coming from the figure. His whole body bruised and bloody, Horace Ida struggled to his feet and staggered to the road. He faintly saw headlights approaching.

As the headlights drew closer, he stepped into the road. Waved his arms in the air.

Then collapsed as the car stopped and its driver rushed to his side.

Chapter Nineteen

The Abduction

"Life is a mysterious and exciting affair."

Thalia reclined on the *chaise longue* at her mother's rented house in Manoa, still in her bedclothes, while her mother sipped coffee at the dining table, a newspaper spread before her. Grace had initially lived with Tommie and Thalia at their home on Kahawai Street, but after a few crowded and tense weeks, she found a bungalow a few blocks away at 2754 Kolowalu Street and moved there. With Tommie preparing to go to sea again, Grace insisted that Thalia move in with her and Helene, at least until Tommie's return.

Thalia's state of mind had gone from bad to worse since the trial, as the newspapers had kept not only the trial but the events leading up to it alive. Thalia insisted on reading them all, and her malaise spiraled downward with each new recounting. She also knew of the rumors that swirled around the military bases, the stories of her infidelities, her quarrels with Tommie, and her penchant for tall tales. The jury hadn't believed her—or at least half of them hadn't—so why should anyone else?

Not even Tommie had believed her when she radioed him aboard his submarine to report the verdict. "They let them go, Tommie," she said. Tears filled her eyes and, she hoped, her voice reflected them to her husband. "They didn't believe me, and now people are saying the most horrible things about me."

She paused to allow him to speak. When he didn't, she added, "But you believe me, don't you, Tommie."

After a long silence, he said, "Everything's going to be all right. I'll be home soon."

And now he was home, but he still hadn't answered her question. She knew that he didn't believe her, just as he hadn't believed her that September night, either.

For Grace's part, although she loved her daughter, she was starting to lose patience with Thalia's mood swings and foul temper, but she knew exactly who was to blame for it: those rapists that the judge had let go free. A white woman's life and well-being meant nothing to savages, who were now rewarded by being set free just because their shyster lawyers had distorted the truth enough to hang the jury. A jury that was itself half made up of savages.

Grace slammed her coffee cup down on the table. Its clatter caused Thalia to jump. "Listen to this," Grace said. "The newspaper says that Ida's family is proud of him for not confessing under duress. They say he showed true . . ." She stumbled briefly then phonetically sounded out the Japanese words. ". . . *yamato damashii*. That means 'Japanese spirit.' Like some kind of samurai warrior. Can you imagine that? Comparing a common rapist to a warrior. That's how they grow up to be the way they are, because their families coddle them."

"Oh, he must have confessed, Mama," Thalia said. "From what Tommie told me about what happened to him, I don't think he'd still be alive if he hadn't. That's the only reason they stopped beating him."

"Seems more likely that he wouldn't be alive if he had," Grace said. "Do you really think those sailors would have stopped if he had admitted what he did? Once they knew that, do you think they'd trust a mongrel jury again?"

"They were trying to get a confession out of him that can be used in court, Mama. Not kill him. They must have gotten one and that's why they stopped."

Their conversation ceased as Tommie entered the living room, dressed in his Navy whites. He didn't look at Thalia, who stared straight at him. Grace assumed he felt shame at not having been able to protect his wife—her little girl—and that's why he avoided her gaze.

"I've got to go," Tommie said, "but I just saw Jones pull up outside."

"Tommie," Grace said, exasperation in her voice, "I've told you before, I don't need a bodyguard."

"He's here on Captain Wortman's orders while I'm away on sea duty again. And it's not just you I'm worried about, Grace. I've got to worry about Thalia while I'm away. We've heard rumors on the base that some of Ida's gang are going to bomb our house to get even for what happened to him. Even if they don't, if they get hold of her now, they'll do whatever they have to do to keep her from testifying. I can't let that happen. I've got to protect my wife."

Grace nodded, but said nothing. What she left unsaid, though, was what could have been the end of the sentence: ". . . like you failed to do before."

"So just consider him a visiting relative, Grace. Besides, I hear he's a helluva card player, like you. Maybe you can teach him to play bridge. Just don't play for money."

Tommie opened the front door before their guest could knock. A short, muscular man in civilian clothes stood on the *lanai*. He wore his brown hair somewhat longish and swept back, with a part in the middle. His face showed miles of wear and his smile stopped short of his eyes. He had spent more than a decade in the Navy, much of it in the Far East. In his spare time, he trained the boxing team at Pearl Harbor. In fact, he was quite proficient with his own fists as well. On one forearm, he wore a tattoo of a naked woman that ran nearly from elbow to wrist; the other boasted a dagger of roughly the same length. His only jewelry was an oversized gold ring featuring a dragon's head.

"Am I on time?" the man asked.

"On the dot," Tommie said. "Come on in."

The man nodded coolly at Thalia, who returned his nod. Grace put down her newspaper and took stock of the newcomer. She was instantly taken by his blue-collar appearance and I-bow-to-no-man arrogance. Just what the doctor ordered. She remained seated as Tommie brought the newcomer to her.

"Grace," Tommie said, "May I present Machinists' Mate Albert O. Jones. But everybody calls him Deacon."

He paused then looked to Jones. "Deacon, this is Mrs. Grace Fortescue of Long Island, New York."

"Pleased to meet you, Mrs. Fortescue," Jones said. He bowed slightly and pulled his lips back in a toothy smile. His eyes locked with hers. Eyes that bespoke strength. She knew instantly that this was a man she could trust, who would do whatever he had to do.

And an instant bond was formed.

* * *

Over the course of the next few weeks, Grace and her new friend Deacon Jones quickly became card-playing buddies and almost inseparable companions. Grace taught him bridge while he taught her poker. They whiled away many an hour over cards, but virtually every conversation sooner or later drifted back to the impending retrial for the Ala Moana Boys, the confession—or non-confession—of Horace Ida, and the worry about when an attack by Ida's gang would occur.

When Tommie went away for sea duty, he left his .45 revolver with Thalia, but that wasn't enough for Grace, even with Deacon Jones on guard.

"Deacon, do you really think one gun is enough protection for three ladies left on their own?" Grace asked shortly after Tommie's departure.

"You're not left on your own. You've got me."

"Yes, but there's just one of you and three of us. And an island full of savages out there."

"Well, I just bought a new Colt .32 at W. W. Diamond Company. If you'd like, I can take you there."

Grace agreed, and so by the time Tommie returned home, she was the proud owner of an Iver Johnson .32—the same weapon that had been used to assassinate President William McKinley in 1901—and Thalia had a .22 of her own. Nothing like a well-armed naval family.

* * *

Christmas came and went, as did New Year's, and 1932 dawned. Despite repeated visits by Grace to the chambers of Judge Alva Steadman, there had been no progress in getting the retrial set. Talk ramped up about whether one would occur at all, much less when. And, if it did, what could be done differently this time to ensure a different result? Following that theme, one of Grace's conversations with Jones took a dark turn one evening shortly after Tommie's return.

Jones was no longer stationed at Grace's home, but he maintained patrols and a vigil in Manoa, keeping a keen eye out for the safety of the women. He even stopped by from time to time for a game of bridge and to keep up the friendly relationship he had developed with Grace. The first week of January, as Tommie watched from a nearby chair, Grace and Jones teamed up against their usual bridge-playing opponents, Thalia and Helene. Grace quickly retreated to her default conversation topic.

"I keep reading in the papers that this Ida fellow's family still says he never confessed," she said. "It's the same thing, time after time. Why don't they just let it drop?"

"That's part of why I asked Deacon to stop by tonight," Tommie said. "We've got some thoughts on trying to get a confession."

"You mean another confession," Jones said. He leaned forward at the table and, in a conspiratorial whisper, said, "Because I can assure you that Ida confessed, all right."

"You never told me that," Tommie said. "How do you know?"

"I heard it with my own ears."

"Oh, Tommie," Thalia said, "do you hear that?" Her tone suggested vindication. His frown in response suggested disbelief.

"You were there?" Grace asked. "When Ida was beaten?"

"Just serving my country, ma'am," Jones said.

"Why haven't you told the authorities?" Thalia asked. "This is exactly what we need: a confession."

"It's not quite that easy," Tommie said. "I talked to Eugene Beebe and he said—"

"Who?" Grace asked.

"The lawyer who worked with the prosecutor on the case. From the private law firm. Anyway, he said even if Ida had confessed—"

"I'm telling you, he confessed," Jones said.

"Nevertheless, it wouldn't stand up in court. Beebe said Ida's lawyers would start flashing those pictures around in front of the jury of Ida all beat up, and they'd say he only confessed because he was tortured."

"So a confession doesn't mean anything?" Jones asked.

"Not one like that," Tommie said. "Beebe said we'd have to get one without leaving a mark on whoever confessed."

"So we grab Ida again and—"

"Not Ida," Tommie said. "They'd still wave those pictures around even if we didn't touch him this time. Besides, I hear he never confessed—"

"I say he did," Jones said.

"I'm just telling you what I heard. And I don't suppose you want to get on the stand and swear that you helped beat a confession out of him."

Jones's silence provided Tommie his answer. "So we need to get it from one of the others," Tommie said. "And we'd have to get him to confess where it would just be his word against ours, and with not one blessed bruise to support his story."

"I don't care what we have to do. We must get another confession," Grace said. Her tone left no room for dissent. "My daughter's reputation is being dragged through the mud by these animals, and I'll not stand for it."

"I hear the big *kanaka* is the one most likely to crack," Tommie said. "Major Ross says he thinks Kahahawai will give it up without too much pressure. He swaggers around like a bully, but I hear it's all show."

"So how do we get him to confess?" Grace asked.

"I've been thinking about that," Tommie said, "and I've got an idea. The first thing we've got to do, though, is find out what time he reports to his probation officer at the courts building. I understand that Judge Steadman makes all of them do that every day, but each of them at different times."

"I think I can find that out easily enough," Grace said. "I've developed a pretty good relationship with Mrs. Whitmore, the court clerk."

"Okay." Tommie turned to Jones. "Can you get someone else to help us?"

"I know just the man."

"Okay. Then here's the plan."

* * *

January 6–7, 1932

Grace stopped by the Judiciary Building on Wednesday morning to plot out the logistics. Her careful eye took in the locations of the clock, the front entrance to the building, the traffic circle, and the statue of King Kamehameha. While there, she spoke with the court clerk, who confirmed that the Ala Moana Boys reported separately, starting with Joe Kahahawai each morning at 8 a.m. From there, Grace stopped by the offices of the *Honolulu Star-Bulletin* and obtained a newspaper clipping with a clear photograph of Kahahawai.

While Grace was doing her part, Tommie met up with Deacon Jones at Pearl Harbor, who introduced him to twenty-one-year-old Edward Lord, a fireman first class and member of Jones's boxing team. Lord, a jaunty, fresh-faced fellow, was more than happy to assist. He had been as outraged by what had happened to Mrs. Massie as had Jones, and Jones vouched for the trustworthiness of his boxing team member.

The next morning, Grace sat in her Durant roadster in front of the Judiciary Building and patiently waited while each of the Ala Moana Boys appeared, entered through the main entrance, then came back out shortly after entering. After a two-and-a-half hour wait, she knew exactly which boy reported at what time. Kahahawai was the first each day, at eight o'clock. If tomorrow was to be anything like that day was, he would be on time.

At roughly three o'clock, Tommie drove Jones and Lord to the Army-Navy YMCA, where they changed into their civilian clothes, and then on to Grace's house for the final preparations. Grace, working with scissors, paste, and a newspaper, put the finishing touches on a prop needed to carry out their plan. By the time they went to bed, the scheme was ready for execution.

* * *

January 8, 1932

On Friday morning, Esther Anito, a heavyset Hawaiian woman, sat on a rickety chair in the tiny kitchen of her hovel of a house and sewed the last of the buttons onto a man's blue shirt. Located on Kukui Street in one of the worst tenements of Honolulu, the house might have been small, but it was neat and tidy. Esther kept it with pride, just as she sewed the buttons with pride. She didn't believe for one minute the terrible things that had been said about her Joseph, and she was determined that, when he went to meet with his probation officer, he would look neat and respectable. Clothes make the man, she believed.

Bare-chested and muscular, Joe Kahahawai leaned against the wall by a cast iron stove and waited patiently. After a while, though, his patience was outstripped by the tedium of his mother's sewing.

"Mama, I got to hurry. Mr. Dixon don't like it if I'm late."

"Just a minute longer." She made a few last passes, then bit the thread in two with her teeth and tied off a knot. She handed it to Joe. "I think I heard Eddie outside a few minutes ago," she said. "He's waiting for you."

"Thanks, Mama." He slipped into the shirt, muscles straining against the worn fabric, and buttoned it up the front. "The buttons look good, Mama." He grabbed a brown cloth cap from a hook and put it on. Then he leaned over and kissed Esther on the top of the head.

"When you come home, I fix you something good to eat for lunch," she said.

"I love you, Mama." Then he hustled out the door to meet up with his cousin, Eddie Uli'i, who had promised to accompany him to his appointment.

Esther watched as the two set off together. Her heart was heavy for the burden it bore. Joseph was a good boy, not a rapist. Not a savage. Not an animal.

* * *

Fireman First Class Edward Lord pulled Grace's blue Durant Roadster to the side of the traffic circle in front of the Judiciary Building and put the car in park. Grace sat in the backseat and clutched her cloth handbag in her lap with both hands. Pinned to the outside of the handbag was the folded newspaper clipping, with the face of Joe Kahahawai on the exposed side. Although she had seen plenty of Kahahawai at the trial, and had even seen him the day before, she needed to be sure they got the right man. All these dark-skinned savages looked pretty much alike.

Neither Lord nor Grace said a word. Grace had not bonded with Lord as she had with Jones, and Lord couldn't quite identify with Grace and her upper-crust attitude. All that held them together that morning was a shared desire to see justice done—justice as they defined it, based upon their own conceptions of the facts.

At eight o'clock on the dot, Kahahawai and Eddie Uli'i walked up the sidewalk, turned toward the main entrance, and disappeared inside the building. Grace glanced at the newspaper photo as Kahahawai passed by, then stared at his back until he was inside. Still without a word being exchanged, Grace got out of the Roadster and walked purposefully to the front of the building, but stepped off the sidewalk near a wall. She pulled back into shadows and waited. She glanced across the way, to the other side of the Judiciary Building, where Deacon Jones stood by the circular driveway. Jones wore a dark blue suit. He had one hand in his coat pocket and patted his breast pocket with the other. He nodded at Grace, who nodded back and then pulled deeper into the shadows.

After a few minutes, Kahahawai and Uli'i exited the building. They chatted and laughed, oblivious, it seemed to Grace, to the pain Kahahawai had caused her family. But not for long. Neither man noticed Grace standing beside the doorway. She glanced at the newspaper photo again, as if the image of the savage wasn't already burned into her brain. With a less than subtle gesture, she looked at Jones and pointed directly at Kahahawai's back. Jones moved into action.

He drifted from his position on the sidewalk to intercept the two Hawaiians as they rounded the circular driveway. He stepped directly in front of Kahahawai. As he did, Eddie glanced back over his shoulder at the Judiciary Building. In the shadows near the front door he saw a *haole* woman standing rigidly, her arm extended, index finger pointed at Joe. He turned back just as the man in the dark suit stopped them.

"Hold on there," the man said.

As he spoke, a dark blue Buick sedan pulled to a stop next to them in the driveway. Behind the wheel sat Tommie Massie, wearing a chauffeur's hat and goggles, hiding his features. Neither Hawaiian seemed to pay any attention to the Buick, so focused were they on the man before them.

Jones pulled a folded page from his pocket, grabbed Joe by the arm, and thrust the paper in his face. "Major Ross wants to see you."

Joe's eyes widened in recognition. Gordon Ross, who had just been appointed to head the Territorial Police, had been his old leader when he served in the National Guard. But why would Major Ross want to see him?

"Get in the car," the man said. He kept waving the paper in Joe's face.

"What is this?" Joe asked.

"This is a summons."

Joe unfolded the document. Sure enough, the paper looked official. It bore the heading "TERITORIAL POLICE, MAJOR ROSS COMMANDING," complete with the misspelling of territorial, compliments of Grace Fortescue. It billed itself as a "SUMMONS TO APPEAR" naming "KAHAHAWAI—JOE," but all Joe could make out was the name of his old National Guard leader and his own name. Had he had time and been able to study the page, he would have seen that the words in the middle had actually been clipped from a newspaper. Far from containing any official legal language, it, instead, contained these almost nonsensical words: "Life is a mysterious and exciting affair, and anything can be a thrill if you know how to look for it and what to do with opportunity when it comes."

He might also have seen that the seal, which looked official, had no reference to the Territorial Police or any other authority in the Territory of Hawaii. Instead, it was a seal that had been cut from a diploma given to Tommie Massie after completing a three-month course at the Chemical Warfare School in Edgewood, Maryland.

Still, it looked like a summons to Joe. Given his legal troubles, and his newfound perpetual state of befuddlement as to what was happening to him, he concluded that it was not out of the realm of possibility that Major Ross did, in fact, want to see him.

Jones opened the door to the Buick. He put the "summons" back in his pocket. When Joe hesitated, Jones produced a .32 from his coat pocket and stuck it in Joe's ribcage. "Get in the car."

Joe froze for a moment. His mind churned. What in the hell was going on? He turned to his cousin and said, "Eddie, you go wit' us."

Jones forced Joe into the backseat and quickly slid in beside him. He slammed the door before Eddie could get in. As Eddie watched, the Buick pulled away with his cousin inside. Another car, a Durant Roadster, followed. He wasn't sure, but it looked like the woman who had pointed at Joe rode in the backseat.

The cars turned right and went up King Street, and then Eddie lost sight of them. What was going on? Joe had just come from his probation officer. Why did he now have to go see Major Ross? Unless Major Ross, who knew and liked Joe, wanted to help. But if he wanted to help, why was a summons necessary? And why did the man in the blue suit have a gun? Something was wrong, but he couldn't quite put his finger on it.

Then it hit him: Major Ross's office was next to Iolani Palace, in the armory building. Right across the street from the Judiciary Building. You didn't have to drive a car to go to Major Ross's office. Not even white people were that lazy. He wondered if the men who had taken Shorty Ida had also told him he was going to see Major Ross before they drove him across the Pali and beat him half to death.

Eddie turned and sprinted back to the Judiciary Building.

* * *

Mary Ann Malu'ihi, a middle-aged *kanaka* known to everyone in her Manoa neighborhood as Aunty Mary Ann, was on her hands and knees, tending to her flower garden at her house on Kolowalu Street. She painstakingly extracted any weed that dared show its head above ground. One of the best things about Hawaii was that you could stick almost any plant in the ground and it would grow. But that meant weeds as well as flowering plants. Her house might not be much, but it was hers, and she was determined to keep it immaculate.

She heard the sound of a vehicle approaching from down the street, slowing at the house across the street shared by Grace Fortescue and her youngest daughter. The day that Mrs. Fortescue had moved in, Aunty Mary Ann carried a basket of island fruit to her front *lanai* as a welcome gift, only to have the door slammed in her face.

Aunty Mary Ann leaned back on her heels and wiped sweat from her brow. A dark-colored Buick sedan turned into the driveway of the Fortescue house and disappeared behind a hedge. She had seen the car before, so she attached no significance to it. She leaned forward on her knees again and dug at the next offending weed. She heard, but paid no mind to, another vehicle approaching a few minutes later.

Then, out of the corner of her eye, she saw a Durant Roadster turn into the driveway across the street. Mrs. Fortescue's car.

The bitch was home.

* * *

Joe felt a rivulet of perspiration stream down his chest. Drops ran along his ribs, tickling him. His pale blue shirt, with the buttons newly sewn on by his mother, had turned dark blue and clung to his torso as if glued on. The goggles on the driver didn't fool him. He knew that the man behind the wheel was the husband of the woman who had accused him and his friends of attacking her. The woman who had accused him of punching her in the face and breaking her jaw. The woman who had accused him of raping her.

It had long since become clear that they weren't going to Major Ross's office, and he also felt pretty sure that Major Ross didn't live in Manoa. He didn't know the identity of the man in the dark suit. Massie had called him Jones, but he didn't need to know who he was in order to understand his plight. An outraged husband—a Navy man—behind the wheel and a man with a gun, also likely a Navy man, were taking him to a strange house in a neighborhood he had never visited. But to do what? To exact revenge? To kill him? Or to try to beat the truth out of him like that group of sailors had done to Shorty?

If it was to kill him, he was already as good as dead. But if it was to beat a confession out of him, he faced a dangerous choice. To confess would likely be to sign his own death warrant. But to hold out would prolong his torture until . . . until what? Until he died? Would he be able to convince them that he had already told the truth and then they would let him go? No, he didn't think so. These men would not believe anything other than a confession that he and the others had beaten and raped the woman, whether it was true or not. Shorty had held out. Shorty had gotten lucky. Could he hold out and, if so, would he be as lucky?

As the Buick turned into a driveway, he saw a woman across the street working in her flower garden. A *kanaka* woman. He had always thought this was a neighborhood for *haoles* and the military, so what was a *kanaka* woman doing here? Unless, of course, she was simply hired help.

If he could see her, could she see him? And if so, would she wonder what two *haoles* were doing bringing a *kanaka* to this place? Would it strike her as strange? Strange enough to call someone?

She glanced only briefly at the Buick, then went back to her yardwork. He lost sight of her as the Buick pulled past a row of hedges and came to a stop next to the side of the house.

"What we doing here?" Joe asked. "Where is Major Ross?"

"Major Ross is inside," Massie said. "He's waiting to talk to you."

But Joe already knew one thing for sure: regardless of what Massie said, wherever Major Ross was, it was most assuredly not here.

Both Navy men got out of the Buick. Jones grabbed Joe by the arm and dragged him out. He kept the barrel of the revolver pressed into his ribcage as he jerked him toward the house. "Inside," Jones said.

Massie opened a side door to the bungalow and entered while Jones forced Joe in behind him. Then Jones entered and closed the door.

The two Navy men pushed Joe into a room at the front of the house, a parlor or living room. Joe couldn't be sure. Houses in his neighborhood didn't have parlors or living rooms. For that matter, they didn't have many rooms at all, to speak of. Rooms, including separate sleeping quarters for family members, were for rich people, not poor *kanakas* like him.

Jones slammed Joe down onto a *chaise longue*. Massie pulled up a hassock close by and sat down, facing Joe. Jones pulled over a dining chair and sat to Joe's right. Massie extracted a .45 from a side table and held it on Joe, while Jones continued to grind his own weapon into Joe's side.

After a moment that seemed like a lifetime, the side door opened again. A middle-aged woman entered, followed by yet another sailor. Joe knew the woman immediately. This was Thalia Massie's mother, Grace Fortescue, whom he had seen at the trial. Her mouth was set, her eyes tightened in a near squint. What little he could see of her eyes chilled him to his toes. This was a woman without mercy. And likely without conscience.

"Eddie," Mrs. Fortescue said, "go out by the car and stand guard. Make sure no one else comes in."

"Yes, ma'am," Lord said, then he left.

She took a seat on a small settee near where Joe sat. The first sailor, the one called Jones, stood and leaned against the dining room table. He was much younger than the woman, but his eyes were as devoid of compassion as Mrs. Fortescue's.

Massie pulled back the catch on the .45 and let it slide into place. He aimed it directly at Joe's heart. "Do you know who I am?" he asked.

"I think so," Joe said. He knew damn well exactly who this man was.

"Well, I got you up here to tell the complete story about what happened in September. On Ala Moana Road. You did your lying in the courtroom but you're going to tell me the truth in this house."

"I don't know nothing about what happened on Ala Moana," Joe said. "I wasn't there." He struggled to maintain his composure, but his words came out in a stammer.

"I know what you and your buddies did. Everyone knows. And you're going to tell me, right here, right now, so you'd better start talking."

Joe remained silent. How could you explain what happened somewhere if you hadn't been there? It was an impossible task, even under the best of circumstances. He had already told the police everything he knew, the same thing he said in court. If they didn't believe him then, these people surely weren't going to believe him now.

"Where were you on the night of twelve September?" Massie asked.

"I was at the Waikiki dance."

"What time did you leave?"

"I don't know. I was drunk."

"How did you go home?"

Drunk or not, Joe knew the way home from the pavilion. It was the way they always went. "I went down Kalakaua Avenue to Beretania."

"Where did you pick up the woman?" Massie asked.

Strange, Joe thought, that he would call his own wife "the woman." But then what did he really know about the relationship this man might have with the woman?

"We didn't have no woman," Joe said. "It was just us."

"You know you're not telling the truth. I'm warning you now that you better start telling it."

"I don't know nothing. I am telling the truth."

"Now tell me again how you went home."

"Down Kalakaua to Beretania. Then we turned on Fort Street—"

"Who kicked the woman?" Massie asked.

"Nobody kicked the woman."

"Now you're lying, and you know you're lying. If you weren't there, then how do you know that nobody kicked the woman? You had to have been there to know that."

Joe's brain froze, and he had no answer to what seemed to be a trick question. Maybe someone had kicked the woman, but if so, it hadn't been him. And it hadn't been Bennie or Shorty or Henry or David. But these two men would never believe him. Nor would the woman with the dead eyes and the grim smile.

"I didn't kick no woman, and I don't know if anyone did."

Mrs. Fortescue stood up abruptly and fixed her gaze on Joe. "There's no use fooling with this savage any longer. We're just wasting our time. Let's do what we have to do."

"Let me ask him one more question, first," Massie said. He leaned forward and locked eyes with Joe. "Jones, here, is on the Navy boxing team. You're a boxer, too, aren't you? A prizefighter? You get money for winning your fights?"

Joe nodded. What the hell did that have to do with anything?

"Well, that explains to me how you knew just where to hit a woman to break her jaw. Did you get any money for that?"

Joe stayed silent.

"Okay, so now you're not going to talk?" Massie asked. "Fine. We'll make you talk. You know what happened to Horace Ida, don't you?"

Joe felt his heart begin to race even faster. Damn straight he knew. Everybody knew. It's why he had his cousin Eddie accompany him to the Judiciary Building each day, so he wouldn't be alone. But a lot of good that had done him.

Massie brandished the gun in Joe's face. "He talked plenty about you, about what you did to the woman. And what he got isn't anything compared to what you're gonna get." Massie took a deep breath then said, slowly and precisely, "This is your last chance. Now, tell the truth about what happened on Ala Moana in September."

"I don't know nothing," Joe said. He knew he was starting to sound like a broken phonograph record, but he didn't know what else he could say to change the minds of these people. He suspected that, not only were they not going to change their minds no matter what he said, they *didn't want* to change their minds. They were out for blood, and harming him was the only thing that would satisfy their bloodlust. The questioning was merely foreplay.

"All right, Deacon, go get Eddie and the boys. They'll make him talk."

Jones straightened up from where he had been leaning on the table. He looked at Joe with a smirk on his lips. "Now you're going to get yours, mutt," he said.

And Joe knew that what had been bad before was now going to get worse.

* * *

It had been only a few minutes since the Durant Roadster disappeared from sight, blocked by the hedge. Aunty Mary Ann hadn't given it a second thought as she continued working with her flowers. What went on at the Fortescue house was none of her business, and she wouldn't give that woman the time of day.

A sharp cracking sound echoed. Aunty Mary Ann stopped her weeding and looked around. It was impossible to tell from which direction the sound had come, although it might well have been from the house across the street.

It was also impossible to tell exactly what had made the sound. It might have been the backfire of a car.

Or it might been a gunshot.

Chapter Twenty

Disposing of the Body

"I then noticed a human leg sticking out of the white bundle."

Officer George Harbottle stood outside his patrol car on Wai'alae Avenue, talking to officer Thomas Kekua about Daniel Lyman, a convict who had escaped from prison on New Year's Eve and who was still at large. As if the tension from the Ala Moana mistrial hadn't created enough problems, an escaped murderer was something else the island did not need. All of the Honolulu Police Department had been enlisted in the search for Lyman, while at the same time it was trying to tamp down the smoldering racial hatred that might combust at any moment.

Both men halted their conversation as Cecil Rickard's frantic voice filtered out from the car radio. They listened very carefully to the excited words, almost unintelligible amid the radio static: "Be on the lookout for a blue Buick sedan driven by a man dressed as a chauffeur, or a middle-aged woman, wanted for questioning in the abduction of Joseph Kahahawai from the front of the territorial courthouse. At least one other man is involved and is reported to be armed."

A few moments later, a fast-approaching vehicle grabbed their attention, sounding like it was going faster than the speed limit allowed. Both officers glanced up Wai'alae. A blue Buick sedan cruised past, without making any effort to slow down. They tried to look inside, but were unable to see anything other than the outline of a woman at the wheel.

A woman at the wheel! And what looked like two men inside. As the sedan passed, the man in the rear seat on the driver's side pulled the car shade down.

"Somebody doesn't want us to see something inside," Kekua said. "You think that might be old Joe in the back?"

"Only one way to find out," Harbottle said. "Ride with me." He and Kekua raced for the patrol car and jumped in. Harbottle pushed the accelerator to the floorboard, and the patrol car jumped forward. "Call it in," Harbottle said.

Kekua grabbed the microphone and radioed the dispatcher. "We're in pursuit of a blue Buick sedan, heading Diamond Head way on Wai'alae. The car matches the description of the vehicle in the Kahahawai abduction."

They headed east, beyond the Honolulu city limits, until the road bent and became Kalaniana'ole Highway just beyond Diamond Head, which loomed majestically to their *makai*, or seaward, side. The highway continued beyond the outskirts of town, close to the shoreline now. This was the main thoroughfare along the coast toward Hanauma Bay and Koko Head, both popular tourist attractions. Harbottle worried that the speeding Buick might strike some unsuspecting tourist gawking at the sights, so he poured on more gas, determined to bring the chase to a halt.

At last, he found himself gaining on the Buick until he was hot on its tail. The driver ahead of him was definitely female, though he couldn't make out her features in the Buick's rearview mirror.

"Is that Mrs. Fortescue?" Kekua asked.

"All I can see is her eyes." Eyes that seemed glued to the mirror.

The Buick increased its speed.

"She knows we're back here. She's been watching me and now she's trying to get away. There's definitely something in that car she doesn't want us to find."

"Where do you think she's going?"

"I don't know. Halona Point, maybe?"

"To the Blowhole?"

"If you wanted to get rid of evidence, can you think of a better place to dispose of it?"

"And if it's a body, once you dumped it there, no one would be able to prove there ever was a body." Kekua licked his lips and looked at Harbottle. "You think they're going to dump Joe there?"

"Not if I can help it."

Harbottle pressed harder on the accelerator. His patrol car jumped forward, again gaining ground. Up ahead, he saw another patrol car coming his way. It passed the speeding Buick and its driver slammed on the brakes. Harbottle stuck his arm out the window and made a circling motion, telling the other officer to turn around and follow. Tires squealed as the patrol car braked and slid its rear end around in a tight U-turn. Then it took its place behind Harbottle's car.

The highway straightened out along the coast, past a series of beach parks. Sunlight shimmered on the ocean and palm trees swayed. A smattering of tourists sprinkled on the white sands perked up at the speeding procession. Some stood and pointed. Harbottle could imagine the excitement in their voices and the stories they would tell once they returned to their lives on the mainland.

He swung into the oncoming lane and, with a sudden burst of speed, pulled up beside the Buick. The Buick's driver kept her eyes straight ahead. Harbottle and Kekua both looked to their right.

"That her?" Kekua asked.

"Definitely Mrs. Fortescue," Harbottle said. "Can you see anything in the backseat?"

"Not with the shade pulled down."

Harbottle edged forward. He hoped he wouldn't run into any oncoming traffic as he raced along parallel to the Buick, scarcely three feet apart.

Kekua strained to look into the backseat through the front side window. "All I can see is that there's some kind of big white bundle. I can't tell what it is."

"All right, enough of this," Harbottle said. He gunned his car again and burst past the Buick as the junction with a cross street loomed ahead, until he was barely a car's length in front. The Buick slowed. Harbottle continued to accelerate, almost as if he was going to simply drive on.

"Hang on," he said.

As he reached the cross street, he suddenly jammed on the brakes. Kekua grabbed the door handle with one hand and braced himself against the dash with his other. The patrol car fishtailed to a stop. Harbottle threw open the door and stepped outside. As the Buick approached, he stepped into the intersection, both hands raised.

The Buick swung wide and zoomed past. Harbottle unholstered his revolver and swung it around. He closed one eye and squinted down the barrel. With the Buick in his sights, he squeezed the trigger twice in rapid succession. A tail-light shattered. A second shot struck metal on the trunk.

But the Buick continued unabated.

The second patrol car, newcomer to the chase, passed Harbottle, blocking any further shooting efforts. Harbottle jumped back behind the wheel and punched the accelerator. Kekua held on for dear life with one hand and, with the other, held the microphone and updated the dispatcher as to their location and that shots had been fired. He glanced over his shoulder to see if any additional cars had joined the chase. No police cars, but there was one civilian vehicle trailing awfully close.

"Who's that behind us?" Kekua asked.

Harbottle glanced in the rearview mirror. His eyes narrowed.

"I've seen him before," Harbottle said. "He's a reporter."

Kekua looked back again. "That's just what we need."

Within minutes, Harbottle passed the second patrol car, but the reporter's car remained on his tail. Harbottle pulled beside the Buick. He and Kekua both looked over at the female driver, who refused to look their way.

"Hold on," Harbottle said.

He jammed the accelerator all the way to the floor, lifting his butt up out of the seat with the force. His car shot beside the Buick. Up ahead was Koko Head and, beyond that, the Halona Blowhole. He suspected that was the Buick's destination, and if he was right, that meant the Buick indeed carried a dark secret. The Halona Blowhole was a tourist attraction that had been formed centuries ago by a lava tunnel. With each surge of surf, thousands of gallons of ocean water forced their way into the narrowing tunnel. At the end, the water exploded skyward as a geyser, then receded. Anything or anyone unfortunate enough to be caught in the opening would be dragged through the tunnel, battered by coral and lava rock, then out to sea, never to be seen again.

Harbottle's car fully cleared the front fender of the Buick. When he had put three or four car lengths' between them, he jerked the wheel to the right. Kekua slammed up against the dash as the patrol car swung in front of the Buick. Just inches from a collision, the Buick driver also swerved right and jammed on the brakes. Both cars skidded to a halt on the side of the road, their noses precipitously close to a drop-off on the *makai* side.

Harbottle drew his gun and bolted from the car. Kekua followed, his gun also drawn. The two officers rushed to the driver's side of the Buick. No one had emerged. They both leveled their weapons at the car. Harbottle aimed at the front seat, Kekua the back.

"Everybody out of the car," Harbottle said.

Seconds passed that seemed like minutes to Harbottle. A drop of perspiration slid down the side of his face. His heart raced and his breath grew shallow. From the angle of the car, he didn't have a clear view inside the front window. The closed shade blocked his view of the back. Would the passengers be armed? Would they exit shooting? He slipped his finger onto the trigger of his weapon and lightly squeezed. Just enough tension to hold it taut but not enough to accidentally discharge it.

"Everybody out of the car now!" he repeated. "With your hands up."

The driver's door unlatched and cracked open a hair. A few more tense seconds passed and then it swung open all the way.

Out stepped Grace Fortescue. Calm. Tommie Massie slid across the front seat and got out behind her.

"You in the backseat, out now!" Harbottle barked.

"Come on out, Eddie," Tommie said.

The rear door opened and Edward Lord got out. Behind him, Harbottle saw a bundle wrapped in a white sheet. The sheet was wet with both blood and water.

A dark-skinned human leg stuck out of the bundle.

"You're all under arrest," Harbottle said.

* * *

Two more patrol cars quickly arrived: the one that been trailing Harbottle and another driven by officer Percy Bond. They pulled up behind Harbottle's unit, and the officers exited, guns drawn. The civilian vehicle that had given chase also pulled to a stop. A reporter for the *Honolulu Advertiser* got out along with a photographer. Harbottle knew that it was just a matter of time before more members of the press arrived. He resigned himself to dealing with the lone reporter who was already present, but hoped to avoid a spectacle by moving quickly. After all, it was the press that had already excited the entire island and likely led to the very result he now had to deal with. He would be damned if he would let this get out of hand.

Harbottle turned his attention from the reporter back to the trio standing before him. "Let me see your hands," he commanded. Dutifully, all three raised their hands to shoulder level. He gestured to one of the other officers. "Search them," he said. He made eye contact with Grace Fortescue. "All of them."

A quick pat-down of Massie and Lord revealed nothing. Grace refused to allow herself to be touched, backing the searching officer away with a look of contempt. Rather than force the issue, Harbottle let it go. If indeed Kahahawai was in the bundle, it was most likely one of the Navy men who had pulled a trigger, not the upper crust from the East Coast.

"What's your name?" Harbottle asked the woman, although he already knew the answer. She remained silent. "Mrs. Fortescue, right?" He looked at Massie. "And you're Lieutenant Massie?" Then his eyes shifted to Lord. "How about you? Eddie, is it?"

Lord kept his mouth shut.

"Fine. You don't have to talk. We'll get you all back down to headquarters and straighten this out." Turning to the other officers, he said, "Put them in separate cars."

As officers moved in to grab the three, the woman stepped away. "I'll wait out here," she said.

Her glare directed at Harbottle sent shivers throughout his body. He had never seen such unbridled hate in eyes before. Near the parked patrol cars, a large flat rock sat on a bluff overlooking the ocean. He pointed at it. "Then wait over there." He glanced at an officer. "Watch her."

Slowly, almost at a saunter, she approached the rock and sat. She turned to face the ocean, as if oblivious to those behind her. The officer followed and stood guard, shifting from foot to foot, as if unsure exactly what he was supposed to do,

Harbottle turned his attention back to the Buick. It was time to reveal what lay hidden in the bloody sheets in the backseat, although he already had a pretty good idea whose leg extended from the bundle.

"Grab hold of that," he said to a couple of officers standing close by, "and drag it over here."

The bundle was tied with a hemp rope, which the officers grabbed as a handle. They tugged, but there was no movement. Whatever was inside had some weight to it. They tried again, and the bundle moved. A third effort, and it slid toward the door. A portion of the rope caught on the door handle as they reached the edge of the seat. An officer struggled to free it. At last, he pulled loose a corner of the bloody sheet. The face of Joe Kahahawai came into view. His mouth was twisted in a grimace, as if he were in pain. His eyes were closed. He looked for all the world as if he were sleeping and experiencing a nightmare. But for Joe, the nightmare was over. Permanently.

The officer pulled the sheet down farther to expose Joe's torso. Blood covered the front, with rivers of red that criss-crossed his sides. Harbottle sucked in a breath. That was an awful lot of blood.

Murmurs behind him got his attention. He turned and grimaced. More reporters had arrived, some also with photographers in tow. "Get that sheet back over him," he told the officers. "We don't need any pictures on the front pages tomorrow."

As all this transpired, Grace sat sideways on the rock, gazing seaward. Close by, within earshot, Tommie sat alone in the backseat of a patrol car where he had been deposited. He intently watched the events unfolding at the Buick. By all appearances, Grace seemed totally unconcerned with the Buick, the bundle, or the police. A reporter, pencil and pad in hand, wandered over, trailed by a photographer. The officer standing guard shifted to block their approach, so they stopped about ten feet away. Grace must have heard their approach, because she turned toward them.

"You're Mrs. Fortescue, aren't you?" the reporter asked.

"I'd rather not say."

The reporter gestured to his photographer, who stepped forward and raised his camera. Grace looked directly at the camera—and smiled just as the bulb flashed. Damned if it didn't appear as if she had actually posed for the picture.

Harbottle hustled over. "Get out of here with that camera."

The photographer started to flash another picture, but the reporter grabbed his arm and led him away.

Harbottle continued to the nearby patrol car. He glared at Tommie, who refused to meet his eyes. Officer Percy Bond approached Harbottle, but before he could speak to his colleague, Grace stood from the rock and strode toward him. She extended her arm, as if to shake hands. Bond stopped and stared at her.

"Haven't I met you somewhere before?" Grace asked. "Didn't you come down from the coast about two months ago, the same time I did?"

"No," Bond said. He refused to take her hand. After a moment, she dropped it and returned to her rock.

Bond turned to Harbottle. "Nice work, kid," he said.

Tommie smiled big, as if the compliment had been aimed at him. He stuck his arms out the window, grabbed his left hand in his right, and pumped it up and down, as if shaking hands with himself. Then, mimicking Grace, he said, "Hello, big boy, haven't I seen you at the police station?"

Harbottle stared at Tommie and then looked at Bond. Both men shook their heads, amazed at how oblivious these two seemed to be of their circumstances. "Get them out of my sight," Bond said.

"Paddy wagon's here," Harbottle replied. "I'll be glad to."

The paddy wagon had pulled up beside the Buick, followed by Deputy Sheriff William Hoopai. Under Hoopai's supervision, two officers unloaded a large wicker basket from the rear and carted it to the Buick. Working in tandem, they extracted the bloody body of Joe Kahahawai and placed it in the basket. Beneath where the body had been, in the rear seat of the Buick, lay a bundle of wet clothing.

Hoopai pointed at the bundle. "Give me that." An officer grabbed it and handed it over. Hoopai carefully unfolded the bundle, which consisted of underwear, pants, a pair of gray socks, black shoes, and bloodstained towels.

And a bloodstained blue shirt. Hoopai lifted the shirt and held it open. A ragged hole had been punched through the left breast. The deputy sheriff put his index finger through the hole. "Probably a lung or maybe the heart," he said.

"I guess that would about do it." He folded up the shirt and tossed it and the remainder of the clothing on top of Joe's body in the basket.

Officers loaded the basket into the rear of the paddy wagon then escorted the three prisoners over. The two men got inside wordlessly and sat on the benches lining the inner walls. Grace balked.

"You need to get in, ma'am," Harbottle said.

She pointed at the wicker basket. "You can't possibly expect me to ride with that . . . that . . . that thing."

"Yes, ma'am, I sure do," Harbottle said. "Now get in."

He grabbed her arm, more tightly than he needed to, and assisted as she stepped inside. With her nose held in the air, and her eyes averted so as not to look at the body, she nestled on a bench next to Tommie, as far from the basket as she could get.

Harbottle slammed the paddy wagon door behind her. He went to the side window and said to the driver, "Get those people away from me."

As the vehicle pulled off, Harbottle said aloud, to nobody in particular, "I need a bath."

Chapter Twenty-one

A Funeral in the Islands

"Poor Kahahawai, these *haoles* murdered you in cold blood."

Admiral Stirling was escorted into Governor Judd's office, where he found the governor in an obvious state of agitation. Judd paced behind his desk, paused briefly to look out the window, and then commenced his march again. He stopped when he realized Stirling stood in the doorway.

"You encourage people to disregard our laws, and this is what happens," Judd said. He grabbed a newspaper from his desk and held it up. "Kahahawai Kidnapped" screamed the headline on the hot-off-the-presses extra edition of the *Honolulu Advertiser*.

"I didn't encourage kidnapping."

"Kidnapping?" Judd tossed the paper on the floor. "You're as far behind as the newspapers are. I'm waiting on the next extra edition any second now. They have killed one of my people."

Stirling stepped forward and picked up the paper. He studied the headline. "They?"

"The police have caught Mrs. Fortescue and Lieutenant Massie with Kahahawai's dead body. And Thalia Massie has even given a statement to the press." He took a notepad from his desk, on which he had written something. "I'm told this will be in the next edition. She said, and I quote, 'I'm sorry this man has been shot, but it was no more than he deserved. I don't think this town is safe for white women.'"

Stirling didn't miss a beat, as if he expected news like this sooner or later. "I told you to keep those animals locked up—for their own safety."

"Those 'animals,' as you call them, didn't kill anyone. And they didn't take anyone out to the *pali* and beat them half to death. Your people did that."

Stirling shrugged, a gesture that infuriated Judd. "When the law doesn't protect our women, American men will always take the law into their own hands. The honor of our women demands it. And now a degenerate sex criminal is dead. What's the loss? That means there's one less for the retrial."

Judd's face reddened and his voice rose. He spoke through clenched teeth. "I don't care about the Ala Moana case, Admiral. I'll bring these killers to trial immediately."

Stirling locked glares with Judd briefly—then shrugged again and turned to leave. He stopped at the doorway and turned around. "You might want to lock up the rest of those boys as quickly as you can. It might just save their lives."

Then he left.

* * *

A subsequent search by the police of Grace's house in Manoa turned up the following:

- A .45 caliber handgun under a couch cushion in the living room
- An Iver Johnson .32 caliber handgun hidden in a basket of eggs in the kitchen
- A coil of rope matching the rope found tying the bloody sheet around Joe Kahahawai's body
- A steel-jacketed .32 caliber bullet on the dining table
- A brown cloth cap
- A purse, inside of which was a newspaper clipping with a photo of Kahahawai
- A wet mop in the recently mopped bathroom
- Bloodstains on the bathroom floor
- Two small buttons, with cloth attached, on the bathroom floor, which matched Joe Kahahawai's undershorts
- A blood-soaked towel with the monogram "USN"

At the Massie house, police arrested Deacon Jones, who appeared to be expecting them. A pat-down search revealed a .32 shell in the watch pocket of his pants, and tucked into his waistband was a small bundle wrapped in paper. The bundle turned out to be a bullet clip. The paper turned out to be the phony summons used to secure Joe Kahahawai at the Judiciary Building.

Grace, Tommie, Lord, and Jones were all booked on the charge of murder in the first degree. Grace's booking sheet contained a more complete statement of the charges against all four:

Joe Kahahawai Jr, one of the defendants in the Ala Moana assault case was kidnapped from in front of the Judiciary Building and taken into a Buick sedan. Kidnapping witnessed by J. Apkins. General Alarm given by Deputy Sheriff, William Hoopai and Chief of Detectives, John N. McIntosh for all Police Officers to be on the look-out for a Buick Sedan probably operated by a White Woman and probably containing two or three men.

A Buick Sedan operated by Mrs. Fortescue noticed by Officer Harbottle, going at a fast rate of speed on Waialae Road near Kahala Road. Officer Harbottle with Radio Patrol Officers Arthur Takei and Manuel Freitas: Louis Camacho and Thurman Black gave chase. Car with all occupants, captured and placed under arrest on Kalanianaole Highway. Sitting in the rear seat were Lieutenant Massie and E.J. Lord, of the U.S. Navy. On the back floor of the automobile the dead body of Joe Kahahawai Jr, covered with a canvas cloth and securely tied with ropes. Victim's body marked at the time of Discovery.

Albert Orrin Jones arrested at Mrs. Massie's residence by Chief of Detectives John N. McIntosh.

Autopsy performed on body of victim by Dr. Robert Faus who stated that victim was shot at the base of the left lung by a 32 cal. steel jacketed bullet. Death was due to bleeding. Defendants taked [sic] to James Gilliland's Office for Investigation. Defendants fingerprinted & Photographed at Police Station.

In short order, the defendants had retained, as counsel, the law firm of Thompson & Winn, which had, at Admiral Stirling's insistence, been hired by the prosecution to assist in the Ala Moana case. Because Jones had been arrested later, he was still being processed when Grace, Tommie, and Lord sat in an interrogation room as Griffith Wight awkwardly read the charges against them and prepared to question them about the events of the day—awkwardly, because not that long ago he had been an ally to Grace and Tommie in pursuing the men whom Thalia claimed had raped her.

A patrol officer stood against the wall behind Wight while Tommie and Grace sat silently, with their hands on the table. Grace wore a look of stunned amazement—her eyes wide and unblinking. It was as if she couldn't believe that she had been arrested for the killing of an animal. Tommie was more stoic, but he said little other than to offer curt, one-word answers to questions from Wight. Lord, an enlisted man, was the only person handcuffed, but danger still seemed to be coiled in his muscular frame.

The door to the room suddenly swung open. All of the occupants jumped at the intrusion. Wight, his back to the door, turned to see who had barged in.

Admiral Yates Stirling.

"Admiral, I'm afraid I'm going to have to ask you to leave," Wight said. "We're in the middle of something."

"They're not answering any more questions without their attorneys present," Stirling said.

"All right," Wight said. "Then we'll have to lock them up until the lawyers can get here."

Stirling's eyes fell on the handcuffs on Lord. "Take those irons off of that man."

No one moved.

"Now!" Stirling barked.

Wight glanced at the officer by the wall and nodded. The officer complied, unlocking and removing the cuffs. Lord rubbed his wrists, which had been reddened by the tight metal.

"The Navy will take custody of these people," Stirling said.

"By what authority?" Wight asked.

"Mr. Wight, I'm sure you know that the military has had an agreement for the past decade with territorial officials to give us jurisdiction over members of the military charged with felonies."

"But not in capital cases. And the agreement applies only to military personnel. Mrs. Fortescue is a civilian."

Stirling spoke sharply. "Mr. Wight, I'll not have my people nor their loved ones spend even a single night inside your miserable little jail."

"Where do you propose to keep them? In the brig?"

"The USS *Alton* is in permanent dry-dock. It has living quarters aboard, and we'll keep these people there. We'll make them available, with their attorneys, as needed for trial or other matters."

Wight pondered the request. It was unusual but, quite frankly, he would be happy to have these people out of his hair until trial.

"I'll agree to it, but only if Judge Cristy signs off on it," Wight said.

* * *

Esther Anito leaned on her husband, Pascual, as detectives escorted them through the police station. All she knew was what she had heard on the radio, that her boy Joe had been kidnapped from in front of the Judiciary Building. The nightmare continued for the Anito family. First Joe had been arrested and charged with raping a Navy man's wife, and then, just that morning, she had sewn new buttons on his shirt so he would look nice when he met with his probation officer. But now someone had taken him, just as they had taken Shorty Ida to the far side of the *pali* and beaten him mercilessly. She held a tissue to her face and tried to stanch the tears, worried about what might happen to her Joe.

In a narrow hallway, the Anitos passed a group of men heading the opposite way: Shorty, Ben, David, and Henry, escorted by men in suits. She made eye contact with Shorty, who nodded at her. Her mother's heart broke as she thought about what had happened to him, and what might be happening that very moment to Joe.

The two groups of people passed without speaking. After they turned a corner, Pascual asked, "Where they taking those boys?"

"Gonna lock 'em up," one of the detectives said. "To keep 'em safe."

Pascual put his arm around Esther. "Where we going?" he asked.

One of the detectives pointed at a sign on the wall that indicated that the hallway they were in led to the morgue. Esther looked at the sign. Her step faltered as she tried to take in the meaning.

They paused at a door with frosted glass, which also bore the word "Morgue."

"We need you to identify your son," the detective said. "We also have some of his things."

He reached in his jacket pocket, took out two items, and held them out to Esther: a wristwatch with a broken crystal, stopped at 9:45, and a gold ring from St. Louis College, class of 1928. Esther took the jewelry and stared at it.

Sobs wracked her body and she crumpled to the floor.

* * *

The funeral director at Nu'uanu Funeral Parlor had dressed Joe in a dark suit, with a yellow lei around his neck and a crucifix on his chest. Esther and Pascual, as well as Joe's natural father, Joseph Kahahawai Sr., kept vigil by the casket the night of Saturday, January 9, as a stream of mourners passed by. The flow continued well into the night and into the morning. Hundreds made their way past the body, most of whom didn't know Joe, but they knew that an attack on one of their own had occurred. Few believed there would be justice for his death.

By the time Sunday morning rolled around, the group of mourners in the chapel and on the streets outside had swollen into the hundreds, maybe even the thousands. Outrage swirled through the crowd, which soon latched on to a catchphrase that percolated from person to person: *Hilahila 'ole keia po'e haole*: "The *haoles* are shameless."

When it became clear that the chapel was not going to be able to hold the crowds, the funeral director made arrangements with Father Patrick Logan at Our Lady of Peace Cathedral to move the service there. While waiting for the body to be transported, Esther, Pascual, and Joe Sr. sat next to the casket and continued their vigil. The men tried to remain stoic, but Esther's tears flowed freely.

About mid-morning, David Kama, a native Hawaiian, made his way with the flow of mourners to the casket. He hugged Esther and shook hands with Pascual and Joe. They knew him from his own troubles a few years earlier. His brother, a Honolulu police officer, had been murdered by a *haole* soldier while he was trying to break up a fight.

Kama stood by the casket for a moment. With his head down, looking at Joe, he spoke in a raised voice so all could hear him. "Poor Kahahawai, these *haoles* murdered you in cold blood. They did the same thing to my brother. The truth will come out. Thank God they were caught. Poor boy, God will keep you. We will do the rest."

The words sank deep into Esther's soul. Kama's pronouncement sent mixed signals. On one hand, he invoked the name of God to guard Joe's soul, but at the same time, he seemed to be calling upon the Hawaiian community to rise up. She hoped not. She didn't know what had happened, if anything, to the sailor's wife, but she knew in her heart that her Joe had nothing to do with it. And she also knew in her heart that more violence was not the answer.

A hush fell over the crowd in the chapel. Then there was a soft rustling sound as the line that filled the middle aisle broke apart, with people moving to the left or right, forming a passageway to the casket. Esther looked down the way and saw Shorty, Ben, Henry, and David approaching. Behind them, at the doorway, police officers waited, obviously escorts from their jail cells.

When they reached the front, each of the men leaned over and hugged Esther. No words were spoken, just tears shed. Then, one by one, they moved to the casket and gazed at the cold, lifeless body of their friend. As all four of them stood in a row, facing the open casket, Joe Sr. stood. He cleared his throat. A tear trickled down his cheek. He looked at his son, and then at the gathered assembly.

"Everybody knows why my boy was killed," he said. "Revenge. But revenge for what? My boy did not do anything wrong, just like these boys here did not do anything wrong. I spoke to Joe many times since he was accused, and he always tell me he is innocent. If he is guilty, then he should be punished. But I asked him. I asked him many times. And he always tell me he and his friends are innocent."

He faltered. Sorrow and tears choked his voice. "I told Joseph to take an oath before God. And he said, 'Daddy, I swear before God that I never did anything wrong.'" Then he broke into sobs and sat back down.

* * *

After the police returned the surviving Ala Moana Boys to their jail cells, it was time to move the funeral to Our Lady of Peace. Motorcycle policemen escorted the procession, with more than a hundred cars, followed by hundreds more on foot, through the streets of Honolulu to the cathedral. There, Father Logan said mass in Latin and offered a prayer in English for Joe's soul. He ended with the words ". . . and thou hast been delivered from the hands of thine enemies."

From Our Lady of Peace, the mourners proceeded on foot to Puea Cemetery on School Street in Kalihi. Esther and Pascual walked directly behind the casket, which was carried by six strong *kanakas*, friends of Joe's. At the cemetery, more than three thousand people crowded around an open grave—the largest funeral in Hawaii since the burial of the overthrown monarch Queen Lili'uokalani fifteen years earlier. Chairs had been set up for Esther, Pascual, and Joe Sr., and Reverend Robert Ahuna delivered a graveside eulogy. He recounted the events that had led to Joe's death only two days before. "I call upon the Lord to pass judgment on those who committed this crime," he said in closing.

After Reverend Ahuna spoke, the mourners chanted in unison a *kanikau*—a death chant—and then sang hymns, followed by the Hawaiian national anthem, "Hawai'i Pono." They finished with "Aloha Oe," a song that had been composed by Lili'uokalani. Among the mourners who stood somberly and sang were Agnes Peeples and her children. One of the voices that rose above the others was that of Lena Machado, a singer of some renown locally, and the wife of Detective Luciano Machado, who had arrested Joe in the first place.

Aloha oe, Aloha oe,
E ke onaona noho i ka lipo,
One fond embrace

A hoʻi aʻe au,
Until we meet again.
Farewell to you, farewell to you,
The charming one who dwells among the bowers.
One fond embrace,
ʻEre I depart,
Until we meet again.

When the crowds departed, Esther waited with Pascual and Joe Sr. while grave-diggers lowered the casket into the ground. A light rain began to fall. Esther turned her face skyward and let the *na waimaka o ke lani*—the tears of heaven—fall on her skin.

PART FOUR

TERRITORY OF HAWAII V. GRACE FORTESCUE, ET AL

Chapter Twenty-two
Turning State's Evidence
"I never should have pulled that shade down."

The arrests of a prominent mainland socialite and three members of the United States Navy outraged the white elite minority, as well as the military as a whole. The furor spread far and wide across the Islands, jumped the Pacific Ocean, and swept across the United States mainland. White newspapers, both in the Islands and across the ocean, launched into commentary mode, proclaiming the right of a husband to avenge his wife, and questioning why the Ala Moana Boys had been out of jail to start with. Had they not been roaming free, the assault on Ida and the shooting of Kahahawai would never have happened. In other words, the Boys had brought misfortune upon themselves. At the same time, the new arrestees were almost universally declared to be justified—assuming they had actually shot Kahahawai.

But it was not only the press that exploded in an uproar. Politicians, intent on grabbing their share of the spotlight, speechified about the sad state of affairs in Hawaii that had led to this inevitable tragedy—the tragedy being the rape of Thalia Massie and the arrest of her husband and mother, not the killing of a Hawaiian.

On January 16, 1932, a hearing was held in the United States Senate before the Committee on Territories and Insular Affairs, on Senate Resolution 81, titled "A Joint Resolution Providing for an Investigation of the Government of the Territory of Hawaii and for Other Purposes." Those other purposes included a discussion of what was now becoming known as the "Massie Case." The Committee, chaired by Hiram Bingham of Connecticut, consisted of Hiram W. Johnson from California, Arthur R. Robinson from Indiana, Gerald P. Nye from North Dakota, Jesse H. Metcalf from Rhode Island, Arthur H. Vandenburg from Michigan, Bronson Cutting from New Mexico, Charles L. McNary from Oregon, Key Pittman from Nevada, William J. Harris from Georgia, Edwin S. Broussard from Louisiana, Carl Hayden from Arizona,

Millard E. Tydings from Maryland, Harry B. Hawes from Missouri, and William H. King from Utah.

Senators speaking at the hearing, mostly from ignorance, expressed amazement that the Territory of Hawaii, by law, did not permit convictions in rape cases based solely on the uncorroborated testimony of the victim. Had that not been the law in Hawaii, the testimony of Thalia Massie, alone, no matter how unreliable, would have been sufficient for a conviction; the Ala Moana Boys would be in prison; and Tommie Massie would not have been forced to take matters into his own hands. Democratic Senator Harry Hawes of Missouri expressed his disbelief this way: "Here are five men identified by the victim, and the jury was eight to four for acquittal, and the men were put on bail and permitted to walk the streets of Honolulu. How can you explain that? It could not be done in our country." Never mind that the actual jury vote was split down the middle at six apiece.

Admiral William V. Pratt, chief of Naval Operations, tried to explain that Hawaii was not the hotbed of crime that the press had conjured up. "I would like to state that with the one exception of these sex crimes, the Hawaiian Islands are as law-abiding as any place I have ever seen, but there is a laxity in that particular matter, which is due very largely just to the nature of things."

It was a version of "boys will be boys": Hawaiians will be Hawaiians. Though he was trying to calm things, Pratt made them worse with his explanation, presuming the guilt of the Ala Moana Boys for the rape of Thalia Massie. "The Hawaiian is a different sort of bird from the average American. I have been there enough to know it. These beach boys are fine, upstanding men, but their attitude toward women is not anything like the attitude of our men toward women. They do not know what rape is, many of them. They think pretty nearly everything is consent."

As the hearing drew to a close, the committee considered Nevada Senator Pittman's inquiry whether to recommend to Hawaii's Governor Judd that he, in turn, "recommend to the legislature that they repeal that peculiar and special act of Hawaii which prohibits the conviction of a defendant charged with rape on the uncorroborated testimony of the victim." Senator Hawes made one final recommendation to Chairman Bingham: "I hope you will make an unofficial recommendation to the governor to get Mrs. Fortescue and Lieutenant Massie back to the United States as quickly as possible."

Typical of the misguided outrage at the state level was a resolution by the legislature in Kentucky, Tommie Massie's home state, passed on January 20 and sent to President Herbert Hoover. It provided:

In September last the wife of Lieutenant Thomas Hedges Massie, an officer in the United States Navy, a native and citizen of Winchester, Kentucky, stationed at Honolulu in Hawaii, was kidnapped, assaulted, beat, mangled, her jaw broken and raped six times by five Oriental native Hawaiians, resulting in pregnancy, confining her to a hospital, and making an operation for abortion imperative, and although she identified four of the five rapists, the jury which tried them, failed to convict, leaving this foul and horrible crime unpunished; prior to this crime six men, natives of Hawaii, were charged with the rape of a Chinese girl and one or more of them were convicted, and one of them, a prizefighter, was pardoned of the offense, and shortly thereafter was in New York City taking part in a prize fight, and that same man is one of the five men charged with the rape of Mrs. Massie, and that following the assault and rape of Mrs. Massie by these five rapists, they were permitted to go at large until one of their number was recently killed, and thereupon the other four of said rapists voluntarily surrendered themselves to the jailer in Honolulu for their own personal safety and protection, and whereas, in connection with the killing of one of the five rapists, Lieutenant Massie, Mrs. Granville Roland Fortescue, the mother of Mrs. Massie and E.J. Lord and A.O. Jones, two enlisted men in the Navy, are held as prisoners in Honolulu.

Now, Be It Resolved by the General Assembly of the Commonwealth of Kentucky, that this Assembly memorializes, petitions and requests His Excellency, the Honorable Herbert Hoover, President of the United States, and Commander in Chief of the Army and Navy, to use the power vested in him as Chief Executive and as Commander in Chief of the Army and Navy, to demand that the repists [*sic*] who so dastardly, beat and raped the Wife of Lieutenant Massie, be brought to justice and to insist that a full measure of the law be meted out to them, and we further memorialize, petition and request that the President as Chief Executive and Commander in Chief of the Army and Navy use every arm of the Government to insure the immediate release of Lieutenant Massie, Mrs. Fortescue, E.J. Lord and A.O. Jones, and to insure this end, we petition and request, if such result cannot otherwise be secured, that the President declare a state of martial law in Honolulu, as has been done, at least, on one former occasion, and thereby exercise direct control from the seat of government at Washington, until such time as the territory of Hawaii can be made safe for women, and especially for the wives of our men in the Army and Navy, who are stationed in Honolulu, not of their own volition, but under orders of the War and Navy Departments, which they must obey.

* * *

Comfortably ensconced in the penthouse-like commander's quarters on the USS *Alton*, Grace Fortescue escorted reporter Russell Owen of the *New York Times* to a table in the officer's mess. Once they were seated, a steward poured tea for both of them.

"Now, Mr. Owen," Grace said, "what can I tell your readers?"

"Well, for starters, I'm sure they'd like to know how you feel."

"Mostly, I'm just glad it's all out in the open. Those days when my daughter's name was suppressed, when people didn't know she had been assaulted but they saw those bruises on her face—well, you can just imagine the whispering and the rumors. But now my mind is at peace. I have to say, I have slept better since Friday the eighth, the day of the murder, than for a long time."

Owen took notes, amazed that she had referred to the killing of Kahahawai as a "murder."

"What was your reaction when the police stopped your car near Koko Head?"

"We thought we were being careful, but now I realize we bungled dreadfully. I never should have pulled the shade down."

If Owen had been amazed before, he now moved into fresh grounds of incredulity. "You mean you think your only mistake was pulling the shade down? Not killing the Hawaiian in the first place?"

Grace took a sip of tea then snorted. "I come from the South, and in the South we have a way of dealing with niggers."

Owen scribbled furiously, making sure to capture her words perfectly. He would later report that he believed Grace incapable of understanding that Southern Blacks had no relation to Hawaiians.

"Oh, look," she said. He stopped writing and looked up. "There are the boys."

She waved over Tommie, Jones, and Lord. Jones carried a thick scrapbook under his arm, which he set on the table as the men took seats. After introductions were made, Grace said, "Mr. Owen is from the *New York Times*."

Jones perked up. "You're a reporter?"

"That's right," Grace said. "He's here to do a story on us. Show him your scrapbook, Deacon."

Jones opened the thick tome and flipped through its pages, crammed with clippings about the case. Inflammatory headlines screamed from the articles: "Honor Slaying"; "Race War Threatened"; "Hawaii: Crater of Racial Hate"; "Bayonets Rule Honolulu as Races Boil in Killing."

"I just pasted in some new ones today," Jones said. "Gosh, I never got my name in the newspaper before."

"It will be in there again tomorrow," Owen said. "Front page of the *New York Times*."

Jones leaned back in his chair. "The *New York Times*? Well, how about that!"

* * *

On January 20, Montgomery E. Winn, of the law firm of Thompson & Winn, filed a motion to dismiss the charges against his clients on the basis that it had been twelve days since their arrest, but no formal indictment had been issued by the grand jury. As Winn stated in his supporting affidavit for the motion, after first bemoaning that his clients have been "in solitary confinement on the *S.S. Alton*," a complaint likely to fall on deaf ears given the *Alton*'s relative luxury compared to the jail cells in which the surviving Ala Moana Boys were lodged:

> That since the 8th day of January, 1932, the Grand Jury of the First Judicial Circuit, Territory of Hawaii, has convened upon two occasions; that on neither of these occasions has the City and County Attorney's Office made any effort whatsoever to place any facts before said Grand Jury to warrant an indictment of the said defendants or either of them, and that the City and County Attorney has, contrary to the constitutional rights of said defendants, made no attempt whatsoever to secure an indictment against said defendants or either of them, and that no indictment has been returned against said defendants.

Winn's affidavit went on to assert that this delay, "prejudiced the rights of all of said defendants to secure a fair and impartial trial." Furthermore, he said, he understood that the grand jury would convene again on January 21, "but that the City and County Attorney will not on said date attempt to secure an indictment against the defendants or either of them."

* * *

In addition to being concerned with the Massie defendants, the prosecution still had to deal with the retrial of the remaining Ala Moana Boys, which had changed its complexion a bit with the death of Joe Kahahawai. While the retrial of the Ala Moana Boys was a political necessity, the Massie case presented a potential time bomb. Maybe that pressure could be eased, the prosecutors thought, with a conviction in the Ala Moana case. After all, if these young men had raped and beaten Thalia Massie, who could blame her husband and mother for what they had done?

The prosecution had tried before the first trial to get David Takai to turn State's evidence, but he had refused, a fact that had been brought out at trial. Now attention turned to trying to get cooperation from one of the others. Each of the men was interrogated individually, in hopes of finding one who would make a deal. When efforts with Horace and Henry failed, Officer D. W. Watson had Ben Ahakuelo brought from his cell to an interrogation room on the afternoon of January 20, where he and a stenographer waited. He had known Ben for a number of years, and had even counseled him in his youth about staying away from bad influences and out of trouble. He hoped his prior relationship might help entice concessions from him.

Ben entered and sat at a small table across from Watson. He narrowed his eyes and looked at the officer, who smiled and nodded.

"Well, Ben. This is a hell of a mess you are in, isn't it?"

"Yes."

If Watson expected more, he was disappointed. He spoke in the friendliest voice he could muster. "I have been thinking a great deal about your case, Ben. I can't help thinking that you may be shielding someone. Are you afraid to tell something? You know I helped you before and I will help you again. You don't need to be afraid to tell me the truth, you know that, don't you? You are going to have a hard time getting out of all this. Lots of people think you boys are guilty."

"All I say is I don't know about this job. I never touched any *haole* woman." A firm nod punctuated Ben's statement.

"You boys have caused lots of trouble. All the *haole* people on the mainland think you boys are guilty and they are blaming the Hawaiians. They're not going to let you boys get off. You know what happened to Joe Kahahawai."

At the mention of Joe's name, Ben grew silent. He dropped his head and stared at the tabletop, and then looked up at Watson. "They killed an innocent boy. Joe didn't know about that case."

"Ben, suppose you had a wife and somebody beat that wife and assaulted her. You would like to kill the man that attacked your wife?" Watson realized that this was the defense likely to be employed should the four killers ever go to trial.

"Sure, but Joe's not guilty of that."

"Suppose after someone attacked your wife, if you saw that man, you wouldn't kill him unless you were sure."

"No, I'd want to be sure."

"The people who killed Joe are not dumb, Ben. They were *sure* before they shot him. They were just as sure as you would be before you shot anyone. And they think the rest of you boys are guilty."

"All I know is Joe was not guilty and I am not guilty," Ben said. "They think Joe was dumb, but he wasn't dumb. This fellow Wight, he's a dirty guy. He puts lies into your mouth. He tried to get Joe to sign a paper of what he said. Just because Joe didn't talk much, Wight thought he was dumb, but Joe read that paper first and when Wight put lies into his mouth about Ida having a jacket, Joe scratched that out."

Frustrated, Watson ended the session but, after giving Ben a night to sleep on their conversation, he returned to the jail the following day to continue his interrogation. Ben's eyes were puffy and bloodshot, his features wan and drawn. Watson supposed Ben had not slept the night before, or maybe not even since Joe Kahahawai's body had been found. In his weakened state, maybe he would be more susceptible to Watson's suggestions that he cooperate with the prosecution.

"I have been worrying about this trouble of yours, Ben," Watson said. "Why try to protect those other boys? You are the only Hawaiian left. These people shot Joe, and now there's only you, two Japanese boys, and one Chinese boy. Those other boys wouldn't help you—they are going to squeal, Ben. They're going to blame you just as sure as hell."

"If I know anything, I tell you. Even if I know about my best friend, I'd tell on him."

"I understand they are going to try you boys one at a time next time." Watson didn't know that for a fact, but some suggestion had been made that separate trials be held. Still, nothing was set in stone. As a practical matter, he doubted that the Territory would be willing to bear the expense of multiple trials.

"If our lawyer wants, they will."

"Ben, they'll try you one at a time whether you like it or not. Do you know why? Because Ida is going to squawk. He's going to tell. What do you think they killed Kahahawai for? Because Ida told."

Ben's eyes flashed anger. "No, I asked Ida many times and he say people tell lies. He say he never told anything. He said these men take him up to Pali and try to throw him over, but they were afraid because an automobile was parked there. They didn't kill him because he never fight back—Joe fought those people, that's why they shot him."

"Ida wouldn't admit to you that he squealed. But those people are not killing Joe for nothing. They *know* he was guilty. That Japanese put the blame on Joe. He's a Hawaiian, Ben, and so are you."

"I know Joe is innocent and I am innocent."

"All the *haoles* on the mainland are blaming the Hawaiians, Ben. And these people that killed Joe blame you fellows. They got one Hawaiian, and Ben—you are going to be next. They're going to get you just as sure as you are alive right now. Even if it takes ten years, you'll never know when you are liable to get it. Joe got off easy—they just shot him. The next time, Ben, they're going to torture you fellows. It's going to be hell."

"I might as well die. I'm not afraid. If I was guilty I'd feel funny, but I don't. I'm going home and if they want to shoot me, all right." Tears gathered in Ben's eyes. He wiped them away on the sleeve of his shirt. He had a tough guy image to uphold, and Watson knew he didn't want to cry in front of him.

"Ben, can't you think of anything that you have not told me? I am afraid you are trying to shield these other boys. Why should you be here in jail when you might just as well be out of here—away from Hawaii?"

Ben banged his fist on the table. "I wouldn't shield even my best friend on a job like this. I know nothing about it." He traced, again, his movements on the night in question, then concluded with, "We never went down Ala Moana."

Watson made one last effort. "Did you see this *haole* woman after the dance?"

"I never saw her. I know what I say is true. I am a Catholic and when the father came down here, he asked me if I touch that *haole* woman and I told him the truth that I never touched her. Joe Kahahawai was a Catholic too, and his father made him go to confession every four days and Joe always says the same thing: that he was not guilty."

Watson made one last plea to practicality. He knew that, when it came to making deals with criminal defendants, sometimes guilty pleas were agreed to for no other reason than it was cheaper and easier than a trial, and the sentence agreed to was less than what a jury might hand out.

"If you tell, you can probably get a short sentence, you will then be free," Watson said. "There is a reward offered in this case, and you can go away and start life all over again."

"It wouldn't be easy for me to go away. I'm just the same as married."

That was the first that Watson knew that Ben had a girlfriend. A girlfriend he likely wouldn't want to believe that he had committed this rape. All the more reason to reach an agreement and serve no time. For all she would know, he had not been involved in the rape, but had simply helped the prosecution to convict the real rapists.

"That's all right," Watson said. "You can get married and take your wife with you."

Ben answered immediately and firmly. "All I know is that I don't know about this job."

And Watson believed him.

Chapter Twenty-three

Judge Cristy and the Grand Jury

"God has not left this world for an instant."

Perhaps Montgomery Winn should have left well enough alone because, on the afternoon of Thursday, January 21, the day after he had filed his motion to dismiss the charges, Judge Albert Cristy convened the grand jury at 1:30 p.m., and Griffith Wight presented evidence to secure an indictment in Cause Number 11891, *Territory of Hawaii v. Grace Fortescue, Thomas H. Massie, Edward J. Lord, and Albert O. Jones.* Wight concluded his evidence at noon on Friday, and right after lunch the grand jury began its deliberations on the charges of kidnapping and first-degree murder.

A thin-faced man with a neatly trimmed mustache and brown hair cropped close on the sides, Albert Cristy was one of four judges in Honolulu's First Circuit. He had obtained his bachelor of arts degree from Brown University, where he was a diver on the swim team and a member of the Glee Club. He went on to Harvard Law School, where he was editor of the *Harvard Law Review*, and graduated *cum laude* in 1914. Although he had been born in Ohio, the son of a minister, he moved to Hawaii immediately upon graduation. The dean of Harvard Law had arranged a job for him there with Frear, Prosser, Anderson & Marx, a prominent Honolulu law firm that boasted a former chief justice of the Territory of Hawaii's Supreme Court, Walter Frear, as one of its name partners. Cristy proved to be a quick study and, after serving in the Territorial legislature, was appointed judge in 1926.

In 1931, criminal matters in the First Circuit had been assigned to Alva Steadman, while Cristy's docket was strictly civil. Now that 1932 had rolled around, though, the rotation moved the criminal docket to his court and tossed this hot potato in his lap. He took his role as judge very seriously, and he was not looking forward to dealing with the sideshow that the Ala Moana case had become in its new and transformed state. It was no longer about the assault of Thalia Massie, but was now about the killing of one of those accused of the crime. He tried not to prejudice himself by reading the daily news stories, but it was impossible to completely block out the furor. And he was no stranger to some of the players, having presided over the Rose Younge assault trial several years earlier, in which Ben Ahakuelo and Henry Chang had been involved.

At shortly before three o'clock that Friday, Judge Cristy was summoned from his chambers by his clerk to the grand jury room to answer questions the jurors had. He had anticipated there might be questions about this case, but he was surprised they came up so quickly. He wondered if they really had questions, or if they simply wanted to take his temperature on the matter. Cristy met the court reporter at the door to the grand jury room and they went inside together. He waited until the reporter was set up before he started speaking. He knew that, in a case like this, everything needed to be on the record.

Cristy explained how the roles of a grand jury and a trial jury differ, with the grand jury simply deciding whether there is enough evidence to send a case to trial, while the trial jury makes the ultimate determination of guilt or innocence. After a few more perfunctory questions, he stopped the discussion and gave detailed instructions on their role as grand jurors and their duty in deliberations.

"In sitting as a grand jury, the primary purpose of the grand jury, as expressed in the original charge, is, in the first instance, to prevent malicious or frivolous charges being brought against innocent people. And the second part of your duty, however, and the graver responsibility, is that every person who, by credible evidence, has been shown to be connected with any crime that is a violation of any statute of the Territory of a criminal nature that has been shown to be committed, and by credible evidence of parties they are shown to be connected with it, if it is shown the charge is not frivolous, that those persons should be compelled to stand their trial in the ordinary course of regular procedure. The duties of the grand jury have been so performed when they so present matters to the Court."

Then he shifted into a trickier area. He did not want to impose his own beliefs and thoughts on the grand jury, but he also didn't want them to buckle to public pressure. The judge didn't want to assume that was what was happening—it appeared that they didn't have any serious questions but, as he had feared, they seemed merely to be taking his temperature.

And so he would give them his temperature.

"On the other hand," he continued, "in connection with the general duties of grand jurors, let me remind you in a cool, unimpassioned fashion"—he hoped his voice was, indeed, calm—"without any desire to interfere with your discretion as representatives of the community, let me remind you of those things in your oath, that you should present no one through envy, hatred, or malice and, on the other hand, you should leave no one unpresented through fear, favor, affection, gain, reward, or hope therefor."

Already the press had saturated the Islands with justifications for the shooting of Joe Kahahawai. It had been described as an "honor killing" in more than one report. *Honor killing* was merely a justification that might be presented as a defense to a crime, not evidence that a crime had not been committed. Cristy feared that his jurors might rely upon that defense to fail to indict, when the application of honor killing as a defense was the province of a trial jury, not a grand jury.

"These are the responsibilities which the community, by drawing you as grand jurors, has placed upon you, and in that same connection they have not suggested you should search for any fanciful defenses for those who have been identified with a crime that has been committed, to your satisfaction on credible evidence, and they should answer therefor, and their guilt or innocence be determined by a trial jury." In other words, don't worry about honor killing. If there was a killing at all, then indict; let the trial jury worry about honor killings. He looked at the faces of the twenty-one jurors and wondered if they had gotten the message.

* * *

It seemed to Cristy as if he had barely gotten seated back in his chambers when his clerk knocked again. "Sir," she said after he invited her in, "Mr. Franson is here to see you."

Harry Franson was the foreman of the grand jury. He worked for Honolulu Iron Works, a company in the corporate structure of American Factors, Ltd., better known as Amfac, one of the Big Five. Cristy pulled out his pocket watch and looked at it: 3:15. Maybe five minutes since he had given his supplemental instructions to the jury, so the speed with which another question followed was amazing. As far as grand jury presentations went, he believed this one was pretty straightforward. A man had been shot, and his body was found in the possession of the defendants. By definition, that constituted murder, and that was all the grand jury needed to decide in order to present the case for trial. As he had instructed them, guilt or innocence was not their province. He didn't know how much clearer he could be.

"Send him in," Cristy said.

A moment later, the fifty-six-year-old foreman stepped inside.

"Yes, Mr. Franson?" Cristy said.

"Judge, we took a vote after you left." He stopped and looked at the floor. His feet shuffled in place, as if he wanted to get out quickly. "Nine to indict, twelve not to indict."

The words stunned Cristy. "Were my instructions not clear a few minutes ago?"

"They were clear. But we took a vote, and it's twelve to nine."

Cristy sat silently, his eyes fixed on the edgy foreman. "I don't see how you could possibly have had enough time to discuss my instructions, much less take a vote."

"To be honest, judge, that's pretty well the way this thing laid out even before you gave those last instructions."

Cristy stood. "Obviously the jury needs more instructions."

"The men are packing their things now and getting ready to go home for the weekend."

"Well, they'll just have to put a hold on those plans." Cristy's tone was even but firm. "Go back in there and tell them to stop packing. I'll be in shortly."

At precisely 3:30 p.m., an angry Judge Albert Cristy reentered the grand jury room, along with his court reporter, to a babble of voices. Talking ceased as soon as the judge stood before them, hands on his hips. Everyone took their seats while the court reporter prepared to take down the judge's words.

When Cristy spoke, he did so almost formally, enunciating as if speaking from the judge's bench in a courtroom full of spectators. He intended his words not only for the grand jury members, but also for the record that was being transcribed. He was speaking for an appellate review, lest there be any misunderstanding as to what he had actually said.

And he was speaking directly to the twelve who had voted not to indict.

"Under the statute," he began, "it is provided that the Court may, at any time, if necessity requires, further charge you upon your duties. From information conveyed to the Court by your foreman—" Cristy acknowledged Franson with a nod of his head. "—at the Court's request, that he thought you were about ready for a partial report, the necessity presents itself to the Court to, in very simple language, further charge you upon the situation in the Territory of Hawaii in regard to crime in general, and in connection with your duties.

"I do not want any juror under any circumstances to feel that this Court is interfering in any respect with your conscience nor with your deliberations or conclusions of fact, but perhaps the structure of the criminal procedure might be placed before you for the enlightenment of those of you whom the Court will ask to think it over."

He emphasized that the grand jury needed to consider ramifications for all other criminal cases that might come before it, telling them to "thoroughly study over the conclusions and after-effects, not on single individuals who may or may not have taken the law into their own hands, but upon the community at large, and the further administration of orderly criminal jurisdiction here."

"The Court at this time is not prepared to receive a report, but is going to ask each one of you jurors that, whatever proceedings you have had before you, and whatever you have considered, that you take that matter with yourselves, with the usual caution of disclosing the same to others, and reflect upon it, and reflect upon the consequences of any actions on your part."

The grand jurors sat silently, faces solemn. They knew they were being chastised, as a parent would lecture a misbehaving child.

Cristy moved into a civics lesson. "After you have determined in your own minds, as grand jurors, whether a criminal statute of the Territory has been violated and a crime has been committed, the only remaining question before you is: Has credible evidence identified those who are prima facie responsible for that crime? The question as to whether they should or should not be convicted, from the matter of personal considerations, the question of whether from some inner feelings of your own you might feel you might have committed the same thing, is not the question, because whether you committed it, or I committed it, if a crime has been committed, we do it with the laws that are there to be administered before us.

"If a crime has been committed and the identity of the criminals known, that is, criminals in the sense of the technical provisions of the law, and the grand jury, for reasons, refused under their oath to present an indictment therefor, I present to you the question of anarchy in the community. Are you willing to take the responsibilities for that situation?"

Cristy hit all of the emotional notes. Knowing that racial tensions were high in the Islands, he said, "You know our racial structure. Whether that is involved in any particular case, and in the particular case before you, is for your consideration and not mine. But really, gentlemen, it is a very serious situation which I want you not to act hastily on, and to reflect upon. If there is any juror who cannot conscientiously carry out his oath of office, he should resign immediately from the grand jury."

With that, he dismissed the jury for the weekend, with instructions to return the following Tuesday at 10 a.m. One of the jurors, Edward Bodge, stood. "Do I understand you are not accepting this report?"

Cristy considered the question. In his conversation with foreman Franson, he had been told that a vote had been taken, and what the vote was, but he had cut off Franson at that point in order to give further instructions, since the grand jury had clearly not followed his previous instructions. So, had a report actually been given to him or not? There was no formal writing of a failure to indict, just an oral statement of the results of a vote.

"There has been nothing presented to me," Cristy said. He looked at Franson, half expecting him to contradict what he had just said, but Franson remained quiet. "The Court refuses to accept any further report until the grand jury deliberates further upon matters of serious import to the Territory. After Tuesday, I will talk to you. I will ask you to seriously deliberate upon it until you return for your deliberations at ten o'clock on Tuesday next."

* * *

When the grand jury resumed its deliberations on Tuesday morning, there had been one change. Edward Bodge, who had challenged Judge Cristy's nonacceptance of the jurors' vote, had received an appointment to the Honolulu Police Commission over the weekend. Although the Commission was made up solely of private citizens, its goal was to protect business interests in the Territory and to, among other things, oversee the city's search for a new police chief.

The grand jury assembled at 10 a.m., with Bodge seated front and center, and Cristy addressed the jurors. "Before you begin your deliberations this morning, there are two or three matters that the Court desires to call to your attention. The first matter is, the Court received, since the last session of the grand jury, a communication from the Police Commission, that was created by an act signed subsequent to your last session, informing the Court that Mr. Bodge has been appointed to the Commission and has accepted it, and suggested the impropriety of a commissioner on that body further deliberating as a grand juror.

Cristy directed his attention to Harry Franson. "So, Mr. Foreman, if you will note on the minutes that Mr. Bodge has been excused."

Cristy knew what was going through everyone's mind. The previous Friday, Bodge had been the only one to verbally object that the judge was not accepting a report from the grand jury, even though a vote had been taken. They also all knew that, in all likelihood, the vote now stood at nine to indict and eleven not to indict. It would only take one swing vote to deadlock the jury and two to indict. Was Judge Cristy weeding out opponents to indictment?

Cristy waited until Bodge left before addressing the jury again. Aware of increased pressure from the mainland, as well as from business interests in the Territory and the press, to turn the defendants loose, Cristy took up another matter.

"Gentlemen, there are matters which the Court, under its prerogative as taken last week, further wishes to charge and instruct this jury. Incidents incurring outside of the grand jury room, and before your consideration of the present cases began, indicate to the mind of the Court the possibility that one or more of you entered upon the grand jury session in the matters now pending with your minds so fixed and determined on personal views of law and fact that you are prepared to prevent any indictment in matters now pending so far as you are able to, notwithstanding what the Court should advise the jury the law might be."

Because much had been said in the press to justify the killing of Joe Kahahawai as an "honor killing," Cristy reemphasized the law on murder. "Under the laws of the Territory of Hawaii, no man may legally take the life of another except in legitimate self-defense, unless he be an officer of the law in the performance of a duty requiring or justifying such action. No person can invoke the law of self-defense who has created the difficulty by his own illegal acts. That is, if I, not being an officer of the law and in the performance of my duty, without authority seek to deprive another of his liberty, I cannot justify the killing of such person in order to prevent his regaining his liberty. Under the laws of the Territory, the taking of human life by private citizens, in the nature of a lynching or its equivalent, is prima facie murder."

He then made one final appeal to reason. "The jury room will be closed and you will proceed with your further deliberations. Before so doing, may I ask you gentlemen, as representatives of the Government and the community, to lay aside all race prejudice, to rise above such trivial or personal matters, and apply yourselves coolly and impartially to the question of whether this government shall exist, and how it shall exist."

* * *

At 10:55, Judge Cristy was again summoned to the grand jury room. A new tally had been taken, with nine votes to indict and eleven not to indict, and the first question he faced was, "If we had several indictments to work on and a vote was taken on one, is it possible after recording that vote to reopen the matter and vote again?"

Judge Cristy understood what the juror was asking, even if he hadn't come right out and said it. Why, they wanted to know, were they still deliberating after they had already taken a vote the week before?

"It is not a question of reconsidering, because from the standpoint of the law, until the matter is reported to the Court in open court and that report filed by the Court, there is nothing finished, and the grand jury can take many ballots before arriving at a final result which the Court accepts and files. Does that clarify the issue or can I state it differently to you? The question is not closed until the report is presented and filed by the Court. The matter is still open, and before the grand jury, until that report is in."

After then reminding them that the three options they were considering for indictment were kidnapping, first-degree murder, or second-degree murder, he paused and waited for more questions. There were none, so he continued. He had already appealed to the law, to their sense of duty, and even to their emotions. Now he appealed to their souls.

"Further, let's get down to common sense on the situation. You are all religious men, as I know, and God has not left this world for an instant, and if you will sit with your God and your conscience under the evidence, your duties will clarify themselves in your own minds."

With that, Judge Cristy left the jurors to their deliberations again. At shortly past three o'clock, Judge Cristy was summoned to the jury room one last time. "We have a report to make," Harry Franson said when the judge came in. "And one other matter."

"And what is your report?" Cristy asked.

"By a vote of twelve to eight, we bring an indictment against the defendants for second-degree murder."

Cristy nodded. "I accept your report. What is the other matter?"

Franson handed the judge two folded sheets of paper. "Here are the resignations of two members of the grand jury."

Cristy nodded again. He assumed they had been part of the losing eight, after having been part of the winning twelve on Friday and the winning eleven earlier that day. But that was fine with him. The indictment that was drawn up on January 26 and signed by H. A. Franson as foreman of the Grand Jury, and by Griffith Wight, as city and county attorney for Honolulu, alleged that the defendants:

> . . . on the 8th day of January, 1932, with force and arms, to-wit, a certain pistol loaded with gunpowder and bullets, a more particular description of which is to the Grand Jury unknown, held in the hands of them, the said Grace Fortescue, Thomas E. Massie, Edward J. Lord and Albert O. Jones, unlawfully, feloniously, willfully, and with

malice aforethought, and without authority and without justification and without extenuation by law, did kill and murder one Joseph
Kahahawai, Jr., a human being then and there being, and did then and
thereby commit the crime of murder in the second degree, contrary to
the form of the statute in such case made and provided.

* * *

One of the grand juror resignations was that of Rudolph Bukeley, a former
banker who had moved into the life insurance business. Prior to his resigna-
tion, he delivered a letter to the grand jury, through Foreman Franson, which
included this complaint against Judge Cristy: "I bitterly resent what I consider
to be a deliberate and unlawful attempt on my rights as a grand juror, and further as a deliberate attempt at intimidation."

As if taking their cue from Bukeley, the next day attorneys from the
Honolulu law firm of Thompson & Winn, who represented the defendants,
filed motions to quash and to dismiss the indictments. The motion to quash
asked the court to find the indictments invalid due to some error or technical
violation of legal rules, while the motion to dismiss went to the merits of the
indictments. Signed by Montgomery Winn, the motions listed a number of
grounds, starting with a claim that Judge Cristy refused to accept the grand
jury's report of a no bill against the defendants, and that, by so doing, "[T]he
Honorable A. W. Cristy usurped the time honored function of the Grand Jury
as the sole and exclusive judge of the facts presented before it and as the sole
and exclusive judge of whether or not sufficient facts had been presented to it to
warrant the finding of a true bill against said defendants . . . ."

Other grounds ranged from the additional instructions Judge Cristy had
given, to the removal of Edward Bodge from the grand jury, and included his
remarks that, according to the lawyers, tended to "cause the members of the
grand jury to believe that unless they voted for a true bill against the above
named defendants, their failure so to do would be subversive of good government and that the government could not exist unless a true bill were rendered
by the members of the Grand Jury." In a supplement, the lawyers also asserted
that, after speaking with Judge Cristy, Harry Franson had read to the grand jury
an editorial in the *Honolulu Star-Bulletin* that said that "it was the duty of the
grand jury to return a true bill."

It was clear to Judge Cristy that the attorneys must have spoken to members of the grand jury because they had access to information that they could

not otherwise have known. Furious, Cristy set both the motion to dismiss and the motion to quash for hearing on Friday, January 29, just three days after the indictments had been returned and two days after the motions had been filed. Montgomery Winn promptly served subpoenas on the individual members of the grand jury, as well as others, to appear and testify at the hearing.

When Judge Cristy took the bench at 1:30 p.m. that Friday, the courtroom was filled with subpoenaed witnesses, as well as members of the press, all anticipating a show. Both Frank Thompson and Montgomery Winn, of Thompson & Winn, appeared for the defendants, while Barry Ulrich, whom the prosecution had hired from a private firm as a special prosecutor, and Griffith Wight appeared for the Territory of Hawaii.

Judge Cristy took up the motion to dismiss first, which primarily included a claim that the defendants' constitutional rights had been prejudiced.

"We feel under our constitutional guaranty," Winn said, "the Sixth Amendment to the United States Constitution, the rights of our clients have been prejudiced."

"Which right?" Judge Cristy asked.

"To a speedy trial."

Cristy shook his head. "The Court is trying to give you one. The motion is dismissed as without merit."

Judge Cristy then shifted gears to take up the motion to quash. As Winn went through the various grounds upon which he insisted the indictments should be quashed, Judge Cristy reached the same decision he had made on the motion to dismiss. He concluded, "The Court is compelled to the solution that the motion to quash the indictments as now before the Court, with the original and additional grounds therein alleged, are wholly without merit and are overruled."

Winn stood and addressed the court. "May we have an exception to your honor's ruling?"

"I want to add one thing to it, so you can have one other exception, Mr. Winn. That the fair-minded reading of the instructions that the Court gave the grand jury, some at their request, some at the urge of the Court itself upon opening court, with the entire context of the statements therein contained of record, and not isolated quotations as the devil may do with Scripture, will convince, I am sure, any reasonable mind that this Court at all times left open and free to the grand jurors of this Territory, and will always hereafter continue to leave open and free, the credibility of witnesses, the weight to be given to their testimony, and the sufficiency of the evidence.

"The errors of law are the errors of the Court, and the remedies are provided by proper appeals and writs of error. The errors of jurors who take the law into their own hands, and who apply their own law, would bring on a state of anarchy in any civilized community."

He paused, stared directly at Winn, and put an exclamation point on his ruling. "You may have an exception to that ruling, Mr. Winn."

Then, almost as a parting shot, Cristy set bail for the defendants at $50,000 each. After impassioned pleas and argument, he lowered it to $5,000 for Grace and $2,500 for the others.

* * *

For all of the surety of his statements in ruling on the motions, Judge Cristy, in private, was not so certain that he had properly followed the law. Less than twenty-three hours later, he wrote a letter to the research bureau of Lawyers Cooperative Publishing Company in New York, asking for research and, hopefully, validation of his actions. He sent along a full copy of the transcript of his instructions to the grand jury. He noted that counsel for the defense "are now attacking the indictment," and he asked for research into, among other things, a court's authority to refuse to accept a report of no bill, the court's power to resubmit a question of whether a crime had been committed, the power of a court to dismiss a grand juror who had been appointed to sit on the Police Commission, and, "Where facts are conceded sufficient and qualifications of Jurors conceded, what rights attorneys of accused have to examine minutes of Grand Jury as to earlier deliberations, when attempts to bring in 'no bills' are admitted in the record."

The whole issue, at least as far as Judge Cristy was concerned, became moot a month and a half later when, on March 9, Montgomery Winn filed affidavits with the Court, asking that Cristy be disqualified and that he "make an order transferring the case to any judge whom you shall select."

Under Act No. 292 of the Session Laws of 1931 for the Territory of Hawaii, a defendant got one automatic bite at the disqualification apple, merely by filing an affidavit accusing a judge of bias. Winn filed affidavits from all four of the defendants, each of which contained the same magic words: "[T]hat the Honorable A. M. Cristy, Second Judge of the Circuit Court of the First Judicial Circuit, Territory of Hawaii, has a personal bias or prejudice against [him/her] and the other three defendants in said cause and matter, and for that reason seeks that he be disqualified from further proceeding therein."

In a bit of irony, Judge Cristy was required to sign the order disqualifying himself based on technical compliance with the statute. In a thirteen-page opinion in which he disputed the allegations of bias or prejudice, he concluded, "A fair and impartial trial can be adequately provided by resolving all doubts in favor of Defendants as to the application of Act 292 invoked by them in the present stage of the proceedings. Therefore, without admitting the correctness of the position taken by counsel for the Defendants as to the construction of technical matters herein discussed, this Court hereby assumes the technical compliance by the Defendants themselves, in invoking said Act. The case will be transferred in accordance with the order attached hereto."

The case was then transferred to the court of Judge Charles S. Davis, Honolulu-born but mainland-educated at Cornell, Harvard, and Stanford. The next bombshell would soon arrive from the mainland.

Chapter Twenty-four

The Heavyweights

"[H]e has a damn fine jury personality—when he's sober."

One evening, shortly after indictments had been returned against the defendants, Clarence and Ruby Darrow dined at an elegant restaurant on Lake Michigan, enjoying the food, the view, and each other. At seventy-four years of age, going on seventy-five, Darrow's health was starting to fail a bit, but his mind remained as sharp as it had ever been. Now retired, Darrow had already experienced a long and storied career that had seen him championing the cause of the underdog in the Scopes Monkey Trial and cases against Communist Labor Party members. He had also outraged the nation when, just seven years earlier, he successfully argued continuously for three straight days that his clients, Nathan Leopold and Richard Loeb, who had brutally murdered a fourteen-year-old boy for the sheer thrill of committing murder, should receive life imprisonment instead of being sent to the gallows. But for all his successes, wealth had escaped him and, on the heels of the stock market crash of 1929, he and Ruby were in precarious financial straits. They were not exactly broke, but reverses in their investments raised the possibility, unlikely though it might be, that they would outlive their money.

As they dined, a young man approached their table respectfully and stood at attention. He hesitated, reluctant to interrupt the conversation between Darrow and his wife. After a moment, Darrow saw George Leisure in his peripheral vision. Leisure was a young lawyer whom Darrow was training in the ways of fighting the good fight.

"George, my boy, pull up a chair and have a seat," Darrow said. "The steaks are rare and tender tonight."

"Thank you, sir, but I can't stay."

Darrow wiped his mouth with a cloth napkin then folded it and placed it on the table beside his plate. "Well, something brings you here."

"I received a cable today, directed to your attention, that I think might interest you. It's about a new case."

"I'm retired."

"You can name your fee."

That piqued Darrow's interest. "Name your fee" was music to any lawyer's ears.

"Where might this case be?"

"Honolulu."

Darrow looked at Ruby, whose attention had also been arrested.

"The Fortescue case?" Darrow asked.

"Yes, sir."

Darrow thought for a moment then nodded. "I hear Hawaii's very charming. I've always wanted to go there."

* * *

Darrow named his fee, which Grace's brother-in-law Julian Ripley negotiated, and they settled for $40,000, plus an additional $10,000 for George Leisure to assist in the case, to be paid out of funds raised by friends of Grace Fortescue. That amounted to the equivalent of half-a-million in today's dollars and topped the previous biggest fee Darrow had ever received. It has been reported that Darrow's fee in the Leopold and Loeb case, paid by the millionaire parents of the defendants, was actually $70,000, but that he had to split it 50/50 with his firm, and that, after paying taxes, he netted $30,000.

To pave the way for Darrow, the Honolulu lawyers for the defendants sought a short continuance of the trial setting. While the case was still pending before Judge Cristy, they filed a motion for continuance on March 2. The affidavit in support of the motion stated that negotiations had been underway with Darrow for the past six weeks and that:

> On Tuesday, March 1st, 1932, said Clarence S. Darrow accepted employment as counsel for the defendants, and on Wednesday, March 2nd, 1932, the affiants for the first time received definite notice that said Clarence S. Darrow had been retained to represent said defendants; that said notice and information was contained in a cable from Julian Ripley to the defendant Grace Fortescue, which cable read as follows:
>
> "Doctor approves stop Darrow arrives March twentyfourth [*sic*] desires at least ten days there before trial"
>
> The affiants further aver that said Clarence S. Darrow has been definitely retained to represent said defendants at said trial; that the

said Clarence S. Darrow is not familiar with the facts of the case other than the facts or information he could have secured through newspaper reports; that in order to properly prepare the case for trial said Clarence S. Darrow should have at least seventeen days after his arrival in Honolulu on the 24th day of March, 1932.

One of Judge Cristy's last acts, prior to transferring the case to Judge Davis, was to grant the continuance and set the case for trial on April 4, 1932.

* * *

On March 24, the Matson liner *Malolo* docked at Honolulu Harbor, greeted by the same kinds of throngs that had greeted Grace and Helene when they arrived the previous fall. Among the disembarking passengers were the Darrows and George Leisure. Ruby wore a flower print dress, while both men were attired for the islands in lightweight linen suits. At the bottom of the gangplank, a hula girl greeted the three with kisses and draped plumeria leis around their necks, while a gaggle of newspaper reporters waited anxiously to speak to one of the most famous visitors ever to set foot in the Hawaiian Islands.

As Darrow approached the reporters, he removed his lei. "Let's get rid of these jingle bells," he said, laughing. "I feel like a decorated hat rack."

"Mr. Darrow, you'll be happy to know your autobiography is on sale in our bookstores," a reporter said.

"I would have thought they'd be all sold out by now. Some of you aren't buying enough books."

Laughter from the reporters told him he had a friendly audience, and he turned on the charm as more questions were fired at him.

"What made you decide to come?"

"I wasn't at first, but the more I thought about these islands, which I have long wanted to see, and the more I investigated this strange and puzzling case, the more I felt I had better go."

"Mrs. Darrow, why do you think your husband took this case?"

"You'll have to ask him," Ruby said. "I'd like to know myself."

"Mr. Darrow, what will your defense be?"

"I think I'll just surprise everybody at trial with that." He winked. "All I know is that you never see a good-looking woman convicted of manslaughter or murder—or refused alimony."

As the reporters laughed, some a little too hard, he said, "Now, if you'll excuse me. I need to go see my clients."

The visitors began to push their way through the group to two naval officers, who waited to transport them to the USS *Alton*. As they shuffled by, one last question was thrown at Darrow. "Do you have any other plans while you're in Hawaii?"

Darrow stopped and smiled. "As a matter of fact I do. I just may become a beach boy."

* * *

Admiral Yates Stirling greeted Darrow and Leisure onboard the *Alton*. Ruby had been left at a hotel on Waikiki Beach while the lawyers went to meet with their clients.

"Welcome to Honolulu, Mr. Darrow," Stirling said. "It's an honor to have you here."

"Thank you, Admiral. This is George Leisure, who will be assisting me with the trial."

Darrow and Stirling walked in front, followed by Leisure as they headed across the deck.

"I understand that Honolulu has a new prosecutor," Darrow said.

"His name is John Kelley. This will be his first case as city and county attorney to earn his seventy-five hundred dollars a year."

Darrow nodded. Kelley's annual salary paled beside the sum he would earn over the next six to eight weeks. "What can you tell me about him?" Darrow asked.

"He's the son of a copper miner from Montana, so he's no stranger to hard work. He was educated at the University of Michigan, both college and law school. Been all around the world since he got his law degree. China. Australia. Even Fiji, just before he came to Hawaii. He's generally regarded as one of Hawaii's finest trial lawyers. The local US attorney told me that he has a damn fine jury personality—when he's sober."

"When he's sober?"

"I've heard that he goes on the occasional bender. I guess we'll see which John Kelley shows up at the courthouse."

Darrow, not above having a nip or two himself, made no comment. As they neared Grace's stateroom, he said, "I would like to meet with Mr. Kelley as soon as possible."

"I'll see to it," Stirling said.

* * *

The meeting between Clarence Darrow and John Kelley took place in the same courtroom where the two would square off in just a matter of days. At forty-seven years of age, Kelley looked old beyond his years, bald and slightly overweight, with a paunch that showed, whether he was sitting or standing. After posing for photographers, the lawyers banished the press so they could talk privately. George Leisure and Barry Ulrich, who would be assisting Kelley, sat behind them, almost in the shadows.

"How do you like our little island, Mr. Darrow?" Kelley asked.

"I think the island is just splendid."

"Let me ask you straight up, Mr. Darrow. Are you intending to utilize an insanity defense in this case?"

Kelley was aware that, after pleading his clients guilty in the Leopold and Loeb case, Darrow had used insanity to mitigate their punishment. He had told the judge in that case that he wasn't actually relying upon insanity, but merely intended to show that his clients were "mentally diseased." Near the end of his three-day closing argument, he said that all of the evidence, "shows that this terrible act was the act of immature and diseased brains, the act of children."

"No one really thinks much of insanity defenses, John," Darrow said. "No one really understands them."

"But you haven't answered my question."

"Haven't I?" Darrow smiled and winked at Kelley. "You know, I had my picture taken with your Duke Kahanamoku the other day. I even watched him put on a surfing exhibition. He's a remarkable athlete."

"He did quite well swimming in three different Olympics for the United States," Kelley said. "Even won a gold medal. And he took a silver in Paris in 1924, right behind Tarzan."

"Tarzan?"

"Johnny Weissmuller. He's the star of a picture that's just come out called *Tarzan: The Ape Man.*"

"I've heard of that picture. I understand it's quite a show." Darrow paused and smiled. "And I guess we're going to give the people here quite a show, too, aren't we?"

"That we are, Mr. Darrow. And I don't intend to lose."

"Nor do I."

* * *

Jury selection started on Monday morning, April 4, was completed on Thursday, and Kelley and Darrow clashed almost from the start. During questioning of a potential juror, Kelley asked, "Are you willing to return a verdict, understanding that the guilt or innocence of Joseph Kahahawai in the Ala Moana case has nothing to do with this trial?"

Darrow stood. "If I have something to do with it, the Ala Moana case will certainly have something to do with this trial. I hardly think counsel should ask the jurors to ignore that matter."

Kelley took note that Darrow had now served notice of his intent to rely on the "unwritten law." He wondered what other tricks Darrow had up his sleeve.

On Thursday morning, a small bit of levity seeped into the case, in the form of questioning of Walter Napoleon, who was clearly trying to avoid being selected as a juror. When questioned by Darrow about his ethnicity, he answered that he was a mixture of Hawaiian, French, Tahitian, Irish, and Scottish, and that he spoke three languages: English, Japanese, and Hawaiian.

"So what does that make your nationality?" Darrow asked.

"League of Nations."

The jury that was ultimately seated consisted of seven whites (including one Portuguese), three Chinese, one Hawaiian, and Walter Napoleon, the League of Nations juror—probably best classified as Hawaiian, making two Hawaiians.

At the end of jury selection, an article appeared in the *New York Times*, under the byline of Russell Owen reporting from Honolulu, with the headline "Alienists to Aid in Trial." The opening line of the article stated: "Two alienists who figured in notorious murder trials of Southern California and Arizona, arrived here tonight to confer with Clarence Darrow, the Chicago lawyer who heads the defense counsel for Mrs. Granville Fortescue and three naval men on trial for second-degree murder."

"Alienist" derived from the French *aliene*, which meant insane. The French term came from the Latin *alienatus*, which meant "to deprive of reason," and alienists were psychiatrists who testified as experts on the issue of mental competence. Now Kelley had learned from the newspapers, when it was too late for him to retain psychiatrists of his own as part of his case-in-chief, that Darrow likely planned to use an insanity defense.

He had also learned that the great Clarence Darrow was not above trickery. The battle lines had been drawn.

Chapter Twenty-five
The Finger of Doom
"Is Joseph alive?"

The presentation of evidence started on Monday, April 11, with intense security at the courthouse; even the attorneys were subject to search. The judge had already banned smoking and cameras in the courtroom, but when prosecutor Kelley received death threats, guns were also banned.

The courtroom was filled to overflowing, its racial makeup pretty close to fifty-fifty, half brown and half white. The United States Navy was well-represented, there to show support for the defendants and also, likely, to intimidate the natives in attendance.

John Kelley and Barry Ulrich sat at the prosecution table, notepads in front of them and a box of evidence on the floor between their chairs. Directly behind them, in the front row, sat Esther and Pascual Anito, and Joe Kahahawai Sr. At the defense table, the lawyers huddled together, while their clients sat in a row of chairs behind them. Their hushed conversation was halted when Judge Charles Davis entered and sat on the bench. He nodded to the bailiff, who opened a side door, and the all-male jury entered. The jurors solemnly filed in and took their seats.

"Mr. Kelley," Judge Davis said, "Are you ready to proceed with your opening statement?"

"I am, Your Honor."

"You may proceed."

Kelley rose and approached the jury box, where he stood directly in front of the jurors. After a few introductory remarks, he began his statement. "Gentlemen, these defendants are charged with the crime of murder in the second degree. In order for you to follow the course of the evidence, I'll briefly outline for you what the Territory will endeavor to prove."

He began to pace as he laid out the evidence. He described the kidnapping, the chase to the Halona Blowhole, the guns, the bloodstained clothes of Joe

Kahahawai, and even the bloody towel with the monogrammed USN—United States Navy. As he drew to a close, he stopped directly in front of them again. He waited until he was sure he had the full attention of all twelve.

"On January 8, 1932, when Joe Kahahawai approached this building to report to probation officers, three persons were outside who were soon to put into action forces that were to end his life. When he arrived almost to the statue of Kamehameha, under the shadow of its outstretched finger, the finger of doom pointed at one of the members of the King's people."

He turned and pointed his own finger squarely at Grace Fortescue. "And we will prove that it was the finger of Mrs. Grace Fortescue that pointed that doom. She was the one who put Joseph Kahahawai on the spot."

Darrow deferred his statement until the start of his case, so Kelley proceeded with his first witness, Eddie Uli'i, who testified about the kidnapping of Joe Kahahawai on the morning of January 8. Kelley followed with Joe's probation officer and then began his presentation of the physical evidence with the arresting officers and introducing Joe's clothes. One by one, he held them up for the jury to see. As he held up Joe's blue shirt, stained with blood and marred by a single bullet hole, Esther Anito began to sob.

Darrow stood. "Your Honor, I request that Kahahawai's mother be removed from the courtroom." Though he didn't say it, he was obviously concerned that the sobs of the victim's mother might arouse sympathy in the jurors.

Stunned by Darrow's transparency, Kelley stood silently at the lectern. Before he could think of a suitable sarcastic response, Judge Davis said, "Your request is denied."

Wanting to end with Darrow's effort to exclude Joe's mother fresh in the minds of the jurors, Kelley said, "Your Honor, this is a good time to adjourn for the day."

* * *

The next day, Kelley continued with witness after witness to testify to events, the scene, the clothes, and the guns. In each instance, Darrow either asked no questions or was very brief in his examination. As an experienced trial attorney, he knew that there was nothing to gain by dragging out the testimony on physical evidence. After all, he was conceding the killing, so he didn't rely on attacking the evidence. His defense was justification.

Dr. Robert Faus, the city and county physician, testified about the autopsy he had performed. He described Joe as "a well-built male, Hawaiian, approximately six feet tall and one hundred ninety pounds. His shoulders and upper torso are particularly muscular."

Kelley placed a medical chart of the human body next to the witness stand. "Dr. Faus, please show us, if you will, the path of the bullet."

"The bullet was fired from the front, at a bit of a side angle. It entered the left side of the chest, approximately two or three inches from his nipple, followed a downward course, and lodged just to the right of the seventh dorsal vertebra."

"What does the angle tell you about the position of the victim at the time he was shot?"

"He was sitting down and the shooter was standing."

And, Kelley hoped the jury would infer, the victim posed no threat to the shooter.

"What was the cause of death?"

"The chest was filled with blood, four or five liters. The cause of death was hemorrhage from a bullet wound penetrating the left pulmonary artery."

Faus was the first witness whom Darrow questioned much, although his inquiries were perfunctory. It seemed to Kelley as if the cross-examination was nothing more than an attempt to dilute the emotional impact of Dr. Faus's testimony by putting some time between it and Kelley's next witness.

That next witness was Vasco Rosa, a young man who had been working in the sporting goods department of Diamond-Hall Company, when Deacon Jones, to whom he had previously sold a handgun, entered with Grace and Helene Fortescue. "Did you sell any guns to Mrs. Fortescue and her daughter?" Kelley asked.

"I sold a thirty-two caliber Iver Johnson revolver and a twenty-two pistol."

Kelley walked to the witness stand and placed a cartridge clip—the one found in the waistband of Jones's pants, wrapped in the phony summons—on the rail. One bullet was missing from the clip. He placed an empty shell, the one found in Jones's watch pocket, next to the clip. He then took an unfired .32 bullet and stood it on its end next to the empty shell. With every eye glued on him, Kelley returned to the prosecution table, where he picked up an envelope marked Exhibit 18. He removed a slug from it and approached the stand again.

He held out his hand with the slug in it. "This is Exhibit 18, which has already been identified by Dr. Faus as the slug that was removed from the body of Joe Kahahawai."

He put the slug on the rail, next to the other items. Wordlessly, he returned to the lectern, while the courtroom waited in silence. Rosa shifted in his seat, wondering what Kelley would do next. Judge Davis and the jurors all looked intently at the items lined up on the rail.

At last Kelley spoke. "Mr. Rosa, will you fit the spent slug into the empty casing, please?"

With trembling fingers, Rosa picked up the casing. Then he picked up the slug and fitted it perfectly into the casing.

* * *

As the prosecution neared the end of its case, Kelley announced, "The prosecution calls Mrs. Esther Anito."

Esther stood and prepared to go forward.

Darrow stood. "Objection. The defense stipulates that the clothes in evidence are those worn by Kahahawai the day he died. There is no need for identification by Mrs. Anito, and she has no other relevant testimony to offer."

"Your Honor, there are two mothers in this case, not one," Kelley said. He barely disguised the contempt in his voice. "I think both of them have a right to be heard."

"Objection overruled," the judge said. "Mrs. Anito, please take the stand."

Fighting back sobs, Esther sat in the witness chair. Kelley waited for a moment to allow her to compose herself before starting his questions. Esther testified about that last morning when she sewed new buttons on Joe's shirt and sent him off to meet his probation officer, never to return home. She identified his bloodstained shirt and torn undershorts. She occasionally dabbed at tears in her eyes, but through it all, she remained dignified. By the time she had finished, there were more tears being shed, even on the white side of the courtroom.

A particularly emotional moment came early in her ten-minute testimony, when she discussed her failed marriage to Joe Sr. "We are divorced now," she said.

"Did you have any children together?" Kelley asked.

"Yes. We had four, but two of them died very young. Only two are now living: Joseph and Lillian."

Kelley blinked in surprise. He waited for a moment for Esther to realize her error, but she remained silent, awaiting his next question.

"Is Joseph alive?" Kelley asked at last.

A shadow fell over Esther's face as the truth dawned. "No. No, he is dead."

"When did you last see him?"

"At the undertaker's."

Chapter Twenty-six

Tommie's Story

"Don't let him get me!"

After the prosecution rested, and following the morning recess on April 14, Darrow called Tommie Massie to the stand. He started his questioning with some introductory inquiries, establishing that Massie and his wife had arrived in Honolulu in June of 1930, and then brought the questioning around to that night at the Ala Wai Inn the past September.

"Do you remember an incident of going to a dance or party?" Darrow asked.

"I can't forget it."

"When was that?"

"It was in September."

"Of what year?"

"Last year."

"Who went with you?"

"My wife, Lieutenant and Mrs. Branson, and Lieutenant and Mrs. Brown."

"Where was this dance?"

"It was at the Ala Wai Inn on Kalakaua, in Honolulu."

As Darrow questioned his client, Kelley shifted to the front of his chair, on the toes of his feet. Ready to stand when he deemed the time to be right.

"Were they your guests or you theirs, or just happened to be together?"

"That afternoon of the twelfth, I think it was, I asked Mrs. Massie if she would like to go to the Ala Wai Inn to dance. I told her I had heard a lot of our friends were going there, and asked if she would mind asking two of our friends to come with us and bring their friends. She said she didn't care much about going that night, but I asked her if she would not, and she said, 'Yes,' I could go ahead and call them up, and I called them up and they said they would be pleased to go."

Kelley slid his chair back, prepared to stand as soon as Tommie finished talking.

"Later, after dinner, Mrs. Massie asked if she had to go to the dance. She said she didn't feel like it, and I told her I thought it was a bit late to call it off, since we had asked some other guests, so I persuaded her to go."

Kelley stood when Tommie paused. "At this time, if the Court pleases," Kelley said, "I would ask counsel if it is his intention, as indicated by the testimony of Lieutenant Massie, to go into the so-called Ala Moana case."

Kelley knew that the events of that September night could only be relevant if the prosecution intended to use them as justification for the killing of Joe Kahahawai. Notwithstanding Darrow's deflection of his question a few days before the trial about an insanity defense, it appeared that this was exactly where Darrow was heading—that Massie or someone else was so outraged by the assault on Thalia Massie as to have gone temporarily insane and killed Kahahawai at a time when he couldn't tell right from wrong.

"I want to make this very brief," Darrow said, "but I intend to go into this Ala Moana case to some extent."

"If counsel intends to go into the Ala Moana case," Kelley responded, "I think the prosecution should be informed as to whether or not as to one or more of these defendants the defense is going to rely upon the defense of insanity. We wish to offer no unnecessary objections to this line of testimony, if the Court pleases, but it is well recognized there are only certain conditions under which it can be admitted, and the prosecution, we feel at this time, has a right to know whether those conditions are going to be met."

"I don't think they have the right to it, but I am perfectly willing to answer the question," Darrow said. "No use of disputing over matters we do not dispute. We do expect to raise the question of sanity of the moving one in the last part of this tragedy—that is, the one who shot the pistol."

"I think that answers your question, Mr. Kelley," Judge Davis said.

Maybe yes, and maybe no, Kelley thought. That was the first time that he knew, for a positive fact, other than what he had inferred from the newspaper article about the arrival of alienists, that Darrow would be relying on an insanity defense. He still didn't know, though, *who* the defense was claiming to have been insane.

"Partly," Kelley responded to the judge. "We object to any further testimony of Lieutenant Massie on this subject unless we are informed that the plea of insanity is to be presented in his behalf."

"I don't think that makes the slightest difference," Darrow said. "Of course, counsel has stated many times to the jury that each one is responsible for what all did, if they were connected in an enterprise of this sort, which, perhaps, would be true if they had reason to foresee what might follow from their act. I don't think we need to go further at this time. The Court is familiar with it, and so is counsel. The statement was made openly and it is just exactly as we stated it."

In other words, since the prosecution contended that all of the defendants were equally guilty of whatever happened during the kidnapping, then if the one who pulled the trigger was excused by insanity, then all of them were excused. What difference did it make, Darrow was saying, which one of them it actually was?

But it made all the difference in the world, as far as Kelley was concerned, for at least two reasons. The first was his right, as he saw it, to have his alienists examine the insane one and reach their own opinions as to sanity. The second had to do with whatever the defense was going to contend caused the insanity. If it was the events of the Ala Moana case, then it didn't make sense that either Jones or Lord, who were not related to Thalia Massie, could have been driven insane. That left Tommie Massie and Grace Fortescue. If the defense was ultimately going to place the murder weapon in Tommie Massie's hand, then that meant they were probably also going to invoke the unwritten law—the right of a husband to avenge the dishonor of his wife—as well as an insanity defense. Kelley needed to be prepared, if that was the case.

"We have the right, if the Court pleases," Kelley said, "at least we feel we have the right, in the event a plea of insanity is relied upon with reference to any of these defendants . . . to know which defendant this plea is going to be presented for, and the right to examine by alienists, doctors, psychiatrists, or other persons of the party who it is claimed was insane at the time the murder was committed."

"Under our law, Mr. Kelley," Judge Davis replied, "the plea of insanity puts in issue the insanity of all. There is no special plea of insanity required."

Darrow interceded at this point, speaking in an almost patronizing tone. Addressing his remarks for Kelley's benefit, he said, "Counsel has been very accommodating to us, and if he says he wants some doctors to come in here and hear the testimony, why, I would be perfectly willing to accommodate him by even calling another witness, although I would rather finish with him as I started. Nobody whom we claim is insane—we may not see fit to submit them to his physician. That will come up later. But certainly they have the right to be here in court, and if he makes any such request, we will try to meet him fairly in the matter."

And Kelley knew he had been completely snookered. While he argued that he was entitled to have his own psychiatrists examine whomever the defense claimed was insane, Darrow's response was that he was too late. Since the prosecution had already rested, while not knowing that the defense was claiming insanity, an examination was no longer in the cards.

As he continued his direct examination, Darrow next took Tommie through the events of the evening at the Ala Wai, then discovering that his wife had left early. After telling Thalia that they had been invited to the Rigbys' house after the dance, Tommie later got ready to leave.

"I started to look for Mrs. Massie and get her wraps, and we were downstairs on the dance floor, and I asked a few people and we couldn't find her. So I looked all over the place, up on top and down below, and Mrs. Rainer was still looking when I got back, and I think Mr. Branson was with her, and he was helping her to see if he could find Mrs. Massie. Then I looked out on the grounds and I couldn't find her there, and I came back and found Mrs. Rainer still looking. I thought she had probably gone home with Mrs. Rigby. I called Mrs. Rigby's and didn't get any answer, and I called my home and didn't get an answer, and I called several other places of people we thought she had left early with, and couldn't find her."

When he finally got to the Rigby house, Tommie said, he called home again. "Mrs. Massie answered. She recognized my voice and said, 'Something terrible has happened. Please come home at once.'"

With a quivering voice, wrenched with emotion, he described Thalia's appearance when he arrived home. "I went into the house, and she was standing in the door waiting for me. She collapsed in my arms and I took her over under the light. Blood was coming from her nose and from her mouth. Her lips were crushed and bruised. Her eyes were swollen and there was a large bruise on the right side of her face."

Darrow paused to allow the jurors time to frame that picture in their minds. It didn't appear that either Darrow or Kelley knew that this description didn't track with the description given by the Clarks and the Bellingers who had picked Thalia up on Ala Moana Road that fateful night. According to her rescuers, although she did appear to have been beaten, the extent of her injuries were a swollen lip—"all puffed up at the mouth" was how George Clark Sr. put it when he testified at the rape trial—and a "mark" on her cheek that might have been made by a ring.

But Tommie's description on the stand of more serious and extensive facial injuries was consistent with reports from police officers who first answered the call and with Dr. Liu's observations. Had Kelley known of this discrepancy between the time Thalia had been dropped off at her home and the time police arrived, it might have raised some questions about what happened to her in between, maybe even at the hands of her husband.

"Did she tell you what had happened to her?" Darrow asked.

"No. I thought a truck had run over her. I asked her what in heaven's name had happened. 'Oh,' she said, 'it is too terrible. It's too terrible!' She couldn't do anything but sob."

Tommie testified that he pressed on with his questioning. "I said, 'Please tell me what has happened.' She said, 'I can't; it's awful; it's horrible.' She kept sobbing and I asked her several times, and she said some men had dragged her into a car and beaten her and taken her to a place and ravished her. I said, 'Oh, my God, no!' She couldn't answer me then. I just sat there dazed. Finally she sobbed and said, 'I want to die! I want to die!' I tried to comfort her but I couldn't. I finally went to the phone and called the police and told them that my wife had been assaulted. I gave them my address and told them to come at once.

"I went back to my wife and got some wet towels and tried to get the blood away, but she wouldn't let me do anything for her. She just stayed there in my arms and cried and sobbed. She was completely broken. I then asked her if she had taken every precaution against conception and disease. She said, 'Yes, I have done everything I can.'"

Moving forward, Darrow asked Tommie about the first so-called line-up, at their home, when the police "brought four of the assailants in for identification."

"I object to the statement of the witness that the 'assailants' were brought in," Kelley said after standing.

"Suppose we say 'four men'" Darrow said. "Change it to that."

"The four people were brought in," Tommie said. "They told Mrs. Massie before they entered not to show while they were in there if she recognized them, before they brought them in. I was there. She questioned them all. She seemed to concentrate her questions on Kahahawai. Finally, about after fifteen minutes, the detectives went out and said, 'Go back and see what your wife says.' I went back in and leaned over the bed and asked her what she thought. She said, 'They are the ones.' I said, 'Please, darling, don't let there be any doubt in your mind, because you know what it means.' The tears came into her eyes and she said, 'Don't you know if there was any doubt in my mind, I couldn't ever draw an easy breath as long as I live.' I went out and told the detectives they were the ones."

To set the stage for Tommie's shaky mental condition, Darrow next asked questions designed to probe at his fragile psyche. Tommie testified that he "wanted to learn something about these people," and that he found out that "several of them had criminal records; that one had been convicted of rape; that another had a criminal record, something to do with robbery, and another was in a sex case."

With prompting from Darrow, Tommie continued his melodramatic tale about his wife. He said that her jaw had to be wired with two splints. "They gave me a pair of wire clippers and told me that if she ever got sick at the stomach to cut all the wires as soon as possible, or she would choke to death.

"One night when I thought she was asleep, I had been lying there and couldn't go to sleep. She had an ice pack on her head, and I thought she was comfortable, but as I was lying there, she suddenly rose up in bed and screamed, 'Don't let him get me! Don't let him get me!' I went over to her and woke her up and said, 'It's all right, darling, nobody is here but me. She said yes there was, Kahahawai was there."

From that moment on, "the whole thing preyed on my mind every minute," he said, and "I began to lose appetite. I couldn't sleep. I had to get up and walk the floor; I couldn't get it out of my mind at all, everything going over and over again, the whole picture of the thing."

"Have you ever got it out of your mind?" Darrow asked.

"Never."

Thalia claimed to hear footsteps under her window at night, he said, and when he checked it out, "I laid there and waited, and I heard footsteps under the window, and there couldn't be any doubt about it."

Darrow then asked Tommie about the phantom pregnancy. According to Tommie, "Dr. Porter explained that we would have to expect two things that were possible: disease and conception." He conveniently left out the part where Dr. Porter specifically told him that Thalia was not pregnant.

"Those were the things that preyed on my mind every minute of the day," Tommie said. "Worse than anything I could imagine. After Mrs. Massie's mother came, we knew that an operation would be necessary to prevent pregnancy. This had a strange effect on my mind."

"Was it done, the operation?"

"Yes, I took her to the hospital, and Dr. Withington performed the operation."

"Did you know or did she know that that pregnancy was due to you or not?"

"There couldn't be any doubt that it wasn't."

With that, Judge Davis adjourned court until the following day.

* * *

Although the trial was scheduled to resume the morning of Friday, April 15, they all had to wait one more day, as Clarence Darrow was under the weather—some thought he was actually hungover. Tommie Massie retook the witness stand at 9:00 a.m. on Saturday morning, April 16. Darrow was finally ready to identify the shooter.

"There seems to have been some misunderstanding between the attorneys on the other side and ourselves, and I want to set it right," he said to Judge Davis. "We believe that a plea of not guilty puts this full question in issue and it is not necessary then or now to say who fired the shot. But we are perfectly willing to do it to save any more time or controversy on the subject. The evidence will show in this case that the defendant Massie, now on the stand, held the gun in his hand from which the fatal shot was fired in this case."

From there, Darrow addressed the Ala Moana trial again, eliciting testimony from Tommie that he was present at the trial, and that, "I would take Mrs. Massie down on the days when she went and I waited outside for her and took her back home."

He seemed to have conveniently forgotten that he had actually gone to sea on maneuvers after the start of the rape trial.

"What was the result of that trial?" Darrow asked.

Kelley immediately stood. "At this time I object to the testimony of the witness and the answer to this question on the ground that it is incompetent, irrelevant, and immaterial, having no bearing on the issues in this case. The only purpose of this testimony, if the Court please, and the only theory under which it is admissible is the insanity of one or more of the defendants. Mr. Darrow has stated this morning that the defendant, Massie, will admit that he fired the shot that killed Kahahawai. Even under that theory or with that admission, this evidence is still inadmissible.

"We contend it is inadmissible to show motive, intent, or in mitigation under our statutes, and that the only theory under which it can be admitted is the basis and theory that Massie or some other one of the defendants was insane at the time the shot was fired. Unless that declaration is made at this time, and unless we proceed on that theory, we object to any further evidence by this defendant and move that his previous evidence be stricken."

"It becomes necessary for the Court to inquire," Judge Davis said to Darrow, "in order to rule on the objection and motion, that counsel for the defense state at this time whether he is relying on the defense of insanity as far as the witness on the stand is concerned."

It appeared that Kelley might finally learn for sure which of the defendants Darrow was going to say was insane at the time of the shooting.

"Your Honor, that is what we are relying on," Darrow said. "We expect the evidence to show that this defendant was insane. I did not say that he would testify that he killed the deceased."

Kelley cocked his head. Hadn't Darrow said exactly that just a few minutes earlier?

"We will show that the gun was in his hand when the shot was fired," Darrow continued, "but that the question as to whether he knew what he was doing at the time is another question."

Ridiculous, Kelley thought. Darrow was simply playing word games.

"It now appears, Mr. Kelley," Judge Davis said, "that the theory of the defense is that the witness on the stand is relying on the defense of insanity, and that the theory of the defense is that the witness now on the stand fired the fatal shot."

At least the judge saw through the word game, Kelley thought. And now that he knew who was supposedly insane, Kelley had another card to play. "Then I would ask this further question," he said. "If the defense is ready to admit at this time that the defendant, Massie, is sane. If he is not, he can't testify."

Insane then, but sane now? Or still insane and, if so, incompetent to testify?

"There is always the presumption that insanity would, of course, exist at this time," Darrow said.

Then, as a precursor to the psychiatric wrangling soon to come from the respective sides' alienists, Kelley said, "We at this time feel that we are entitled to know the type of insanity that the defendant is alleged, or was laboring under at the time he fired the shot, in order that we may meet any medical testimony that may be produced as to his condition at that time. We have in court doctors whom we intend to use. They are entitled to know the type of insanity that the defendant and defense claims that this man was laboring under at the time he fired the shot in order that we may adequately meet that when the time arises."

It may have seemed like an imminently reasonable request, but Darrow was not inclined to agree to anything. "I don't think anybody on earth can tell," he said to the judge. "People who are familiar with books and have made a study of the question know that doctors disagree as to type. There is nothing in the type except the name that different doctors give different symptoms. Of course, this may have occurred before but I have never heard any such request made.

Doctors almost always disagree as to the name because they give the name that they think are the symptoms. There is no rule whatever as to that question."

After several more minutes of arguing, with no consensus being reached, Kelley ultimately withdrew his request to know the type of insanity the defense was claiming, and the testimony of Tommie Massie continued. Soon enough, Darrow turned to the morning of December 8 in Grace's rented house at 2574 Kolowalu Street in Manoa.

* * *

Tommie brandished the .45 at Kahahawai, who sat on a chaise longue across the table, while Lord leaned against a door frame and smirked. Jones stood next to Kahahawai, and Grace perched tautly on a nearby settee, her back rigid and her face blank, with her hands in her lap.

"You know what happened to Horace Ida, don't you?" Tommie asked. "He talked plenty about you, about what you did. And what he got isn't anything compared to what you're gonna get." Massie took a deep breath then said, slowly and precisely, "This is your last chance. Now, tell the truth."

"I don't know nothing," Joe said.

"All right, Eddie," Massie said, "go out and get the boys. They'll make him talk."

Lord went to the door and outside. As Kahahawai watched him leave, his breath came in gasps.

"If you don't talk before he gets back with those men, they'll beat you to ribbons," Tommie said. "This is your last chance."

Kahahawai's whole body trembled. Tears welled in his eyes. "All right," he said. "Yes, we done it."

Tommie's face went slack. The gun barked in his hand.

Kahahawai pitched sideways and sprawled on the floor next to the chaise longue. Blood flowed from his chest and pooled on the floor.

* * *

The courtroom had gone deathly silent as Tommie recounted what happened.

"The last thing I remembered was that picture that came into my mind, of my wife when he assaulted her and she prayed for mercy and he answered with a blow that broke her jaw."

"Did you have a gun in your hand when you were talking to him?" Darrow asked.

"Yes, sir."

"Do you remember what you did?"

"No, sir."

Darrow paused to let that soak in on the jury. "Do you know what became of the gun?"

"No, I do not, Mr. Darrow."

Darrow paused again, letting the drama mount for his next question.

"Do you know what became of you?" Darrow asked.

"No, sir."

With that, Darrow addressed Judge Davis. "That's all, Your Honor."

Chapter Twenty-seven
The Man Who Fired the Gun
"We can trace those impulses back to the cradle."

As Darrow returned to his seat, Kelley stepped confidently toward the witness stand, almost as if attacking the witness. "I believe you stated you were born in Kentucky?"

"Yes, Mr. Kelley."

"And you are proud of your native state?"

"Very proud of it."

"And you are very proud of being a Southerner, aren't you?"

"I would not say that."

Darrow sprang to his feet. "Objected to."

Tommie continued his answer, "Now there is—"

Darrow shut his client down. "Wait a minute."

"The answer may go out for the purpose of ruling on the objection," Judge Davis said. "What is the objection?"

"What has a Southerner got to do with it?" Darrow asked. "Why he is proud of being a Southerner over a Northerner. What is the purpose of it?"

"I don't know," Kelley said. "I just want to find out."

Darrow knew that Kelley was being coy about asking the question, and he called the prosecutor on it. "Yes, but I think I do know, and I think he has a very definite reason for it."

Kelley looked at the judge, innocence on his face. "Is the question admissible or inadmissible, Your Honor?"

"I think it is entirely inadmissible," Darrow said, though he was not the proper person to rule on his own objection. He turned and spoke directly to Kelley. "I am making my statement to the Court and asking you, quietly, what is the purpose of it?"

Kelley refused to meet Darrow's look but instead kept his eyes on the judge. "If Mr. Darrow knows what the reason is, the Court and the jury are entitled to know it."

"That is not correct," Darrow said. "The jury is not entitled to hear it. I think that the purpose of the question is perfectly evident, and it has no place in the case. I think the purpose of it is to create prejudice."

"What are the grounds of your objection?" the judge asked.

"It is irrelevant, immaterial, and asked for the purpose of creating prejudice in the mind of some of these jurors, and it has no bearing upon this case."

Judge Davis thought for a brief moment then made his ruling. "Although great latitude will be allowed on the cross-examination of this witness, the objection will be sustained on the grounds made, for that reason that, whether or not, especially upon the ground that whether or not the witness be proud of any definite fact has no bearing and is immaterial to the issues in this case."

Kelley spread his hands and faced the judge. "We are concerned here with a man who claims he killed a man by reason of insanity. We have given every latitude to counsel for the defendant in his examination. In fact, I felt at times too much latitude. On the motivating impulses that led this man to become insane, we can trace those impulses back into the cradle, and we so desire. I submit this is entirely proper cross-examination, under the theory that the defense is based upon."

"I am inclined to agree with you," Judge Davis said, "but as to his attitude and as to whether or not the witness is proud of any given fact in his life, Mr. Kelley, I don't think it has a bearing on that particular issue, unless you can show me that it has. I don't think you should pursue the question of whether or not he was or is proud of any particular thing."

"Doesn't that create a condition of the mind?" Kelley asked.

"I think that is rather remote from the issue, Mr. Kelley."

Kelley nodded and glanced at this notes. He was sure that the jury had already gotten his point: Massie was a Southerner and racial animus played into his treatment of Joe Kahahawai, a dark-skinned Hawaiian. Now he was content to move on.

Referencing testimony that Tommie had given on direct examination, he said, "You referred to some other plan that you had in mind and stated that if the plan to force a confession out of Kahahawai did not succeed, you were going to put in effect this other plan."

"That is right, Mr. Kelley."

"What was that other plan?"

"To threaten him by sending Lord out to get a bunch of boys that we had waiting there, and to impress in his mind that they were going to cut him to threads by a beating."

Just as had been done to Horace Ida. Kelley glanced at the jury to see if they had made that connection. All he saw were twelve poker faces.

"You had no plan in mind of tying him up and torturing him?" Kelley asked.

"No, Mr. Kelley." Tommie's tone of voice was almost one of righteous indignation at the very suggestion.

Kelley moved on to the abduction and the steps taken to effectuate the plan. "Your .45 was in the Fortescue house that morning, was it not?"

"I am almost sure it was."

"What was the purpose of bringing it over and leaving it there?"

"That was to scare him."

"And a .45 is a very impressive looking weapon, isn't it?"

"I imagine a lot of people would think so."

When discussing the fake warrant, Kelley asked, "Did Mrs. Fortescue tell you that she had seen something in the newspaper that morning that was rather appropriate to the purpose of this warrant?"

"No, Mr. Kelley, she hadn't mentioned it."

"Was it just by chance that this article here, 'Life is a mysterious and exciting affair,' was put on this warrant?"

"If you are asking for my opinion, I would say yes, it was entirely by chance."

Kelley then moved to Tommie's memory lapses, looking for ways to poke holes in his testimony. He showed Tommie a photograph that had been taken when he and his cohorts had been stopped while trying to dispose of Joe's body in the ocean.

"Is this I?" Tommie asked.

"Is it?"

"I don't know. It looks something like me."

"You don't remember hiding your face when that photograph was taken?"

"No, I do not."

"Do you recall the body of Kahahawai being taken out of the car, that Buick car?"

"Here is the way it was, Mr. Kelley. It was all vague. I could see figures and I think I knew they were people, and I could tell something about the distinction in dress, but it was all very vague."

"Do you remember Percy Bond coming up and talking to Harbottle?" Kelley asked.

"No, sir."

"You don't remember congratulating yourself when he said, 'Nice work, kid' to Harbottle?"

"No, sir."

Hopping around in time, to try to keep Tommie off balance, Kelley moved back to conversations that Tommie had with attorney Eugene Beebe that prompted the effort to obtain a confession. "You had been advised by Mr. Beebe that a confession obtained from any of these defendants by force could not be used, is that correct?" Kelley asked.

"He made particular reference to not beating him."

"And did he say anything about not threatening him with a gun?"

"I don't remember."

"Did he tell you that force could be exerted by the threat of killing?"

"I don't recall that."

As Kelley continued to press Tommie on his conversations with Eugene Beebe, and started to tread into Clarence Darrow's legal theories, Darrow got a little antsy and finally threw in an objection, for no apparent reason other than to disrupt Kelley's rhythm.

"Did you ask Mr. Beebe if the unwritten law could be invoked in the Territory of Hawaii?" Kelley asked.

"I don't think so."

"Will you deny that you did?"

"I couldn't deny it and be accurate because I do not know."

"Will you affirm that you did?"

"No, for the same reason."

"You might have?"

Darrow stood. "I object to the question as being answered. He said he didn't know. He says he doesn't know either way."

Judge Davis responded, "Well, counsel has the right to press the witness for an answer on cross-examination. The objection will be overruled."

But Kelley had already accomplished his purpose. When Darrow argued the unwritten law to the jury at closing, and surely he would, the jurors would at least have had questions raised in their own minds about whether Massie had been aware of the unwritten law at the time of the killing and whether it might have entered in to a calculated plan to rely on it and to kill Joe Kahahawai.

Moving on, Kelly asked, "Now, Mr. Massie, do you want us to understand that all that Mr. Beebe told you was that if you got a statement or confession of any of these defendants, and you used no force in getting it, it could be used to stop these vile rumors that were going on about you and your wife?"

Rumors of Thalia's infidelities. Rumors that Thalia had lied at the first trial to hide the evidence of yet another infidelity.

"That's practically what I remember, Mr. Kelley."

"Then you never had at any time any intention of getting any confession to use in a subsequent trial of the Ala Moana case?"

"I was interested in one thing in those days and that was to clear the name of my family. You would have been, too."

"Did you ever consider that the most effective way of doing that would be to get a confession that could be produced in the trial that would result in the conviction of the defendants?"

"I wasn't worried about the trial. I was worried about my wife."

At last Kelley arrived at the actual shooting. "Now, when was it, Mr. Massie, that the plan with reference to threatening Kahahawai with a gun in order to get a statement out of him was discussed with the other defendants?"

"I think the afternoon before."

"So it was agreed that a gun would be used in order to scare him into talking?"

"Yes, sir."

"You felt it would be more impressive and he would become more frightened if you, in front of him, went through the motions of loading that gun?"

"I hoped it would. That and his recognizing me."

After a series of questions about Tommie's lost memory, Kelley then asked, "Now, Mr. Massie, will you just tell us what was the last thing that Kahahawai said before you had this mental lapse?"

"I will, Mr. Kelley. I will never forget it."

"Will you tell us?"

"'Yes, we done it.'"

"That's all he said?"

"That's all I can remember."

"And then what happened?"

"I don't know."

"Did you ever have one of these spells before?"

"No."

"Will you kindly tell us what was the first thing that you recall after this lapse that you had up at Mrs. Fortescue's house that day?"

Tommie pursed his lips and looked at the ceiling, as if thinking. "That is something that has baffled me. I can't recall the first thing. I have thought a great deal about it. Everything was vague and blurred at times, and then I would clear up and blur again."

Kelley frowned, his demeanor intended to communicate skepticism to the jury. "Of course, you make no claim that you are laboring under any mental hallucinations at this time?"

"I don't know how I am at this time."

"Are you the same you were when you went into this lapse at the Fortescue house?"

"My opinion is I am not."

"You don't feel the same?"

"No, I don't think I do."

"You are able to understand everything that is going on here?"

"Yes, sir."

"And you understand the nature of the testimony you are giving?"

"Oh, yes, sir."

"No question about that?"

"Well, I can understand English words, Mr. Kelley."

"And the thoughts you are expressing in words, you understand those?"

"I hope so."

Having established that Tommie was now competent to stand trial, Kelley moved back to Grace's house the morning of January 8. At Grace's instruction, Tommie said, Joe moved from the chair where he had been seated to the *chaise longue.*

"Did you keep him covered with the gun when he moved?" Kelley asked.

"All the time."

"Did he turn his back to you when he walked to that *chaise longue?*"

"I don't recall."

"He didn't make a break for the front door?"

"No."

"Did he say anything?"

"No."

"You say he was trembling?"

"Yes."

"Appeared very much frightened?"

"Yes."

"Did he plead for mercy?"

"No."

"Didn't beg you not to shoot?"

"No."

"Do you recall his saying anything else that morning except the words, 'Yes, we done it'?"

"No, I don't, Mr. Kelley."

"And he was sitting on that *chaise longue* when you shot him?"

"He must have been."

"He didn't make a break for the front door?"

"No."

"He didn't put up any fight?"

"No."

Kelley paused to let the jury understand that Joe Kahahawai was unarmed, in a hostile environment, and surrounded by those who meant him harm. No matter how big he was, no matter how much bluster, no matter his reputation as an athlete, at that moment in that house, he was a scared little boy, all alone, probably knowing that he faced death.

"You remember Kahahawai saying, 'Yes, we done it'?"

"I remember that."

"You don't recall hearing any noise, like the gun going off?"

"No."

"You do recall, however, loading that gun, that is, working the mechanism so a shot went into the magazine?"

"Yes."

Kelley paused before his next questions. He studied his notes for a moment then asked, "So you were standing there with a loaded gun, with the hammer back, when you were talking to Kahahawai?"

"From everything that happened, I must have been."

"Do you remember having your finger on the trigger?"

"I cannot recall it."

Unable to shake Tommie from his memory lapse, Kelley moved back to the night of the dance at the Ala Wai Inn and his drinking habits. "You take a drink occasionally, do you?"

"I have been known to."

"Being from Kentucky, I would naturally expect that you would. You are, in fact, a drinking man, are you?"

"I don't think so."

Then Kelley sprang rapidly forward in time to the events immediately following Joe's death. "Do you know who undressed the body of Kahahawai?"

"I know what I have heard."

"Were you told who stripped Kahahawai's clothes off him?"

"Jones told me."

"What did he tell you?"

"He said, 'The stains wouldn't come out, so we took the clothes off.'"

"Did anyone tell you where he died?"

"Yes."

"Who told you?"

"Mrs. Fortescue did."

"Where was it? On the *chaise longue*?"

"Yes, sir."

"Did she or anyone else tell you how long it was after he was hit with this shot that he died?"

"Not that I recall."

"Did any of the three defendants ever tell you what you did after this shot was fired?"

"Yes, they spoke of it, yes, sir."

"Who?"

"All three of them did."

"Well, what did Mrs. Fortescue tell you in that respect?"

"She said I just stood there like a bump on a log, and she talked to me and I would not answer her, and she finally took me into the kitchen and tried to make me drink some *oke* and I would not do that and she sat me down on a chair and I think she said I stayed there." The words came out shotgun style, in a nervous stream of consciousness.

"Did Jones tell you what your actions were after the shot was fired?"

"Jones was not very complimentary," Tommie said. Disgust registered in his voice.

"Why? Because you shot him only once?"

"No, sir."

"What did he say?"

"He said I acted like a damn fool."

"Jones, by the way, is an enlisted man in the Navy, isn't he?" Kelley asked.

"I resented it just as much as you are going to say I did."

"I don't know whether you did or you didn't."

Tommie hesitated a moment then said, "I did."

Kelley's questioning of Tommie about the shooting and the events following it, the supposed blank in Tommie's memory, was intense and unyielding. He knew he wasn't going to get any concessions out of the witness that would contradict his "insanity"—Massie had been too well coached by Clarence Darrow for that. However, he hoped he could score points with the jury by calling into question the total absence of memory that, to Kelley's mind, seemed unbelievable. By his questioning, he hoped he could keep the jurors focused in reality and to prevent them from suspending their disbelief at the request of the famous lawyer from Chicago.

To accomplish that, Kelley sometimes resorted to sarcasm, to emphasize his own feeling that the witness was lying and that his missing memory was merely a convenience. At one point, talking about disposing of the body, he asked, "Do you remember getting into the Buick sedan?"

"No, sir. For all I know I might have gone to China and back."

With barely disguised contempt in his voice, Kelley said, "Too bad you didn't."

Finally, as Kelley neared the end of his cross-examination, he harkened back to an event that had occurred less than five years earlier that might raise questions in the jury's minds about the character of Tommie Massie and the credibility of Thalia Massie.

"Mr. Massie," Kelley said, "have you ever been implicated in a kidnapping plot before?"

Tommie appeared stunned, as if the question had come out of the blue.

"No, sir," Tommie said.

"Quite sure?"

"Quite sure."

Darrow, hoping to head off the questioning, objected. "I want to take an exception to that question. It is directly prejudicial, irrelevant, and should not have been asked. I simply want to take an exception to it."

And, from the reaction of the jurors, it was also incredibly intriguing. Apparently it was to Judge Davis, as well. "Exception may be noted," he said.

After establishing that Tommie was visiting the Fortescue home on Long Island on August 27, 1927, while he was still at the Naval Academy, Kelley asked, "State whether or not on or about that date, near Bayford [sic], Long Island, you assisted in the kidnapping of a baby."

A buzz moved through the crowd in attendance, and jurors sat up straighter, eyes focused on the man on the witness stand.

"I would rather tell the whole thing," Tommie said.

"Answer my question, 'yes' or 'no'."

"I was not implicated in any kidnapping of a baby. Never have been and never will be." Tommie's tone spoke defiance, but an uneasy shift in his posture betrayed his tone.

"Were you arrested?"

Darrow sprang to his feet. "That is objected to."

"I was asked to come to—" Tommie started, but Darrow cut him off.

"I object to the question 'Was he arrested'."

"Were you arrested on a charge of kidnapping?" Kelley repeated.

A furious Darrow retorted, "Objected to on the ground that arrest does not mean anything."

"Objection overruled," Judge Davis said.

Everyone in the courtroom knew exactly what "arrest" meant, and they also understood that Darrow's real objection was that the very question, and the events inquired about, might taint his client. For his part, Tommie squirmed in the witness chair, obviously trying to figure out the best way to explain what happened that day in 1927. To buy time to think, he settled on evasiveness.

" 'Yes' or 'no,' Mr. Massie?" Kelley asked.

"The question again, please, Mr. Kelley."

"Were you arrested on a charge of kidnapping?"

"What was or what might have been a charge of kidnapping was later proved to be not that."

Making a show of great patience, Kelley said, "All right. Before we get to that later period, were you arrested on a charge of kidnapping?"

"I don't think it was an arrest."

"Were you taken to a police station?"

"We were taken to an office." Tommie paused, then spilled out the story he wanted to tell in a near stream of consciousness. "Miss Fortescue, then, and I were at a movie in Patch Hall [*sic*], Long Island. The movie was quite dull. We left and decided to take a drive. When we came outside, there was a little baby sitting by the box, the ticket box, in a carriage, crying. Mrs. Massie said something about 'Oh, the poor little thing. I will roll it down to the block and back and maybe it will hush crying.' When we got about halfway down there, a woman came screaming and shouting and said, 'You are kidnapping my baby.' We went to the police station, as you call it. It might have been, and we were questioned.

"I think she was an Italian lady was up there and found out what it was all about, and Mrs. Fortescue was called and, as I remember, the Italian lady came up to Mrs. Fortescue and said, 'Well, you give me five dollars and I won't say anything about this,' and Mrs. Fortescue laughed at her. She knew there was not going to be anything to it, and the next morning they held an investigation and dismissed the charge that you call kidnapping."

Tommie then fell silent. Kelley just stared at him for a moment as all in the courtroom tried to digest what the witness had said. It was a story that didn't make much sense, and probably raised more questions than it answered, but Kelley was satisfied that he had landed a body blow to the credibility of Tommie and Thalia Massie. After a few more follow-up questions, he ended his cross-examination of the man who fired the gun.

Chapter Twenty-eight
Delirium with Amublatory Automatism
"What right does he have to say that I don't love you?"

Having now introduced evidence that Tommie Massie had been the one to fire the fatal shot, Darrow set about trying to justify Tommie's conduct with testimony from his two alienists, Dr. Thomas Orbison and Dr. Edward H. Williams. Hoping to convince the jury that Tommie was temporarily insane when he shot Joe, all the two alienists actually succeeded in doing was to bore the jury into a near collective coma.

Dr. Orbison testified first, listing his medical credentials and affiliations with Los Angeles General Hospital, Whittier State Institution for Delinquent Boys and Girls, and the Los Angeles Lunacy Commission. He then launched into a detailed, highly technical discussion of what he termed "delirium with ambulatory automatism." Putting it in layman's terms, he said that Tommie "was mentally deranged. He was insane." Orbison said that the stage had been set by rumors floating around that Thalia had not actually been attacked and that it was Tommie who had broken her jaw.

As Darrow's questions became increasingly technical, Judge Davis interrupted. "The questions are becoming interminably long, Mr. Darrow. I wish you would shorten them." Several appreciative jurors nodded their agreement.

When Darrow asked for further explanation of Tommie's mental condition, Orbison said, "It originates in the internal glandular apparatus, specifically the suprarenal gland. In effect, it plants a kind of mental time bomb inside its victims. A bomb that can be set off by any number of triggers."

"And what was that trigger in Lieutenant Massie's case?"

"The important thing was what happened to him just before the shooting. He told me, 'The last thing I was conscious of was the image that came to my mind of all that happened to my wife when Kahahawai said 'We done it.'"

When Darrow passed the witness, John Kelley's assistant, Barry Ulrich, stood to cross-examine. He perked up the jury with his crisp, direct questions.

"Couldn't Massie's delirium have been merely an irresistible impulse? Can't you understand that a man might kill a man whom he believes to have caused him worry in a fit of anger?"

"That is improbable because all his plans under this stress led up to his getting a confession, and he killed the very person necessary to this purpose."

"The question of the truth or falsity of Lieutenant Massie's testimony is for the jury, not you, to decide. We believe your testimony is based on the assumption of the truth of Lieutenant Massie's story."

For the first time, emotion invaded Orbison's answer. "It is not." Just as quickly as it flared, his temper subsided. "I revise that answer. We learn facts only from what is told us."

"You recognize that there would be every motive to invent this story?"

"I do, but this man has told the detailed truth, and money wouldn't buy my opinion."

As Ulrich and Orbison traded jabs, Judge Davis finally got into the act. "Did I understand that the defendant became insane at the last words of Kahahawai?"

"No," Orbison said. "The mental picture of his wife set him off."

"Before that time he was not insane?"

"No."

For his part, Dr. Williams offered nothing new, and bored the jury just as much as Orbison had, until Barry Ulrich raised not only his ire, but also that of Darrow. Turning Williams's attention to page 74 of a book entitled *Crime, Abnormal Minds and the Law*, which Williams had coauthored, Ulrich read aloud, "'Under the present system in force in most states, Justice Wilbur of the supreme court of California has recently stated, most pleas of insanity are made by sane people, who frequently go free, while most insane criminals make no insanity plea and are duly convicted and sentenced.'"

Williams listened to his own words carefully, appearing ill at ease by what he heard. "As I understand it, that is to introduce testimony that otherwise could not be."

"Then they are faked cases?" Ulrich asked.

"No. I don't like the word 'fake.' People may think they have been insane."

"Isn't it true that insanity pleas are interposed to allow counsel to introduce evidence that could not be brought in otherwise?"

Darrow rose quickly. "Objection."

"Overruled," Judge Davis said.

"Yes, it is true," Williams said. "By lawyers."

"As in this case," Ulrich said, taking a shot at Darrow.

Realizing what he had said, Williams tried to change course. "This case doesn't come into the argument at all."

But the damage had been done.

* * *

On Wednesday, April 20, Thalia Massie took the stand. As was true in the Ala Moana case, her appearance was the main event that most of the spectators, and the press, had been waiting for. After she was sworn in, Darrow almost immediately directed her, as he had Tommie, to the night of September 12 and the outing at the Ala Wai Inn. After testifying that she had gotten bored and left the party, she described her conversation with her husband that had, according to the defense, resulted in the shooting of Joe Kahahawai.

"I left the Inn about a half hour before midnight, when this terrible thing happened, and I finally reached my own home. Lieutenant Massie telephoned. I told him to please come home, that something terrible had happened."

Before she could finish her answer, she lowered her head and burst into almost uncontrollable sobs. Her crying appeared to be contagious, and soon it spread to others in the courtroom. The only persons seemingly unaffected by the contagion were the jurors, who kept poker faces while Thalia sobbed.

Grace poured a glass of water from a pitcher at the defense table. While Darrow waited, she approached the witness stand and handed it to her daughter. After a moment, Thalia looked up and took a sip of water. Grace returned to her chair, and Darrow resumed his questioning.

"What did you tell Tommie when he came home?"

"I did not want to tell him what had occurred because it was all too terrible. He asked me, 'Please, what happened?' And I cried and said they had beaten me up and assaulted me."

"Did you tell him who had assaulted you?"

"I told him it was some Hawaiian boys. I told him Kahahawai would not let me pray. He hit me as hard as he could."

"How did Tommie take all this?" Darrow asked.

"Oh, he was so good to me. Kind and considerate—just like he always was. But he got so that he couldn't sleep or eat. He lost weight and got very thin. And then he started hearing all the rumors about me. I could see that it was affecting his mind."

With impeccable timing, she broke down in sobs again.

"Your Honor," Darrow said, "perhaps this is a good time to recess."

After Judge Davis called for a break, Tommie rushed to the witness stand. With her head lowered, tears running down her cheeks, Thalia stumbled from the stand almost as if drunk. Tommie put his arm around her and led her to a chair by the defense table. They sat side by side, Tommie with her hand in his while his wife wept. Next to her, Grace stared straight ahead, her own cheeks streaked with tears.

* * *

In the late spring of 1931, just a few months prior to the events of the Ala Moana case, Thalia Massie had learned that she was pregnant, but she lost the baby in midsummer. After the miscarriage, she sought counseling with Dr. Lowell Kelly, a twenty-five-year-old assistant professor at the University of Hawaii, who was in the process of designing what would ultimately be a twenty-year longitudinal analysis of marital compatibility among 300 married couples. It became known as the Kelly Longitudinal Study and was based on a battery of psychological tests, plus a questionnaire he had designed. As part of his counseling of Thalia, she answered that questionnaire.

In his analysis, Dr. Kelly wrote that Thalia's "personal and emotional problems were beyond his competency" and that "I became convinced that she was in need of psychiatric treatment and so advised her husband by telephone." After Professor Kelly spoke to Tommie, Thalia canceled her next appointment, and Kelly never spoke to her again.

Professor Kelly had been present in the courtroom the day that the prosecution rested and Darrow started with the defense case. He had been keeping up with case through the press. At first, he didn't know who the victim was in the previous assault case, but when he learned that it was Thalia Massie, as he wrote years later in a letter to Governor Judd, "I could not but doubt the validity of her accusations."

Two days after Dr. Kelly's attendance at the trial, a deputy attorney general named Harold Kay showed up at the office of the university president, David Crawford, and said that Professor Kelly was on Maui but that the authorities needed some materials of his. Crawford retrieved and turned over Professor Kelly's file on Thalia Massie to attorney Kay. From there, it made its way into the hands of John Kelley. And from there, it made its way into the courtroom.

* * *

John Kelley's cross-examination of Thalia Massie lasted all of eight minutes. After a few preliminary questions, he approached the witness stand. Thalia watched him warily, as if expecting a trick. Kelley withdrew a folded piece of paper from his breast pocket.

"Did you have a psychopathic examination at the university last summer?" he asked.

"Yes. I went to see Professor Kelly." Her voice trembled. She still appeared emotionally fragile from her crying jags, and tears poised on her eyelids for another onslaught should the circumstances require it.

Kelley unfolded the paper and held it up for her to see. "Is this your handwriting?"

She leaned forward and squinted at the paper. In a twinkling, she transformed from weak and fragile to furious. The tremble left her voice, replaced by a sharp bite.

"Where did you get this?" she asked.

"I'm asking the questions, not answering them. Has your husband always been kind to you?"

In a rage, Thalia grabbed the page from Kelley's hand. Before he could react to snatch it back, she began tearing up the paper into pieces. Her voice rose to a shout. "Don't you know this is a confidential communication between doctor and patient? I refuse to say whether that is my handwriting or not."

She dropped the torn shreds on the floor and glared at Kelley, who met her gaze evenly.

Someone in the audience started clapping. Then the clapping spread to others, including the defendants. Judge Davis banged his gavel, in an attempt to restore order to the room. "Quiet or I'll clear the courtroom!" The clapping quickly subsided.

"Thank you, Mrs. Massie," Kelley said. "At last you have shown yourself in your true colors."

Thalia lurched from the witness stand, bent at the waist as if in pain. She stumbled toward Tommie, who rushed to catch her.

"Oh, Tommie," she cried, loud enough for all to hear. "What right does he have to say that I don't love you? Everybody knows I love you."

And the mystery of what she had written on the torn page was revealed to all.

* * *

After Thalia Massie testified, Darrow rested the defense case. The prosecution then put on their own psychiatrists in rebuttal, who controverted everything Darrow's alienists had said. Dr. Paul Bowers, another alienist from Los Angeles, had been flown in on short notice when Kelley realized he had been tricked by Darrow. After establishing the bona fides of Bowers and the work he had done to prepare for his testimony, Barry Ulrich asked, "Was there anything in the case which indicated that Lieutenant Massie was suffering from delirium?"

"I found nothing in the records that I read that he was suffering from any delirium."

"At the time of the killing of the deceased?"

"At the time of the killing of the deceased or at any time of which I have read," Bowers said.

Ulrich had Bowers establish what he understood ambulatory automatism to be and whether extraordinary or unusual acts of violence might be expected as a result of it. Bowers said that it depended upon the person's normal behavior. "In a state of automatism, the individual carries an act or movements which resemble acts, or movements or behavior which the individual carried out when he was in a state of normalcy." If the person acted abnormally, that would not be characteristic of automatism, he said. For example, you could expect a carpenter to "use a saw or hammer or the tools which carpenters employ during a state of automatism," but if he should do other acts, "such as going to a library to study a book on anthropology," then that would not be an act due to automatism.

But, he said, "An individual who suffers from epilepsy—say he was a butcher and suffers from epilepsy, he might in a state of automatism kill and dismember the body as he might dismember the body of a hog."

"Have you seen any indication of epilepsy?" Ulrich asked.

"There was no indication of epilepsy in the case, as far as I saw."

"Have you ever found automatic acts to be the sole symptom of hysteria?"

"No, you would never expect to find automatic acts to be the sole symptom of hysteria or any other mental disorder."

At last Ulrich got down to the key question. "In your opinion, was the defendant, Massie, at the time of the killing or shooting of Kahahawai, the deceased in this case, sane or insane?"

"He was, in my opinion, sane." He went on to explain, "I have concluded that the individual was in a normal state of consciousness, that he knew what he was doing at the time he did it."

Following a brief recess, Darrow's cross-examination of Bowers consisted of one question. "Doctor, I assume that you have either been paid or expect to be paid for coming down here and giving your testimony?" he asked.

"Yes, I expect to be paid."

"That is all."

* * *

Darrow was not nearly so agreeable with the prosecution's next witness, Dr. Joseph Catton, a physician from San Francisco, who announced, "I specialize in nervous and mental disorders." A spectacularly verbose witness, he gave answers that sometimes went on for pages, as opposed to mere paragraphs. Darrow periodically objected to Catton's answers, far more than with previous witnesses, sometimes seemingly for the sole purpose of disrupting Catton's lecture style of answering questions.

Catton was also quite expressive, gesticulating emphatically with his hands as he turned in his chair, perched on the edge, and spoke directly to the jury. It didn't take long for him to irk Darrow. After several lengthy answers, Catton finally got to his opinion, which he said consisted of four parts.

"Number one, it is my opinion based upon the data that I have received that at the time of the killing of Kahahawai, Lieutenant Massie was sane in the medical sense. That is, he had no psychosis, that is the medical man's term for insanity. Number two, it is my opinion that at the time of the killing, Lieutenant Massie had no brain disease which led to mental derangement which prevented his ability to discern the nature of the criminality of the act, action, of the transaction out of which came the killing of Kahahawai.

"It is further my opinion that Lieutenant Massie's mental state was such at that time that he is in a mental condition in which he might orient himself or understand himself in relation to the crime with which he is charged, and that he might prepare a just and rational defense through his attorneys. Number four, there is much in the evidence that explains exactly the mental condition of Lieutenant Massie and the manner in which the unfortunate episode could happen and the manner in which they pull down his mental reserve, and the manner in which this occurred was apparent to him."

As Catton droned on, Darrow could take it no longer. "I object to the manner of the witness. Why can't he sit in his chair like any other witness instead of making an argument to the jury? He might just as well stand up.

This is not the manner of a witness who is trying to enlighten the jury or who is trying to give honest testimony before a jury."

The words seemed to strike Catton like a punch. With his eyes focused on Darrow, he asked the judge, "Have I any right to say anything in reply to an allegation made that I am not honest in offering this proof?"

"I did not say you were not honest," Darrow replied. "I said that is not the proper attitude to take on the witness stand."

"You used the word 'honesty' and I resent it."

Darrow stood. "All right, come down and resent it."

Judge Davis, sensing things were getting out of control, tried to calm the two before one of them invited the other to step outside. "Cease arguing back and forth. That will accomplish nothing."

But bad blood continued to boil between the witness and Darrow. At one point, after Darrow objected to one of Catton's answers, Ulrich said, "That can be brought out on your cross-examination."

"I think we will let the witness finish first, Mr. Darrow," Judge Davis said.

"But he will never finish," Darrow snapped.

Later, when Darrow again objected to Catton's demeanor, the judge admonished the witness, "I will ask the doctor to compose himself as much as possible and give the testimony without gestures. Perhaps that will be better."

"I will make the effort, Your Honor," Catton said. "Part of my speech comes out through my hands as well as my tongue."

"You might put them in your pockets," Darrow growled.

* * *

The final witness to testify at the trial was Dr. Robert Faus, who had previously testified as part of the prosecution's case in chief. This time he testified for less than three minutes.

"In your opinion, how long after Kahahawai was shot would it take for death to ensue?" John Kelley asked.

"It was reasonable to believe that he retained consciousness from three to five minutes, and it would be from fifteen to twenty minutes before he could be pronounced dead."

From various places in the courtroom, as well as the jury box, audible gasps could be heard as people focused on what it must have been like for this young man to lie on the floor, bleeding and dying, while no one came to his aid.

"And during that three to five minutes of consciousness, would he be able to move about?"

"He might be."

"A man of Kahahawai's build, as you found it, would he be able to struggle?"

"He would."

With this last bit of dramatic testimony, and only a cursory cross-examination by Darrow, Kelley closed his case with the image of a gasping Kahahawai, struggling for life, fresh in the minds of the jurors.

Chapter Twenty-nine

Closing Arguments

"Three able men and a cold calculating woman . . ."

The night before closing arguments were to begin on the morning of April 26, John Kelley sat alone in the courtroom. Spread before him on the prosecutor's table was the physical evidence from the case: Joe Kahahawai's bloody clothes; the guns; the spent cartridge and casing; the rope that had bound Joe's body. The people of the Territory of Hawaii had entrusted him with a solemn job: to obtain justice for even the least of them, no matter the odds or the opposition, and no matter how much money, prestige, and influence were aligned against him. He felt for Thalia Massie. If indeed she had been raped, she deserved justice. But even if Joe Kahahawai had been guilty of her rape, justice was not a right that belonged solely to the privileged, and that excused them if they took the law into their own hands to mete out retribution as they saw fit. And if Joe Kahahawai was innocent of the charge of rape, as many believed, then his killing had been a massive *in*justice.

Kelley felt a heavy burden weigh on his heart as he held Joe's shirt and put his index finger through the bullet hole.

God! He needed a drink.

* * *

Clarence Darrow and George Leisure sat at a table in Darrow's hotel suite, with the remnants of a half-eaten meal on a room service tray in front of them.

"It's a very simple matter, George," Darrow said. "We must convince this jury to apply the unwritten law."

"Unwritten law?"

"It's indelibly stamped in men's hearts, and has been since the beginning of time. A man has every right to avenge an attack on his wife. And that's all that happened here. Tommie Massie simply avenged his wife, who had been raped."

Leisure was troubled by what Darrow said, espousing justification for murder. Troubled, because it was hard to believe these words were coming from the same man who, in arguing for the lives of thrill killers Leopold and Loeb, had argued, "I am pleading for a time when hatred and cruelty will not control the hearts of men, when we can learn by reason and judgment and understanding and faith that all life is worth saving, and that mercy is the highest attribute of man."

"If she truly was raped," Leisure said.

"It is enough that he believed she was raped."

"And if she truly was raped by Joe Kahahawai."

Darrow remained silent.

* * *

In both criminal and civil cases, the party with the burden of proof is permitted to "open and close." In criminal cases, that means that the prosecution goes first in presenting its case, and in making closing argument to the jury. The defense goes next, and the prosecution is then given one last crack at the jury, to rebut whatever the defense's case or argument might have been.

In a little bit of a departure from the norm, the first day of argument in the Massie case was devoted to the understudies. Barry Ulrich commenced for the prosecution, followed by George Leisure, who made the "opening" closing remarks. Clarence Darrow would speak the next day, with the "closing" closing remarks for the defense, and then John Kelley would finish. No one really paid much attention to the words of Ulrich and Leisure. Everyone, including a nationwide radio audience, was waiting for the two heavyweights the following day.

The heavyweights did not disappoint. Darrow took to the floor first, on the morning of April 27. He paced in front of the jury box and made eye contact, one by one, with all of the jurors.

"Gentlemen," he said, "this case illustrates the working of human destiny more than any other case I have handled. It illustrates the effect of sorrow and mishap on human minds and lives, and shows us how weak and powerless human beings are in the hands of relentless powers. Eight months ago Mrs. Fortescue was in Washington, respected and known like any other woman. Eight months ago, Lieutenant Massie worked himself up to the rank of lieutenant in the Navy, respected, courageous, and intelligent. His young wife, handsome and attractive, was known and respected and admired by the community.

"In that short space of time they are in a criminal court and the jury asked to send them to prison for life. What has happened is a long series of events, beginning at a certain time, ending we don't know where. A whole family—their life, future, name—bound up in a criminal act committed by someone else in which they had no part."

Darrow had the jury's attention. Having planted the seeds of insanity at trial, Darrow watered them as he continued his argument.

"We contend that for months Massie's mind had been affected by all that was borne upon him: grief, sorrow, trouble, day after day, week after week, and month after month. What do you think would have happened to any one of you under the same condition? We measure other people by ourselves. We place ourselves in this place and say, 'How would we have acted?' We have no further way of telling, except perhaps from the conditions of the life in which we live."

Another pause, to ensure that his audience of twelve was listening. "Is there a more terrible story anywhere in literature? I don't know whether there is—or who it was—or where I can find that sad tale but right here. You and all the other people in the city have been chosen to take care of their fate. I hope you will in kindness and humanity and understanding—no one else but you can do this."

He moved from topic to topic, touching on insanity, appealing to sympathy for Thalia Massie, and sparking outrage at vicious rumors that surrounded her. "There have been people who spread around in this community stories I don't believe true. They concocted these terrible stories, and what effect did they have on Massie? May I ask what effect they would have had on you and how you would have stood them? Massie attended to his days' duties as best he could. He went back and forth, nursing his wife, working all day and attending her at night for weeks. It was all that any husband could do, or any man could do. He lost sleep. He lost courage. He lost hope. He was distraught. And all this load was on his shoulders.

"Any cause for it? Our insane institutions are filled with men and women who had less cause for insanity than he had. Everyone knows it. The mind isn't too easy to understand at the best. But what happens to the human mind? It does one thing with one person and another thing with another. You know what it did to Massie's. Do you think he is responsible, or has been, from that terrible night?"

Back, once again, to the insanity that sparked Tommie Massie's act and the phony pregnancy of Thalia. "Here is a man—his wife—she is bearing inside of her the germs of—who? Does anybody know? Not he, but some one of the ruffians who assaulted her and left a wreck of her."

Now it was time to move on to Grace Fortescue, whose beloved daughter had been so brutally attacked. Darrow was perhaps at his most eloquent—and bombastic—on this point. "Gentlemen, I wonder what Fate has against this family anyhow? And I wonder when it will get through taking its toll and leave them to go in peace, to try and make their own life in comfort for the rest of their days.

"Here is the mother. What about her? They wired to her and she came. Poems and rhymes have been written about mothers. I don't want to bring forth eulogies which are more or less worthwhile, but I want to call your attention to something more primitive than that. Nature. It is not a case of the greatness of a mother. It is the case of what nature has done. I don't care whether it is a human mother, a mother of beasts or birds of the air, they are all alike.

"To them there is one all-important thing and that is a child that they carried in their womb. Without that feeling which is so strong in all life, there would be no life preserved upon this earth. She acted as every mother acts. She felt as your mothers have felt, because the family is the preservation of life. What did she do? Immediately she started on a long trip to her daughter. The daughter was married and a long way off, but she was still her daughter. I don't care if a mother is seventy-five and her daughter fifty, it is still the mother and the child.

"Everything else is forgotten in the emotion that carries her back to the time when this was a little baby in her arms which she bore and loved. Your mother was that way and my mother, and there can be no other way. The mother started on a trip of five thousand miles, over land and sea, to her child. And here she is now in this courtroom waiting to go to the penitentiary.

"Gentleman, let me say this: if this husband and this mother and these faithful boys go to the penitentiary, it won't be the first time that a penitentiary has been sanctified by its inmates. When people come to your beautiful islands, one of the first places that they will wish to see is the prison where the mother and the husband are confined because they moved under emotion. If that does happen, that prison will be the most conspicuous building on this island, and men will wonder at the injustice and cruelty of men and will pity the inmates and blame Fate for the cruelty, persecution, and sorrow that has followed this family.

"Gentlemen, you are asked to send these people to the penitentiary. Do you suppose that if you had been caught in the hands of Fate, would you have done differently? No, we are not made that way. Life doesn't come that way. If comes from a devotion of mothers, of husbands, loves of men and women, that's where life comes from. Without this love, this devotion, the world will be desolate and cold and will take its lonely course around the sun alone! Without a human heartbeat, there will be nothing except thin air. Every instinct that moves human beings, every feeling that is with you or any of your kin, every feeling that moves in the mother of the animal is with us in this case. You can't fight against it. If you do, you are fighting against nature and life. If on top of all else that has been heaped upon the devoted heads of this family, if they should be sent to prison, it would place a blot upon the fair name of these islands that all the Pacific seas would never wash away."

Turning back to Tommie Massie, he appealed to the unwritten law, the imprimatur on every husband's heart to avenge his wife. "Poor Massie, strong and vigorous, when all of these things were heaped on him. What did he do? He began to rid his mind somewhat of his own troubles and of the persecution of the men who performed this deed. He began to think of vindicating his wife from this slander. She had been lied about, she had been abused with talk.

"He wanted to get a confession. For what? To get somebody imprisoned? No—that did not concern him—he was concerned with the girl, whom he had taken in marriage when she was sixteen—sweet sixteen. Mrs. Fortescue was worrying about the delay of what she thought was justice, and what other people thought was justice. I fairly well know what law is, but I don't often know what justice is. It is a pattern according to our own personal conceptions. Mrs. Fortescue, too, believed it necessary to get a confession. The last thing they wanted to do was shoot or kill."

Then back to Tommie's mental state. As the saying went in the sport of boxing, "If the left don't get you, then the right one will." Darrow was relying upon a left-right combination of justification and insanity.

"It is of no consequence who fired that shot. I am arguing the facts, and the only facts as you get them. Is there any reason in the world why Massie, on top of all these other troubles, should assume the added burden of assuming the responsibility of this killing? When Kahahawai said, 'Yes, I done it,' everything was blotted out—here was the man who had ruined his wife. No man can judge another unless he places himself in the position of the other before he pronounces the verdict. If you can put yourself in his place, if you can think of his raped wife, of his months of suffering and mental anguish, if you can confront the unjust, cruel fate that unrolled before him, then you can judge—but you cannot judge any man otherwise.

"If you put yourself in Tommie Massie's place, what would you have done?" He pointed a finger from juror to juror. "I don't know about you, or you, or you, or you, but at least ten out of twelve men would have done just what poor Tommie Massie did. The thing for which you are asked to send him to prison for the rest of his life."

He let that soak in. It was known as the Golden Rule argument, and would later be outlawed in virtually all states, but in 1932, it was fair game to ask jurors to put themselves in the shoes of a party and to decide the case based upon what they, themselves, might have done had they been in the same position.

"I shan't detain you much longer," Darrow said as he neared the end of his argument. "Again I say I cannot understand why the prosecution raises a doubt as to who fired the shot and how. Massie was there! He rose! The picture came before him! He doubtless shot! One bullet was shot and only one. Massie saw the picture of his wife pleading, injured, raped—and he shot. There could have been nobody else.

"You are a people to heal, not to destroy. I place this in your hands asking you to be kind and considerate both to the living and the dead."

* * *

By the time he finished, Darrow had spoken for four hours and twenty minutes, lengthy by some standards, although it paled in comparison to his three-day closing argument in the Leopold and Loeb case. He rested at 2:23 p.m., and the court took a brief recess. John Kelley shifted in his chair as he waited for the judge and jury to return. His white linen suit had wilted in the heat and humidity, and he was weary, but knew that he was not alone. He figured that Darrow had pretty well worn out the jury. Were they still alert? They had listened, raptly, to Darrow, but even with a lunch break, four hours can wear a man out. Would they even care what he had to say? Part of him wanted to ask Judge Davis to grant an extended recess, rather than a mere ten minutes, and resume in the morning, so the jurors, and he, would be refreshed and rested. But he also didn't want the jurors to go home for the night with the words of Clarence Darrow the last thing they had imprinted on their minds.

He rose to his feet at 2:38 p.m. He faced the jury and cleared his throat. "Gentlemen of the jury, I would imagine that you are approaching a state of argument amnesia, or verbal psychosis. I will not detain you with a long plea." Legalese for "I know you're tired and I won't take long."

"I stand for the law and opposed to those who have violated the law, and I ask you to do so."

With that introduction, he began pacing in the well, the portion of the courtroom between the judge's bench and the lawyer's tables, in front of the jury box. "Are you going to decide the case on the plea of a man who for fifty years has stood before the bar of justice which he belittles today, or are you going to decide this case on the law? Are you going to follow the law of the Territory or the plea of Clarence Darrow and George Leisure?"

Kelley spoke with every bit as much passion and zeal as had Darrow, with every bit as much indignation and outrage. Where Darrow urged that the defendants be excused from the law, Kelley demanded that they be held accountable under the law. Innocent until proven guilty, a primary tenet of American justice. And a tenet that applied to Joe Kahahawai just as much as it did to Grace Fortescue, Tommie Massie, Edward Lord, and Albert Jones. It applied just as much to the *kanaka* as it did to the *haoles*.

"The same presumption of innocence that clothes the defendants in this case also clothes Joseph Kahahawai, way down deep in his grave," Kelley said. "They have removed, by their act, the possibility of his ever being anything but innocent in the Ala Moana case and 'not guilty' on the records of this court."

He moved from passion to ridicule, as necessary. "They ask you why should Massie take upon himself the blame for shooting Kahahawai. Because he couldn't hide behind the skirts of his mother-in-law. He couldn't stand up and blame these two men whom he had inveigled into this affair."

For each point Clarence Darrow had made, Kelley had a counterpoint. Where Darrow asked the jurors to put themselves in the shoes of Tommie Massie, to ask if they would have done anything different, Kelley said, "Are you going to give Massie a free pass in this case? If you do, they'll make him an admiral. I say, to hell with the admirals."

Where Darrow begged the jurors to listen, with sympathy, to the testimony of Tommie Massie—"How could you sleep, hearing the words of Lieutenant Massie?"—Kelley attacked. "The best you can say for Massie is that he lied like a gentleman and has a very convenient memory."

Where Darrow proclaimed that visitors to Hawaii would clamor to see the building "where the mother and husband are confined," Kelley countered, "Hawaii is on trial. Is there to be one law for strangers and another for us? Are strangers to come here and take the law into their own hands? As long as the American flag flies on that staff, without an admiral's pennant over it, you must regard the Constitution and the law."

Where Darrow begged for mercy for the poor defendants who have "suffered enough," Kelley called them out for what they were. "Three able men and a cold calculating woman let a man bleed to death in front of them." His voice crescendoed with outrage. "They aren't kids. They're brought up in an atmosphere of guns. They're taught the art of killing, also of first aid. But they let him die. They dragged him into the bathroom and let him die like a dog."

He turned briefly toward Darrow, the great orator of the courts. "In the Leopold-Loeb case, Darrow said he hated killing, regardless of how it was done. Always had, always will." Kelley paused to let that sink in. "And now he comes before you and says a killing is justified and is not murder."

Where Darrow pleaded for healing, to bind up the wounds of racial strife, Kelley warned that God has a say-so in the affairs of man. "They almost got away with it. Another five minutes, a shade up in the window of the car, and the body of Joseph Kahahawai would have been consigned to the deep forever. But an omnipotent God said, 'Thou shalt not kill,' and the hand of fate saved Kahahawai's body from the sea so that it might rest in a Christian grave."

And lastly, where Darrow talked of mothers sanctifying the penitentiary, Kelley had another reminder of motherhood. "Mr. Darrow has spoken of mother-love. He points to Mrs. Fortescue as 'the mother' in this courtroom. Well, there is another mother in this courtroom." He paused for his point to soak in.

"Has Mrs. Fortescue lost her daughter? Has Massie lost his wife?" He pointed to Thalia Massie. "No, she sits there between them."

He turned and looked at Esther Anito, then back at the jury. "But where is Joe Kahahawai?"

When he paused, the only sound in the courtroom was Esther weeping for her son.

Chapter Thirty

Custody of the High Sheriff

"We, the jury, in the above entitled cause find the defendant . . ."

After the lawyers had finished their closing arguments, Judge Davis read the multipage charge to the jury, which included definitions and instructions that they were expected to follow.

"You are instructed that the defendants are, and every one of them is, presumed by the law to be innocent of the crime charged against them. Moreover, I instruct you that this presumption of innocence is not a mere form to be disregarded by you at pleasure, but it is an essential, substantial part of the law of the land, and is binding upon you in this case."

Kelley wondered whether the jurors would take that to heart and remember his own argument that Joe Kahahawai had been entitled to that same presumption, but that these defendants had felt free to disregard it in his case.

Judge Davis reminded the jury of the burden of proof in a criminal case—proof beyond a reasonable doubt. "A reasonable doubt is that state of mind which, after a full comparison and consideration of all of the evidence both for the Territory and the defense, leaves the minds of the jury in that condition that they cannot say that they feel an abiding faith amounting to a moral certainty, from the evidence of the case, that a defendant is guilty of the crime as laid in the indictment.

"And in this connection, I instruct you that the doubt which will entitle a defendant to an acquittal must be a reasonable doubt, not a conjured-up doubt, such a doubt as you might conjure up to acquit a friend, but a doubt that you can give reason for. A reasonable doubt is not a possible doubt, not a conjectural doubt, not an imaginary doubt, not a doubt of absolute certainty of the guilt of the accused, because everything relating to human affairs and depending upon mortal evidence is open to conjectural or imaginary doubt, and because absolute certainty is not required by law."

The judge then laid out the differences in the crimes with which the defendants had been charged, and what the jury had to consider in determining whether any of those crimes had been committed. He distinguished first-degree murder, which required "deliberate premeditated malice aforethought," from second-degree murder, which "is committed with malice aforethought," but "the elements of deliberateness and premeditation are lacking." He then distinguished second-degree murder from manslaughter, which lacked the malice aforethought element. "Before you can convict the defendants of murder as charged, it is necessary for the Territory to prove to your satisfaction, beyond all reasonable doubt, first, that the defendants killed Joseph Kahahawai Jr., and second, that they intended to kill him. The fact alone that Joseph Kahahawai Jr. has been killed is not a sufficient basis for you to convict the defendants upon."

He defined "malice" as including not only "hatred, ill-will, and desire for revenge," but also "the acting with a heedless, reckless disregard, or gross negligence, of the life or lives, the health or personal safety of another." He told them that they didn't have to find a specific intent to kill Kahahawai, but it was sufficient to show that "the defendants entered into an agreement to commit a criminal act, and second, that the natural and probable consequence of the carrying out of that criminal act might be the death of Joseph Kahahawai Jr."

Maybe most importantly, the judge instructed the jury on the insanity issue. After reading from the statute on insanity, he said, "The Court instructs you that under our statute, a man is considered insane if, at the time he does an act, his mind is so deranged or unbalanced that he does not for the time being realize the nature and criminality of his act. He need not be violently insane, nor need he be a maniac or lunatic, as those words are commonly understood. It is sufficient if he does not comprehend what he is doing at the time he does the act."

Once that had been made clear, he went on to say that if the jury believed that the insanity defense was "false and fabricated," and if it was "purposely and intentionally invoked" by a defendant, then the jury "may take such action as the basis of a presumption of guilt."

Then, as he neared the end of the charge, Judge Davis blew the "unwritten law" defense right out of the water: "I instruct you, Gentlemen of the Jury, that no man may take the law into his own hands, and that no amount of mere mental suffering or worry, no amount of mental harm, injury, or shame caused to one man by another, not causing insanity, can or will furnish legal justification for the taking of the life of that other, and that the alleged fact, if it be a fact, that the deceased in this case had assaulted or ravished the wife of one of the defendants in this case, cannot and does not furnish any legal justification to any of the defendants to kill said deceased and furnishes no defense to any of them."

After more than a half hour, Judge Davis finished reading the charge. The fates of the defendants were now in the hands of the jury.

* * *

Honolulu had been on high alert ever since the hung jury in the Ala Moana case, and the tension had ratcheted ever higher during each day of the Massie trial. The entire city braced for the verdict. Armed police officers tightly cordoned off the courthouse proper, while hundreds of spectators gathered on the lawn and the streets. And they waited.

And waited. And waited.

By noon on Friday, April 29, the jury had been out for over forty hours. A long time, but still less than half the time the Ala Moana jury had been out before a mistrial was declared. People whispered among themselves as the hours passed, worried about what would happen if there was another mistrial. There were reports of raised voices in the jury room. Speculation was rampant, as it had been in the Ala Moana case, that the jury was split along racial lines. This theory was bolstered by reports that, at one point, while a light rain fell, the seven *haole* jurors stood outside on the balcony while the five native jurors remained inside.

Friday afternoon, at 5:30 p.m., the lawyers and their clients gathered inside the courtroom after being informed a verdict had finally been reached. Judge Davis took his place on the bench and called in the jury. When they were seated, he said, "Will the defendants please rise?"

Tommie, Grace, Jones, and Lord stood, as did their lawyers. Along with them stood Thalia Massie. A bailiff motioned for her to be seated. Appearing unsure, and somewhat embarrassed, she sank back into her chair next to her standing husband.

At the prosecution table, Kelley and Ulrich both kept their eyes on the judge.

"Gentlemen of the jury, have you reached a verdict?" Davis asked.

John F. Stone, the jury foreman rose. In his hands, he held a thin sheaf of papers that contained their verdict. "Yes, we have, Your Honor."

Judge Davis motioned for his clerk to retrieve the verdict sheets. Stone handed them to the clerk, who moved to the front of the courtroom, just in front of the judge's bench. With trembling hands rattling the pages, he began reading the verdict.

"We, the jury, in the above entitled cause find the defendant, Grace Fortescue, guilty of manslaughter; leniency recommended."

Thalia shrieked, a loud, high-pitched wail. Tommie reached over and grabbed her hand, as the clerk continued reading.

"We, the jury, in the above entitled cause find the defendant, Thomas H. Massie, guilty of manslaughter; leniency recommended."

Tommie grimaced and clenched his teeth. Thalia sobbed.

"We, the jury, in the above entitled cause find the defendant, Edward J. Lord, guilty of manslaughter; leniency recommended. We, the jury, in the above entitled cause find the defendant, Albert O. Jones, guilty of manslaughter; leniency recommended."

When the clerk finished reading, a hush fell over the courtroom, with the exception of the loud, histrionic sobbing of Thalia Massie and the soft sniffs of Esther Anito.

"We will reassemble here in one week, on May 6 at 10:00 a.m. for sentencing," Judge Davis said.

"Your Honor," Darrow said, "we ask that the defendants remain in the custody of the United States Navy, under the same arrangements, pending sentencing."

"I have no objection," Kelley said.

"So ordered," Davis said. With that, he excused the jury and retreated from the bench. As soon as the judge was gone, bedlam exploded in the courtroom. Darrow flopped in his chair, appearing dazed, as if he believed himself incapable of losing. He also knew something that his clients did not: under territorial law, the judge had no discretion in imposing a sentence, notwithstanding the recommendation of the jury for leniency. The law of manslaughter required him to sentence each of the defendants to the maximum of ten years at hard labor.

After a moment, Darrow approached Kelley. Both men extended their hands and clasped a firm handshake. "Congratulations, John," Darrow said, although his heart wasn't in it. "You tried a damn fine case."

"As did you."

Tommie Massie, with Thalia clutching his arm, approached Kelley. Following the lead of his lawyer, he stuck out his hand. Kelley hesitated for a moment then shook hands.

"No hard feelings," Tommie said. "If I ever had anything against you—"

"I never had anything against you, sir," Kelley said. He looked at Thalia. "Or your wife."

Thalia suddenly snapped, much as she had when she tore the evaluation to pieces. Her voice was full of venom and sarcasm as she said, "No, of course not. You never had *anything* against me."

Kelley stood silently, unsure of what to say in return, so he opted to say nothing. Tommie put his arm around Thalia and escorted her away.

* * *

Outside the Judiciary Building, Darrow stood beside his clients and addressed the press. "The verdict is a travesty of justice and on human nature, and on every emotion that has made us what we are from the day the human race was born."

Grace was even more blunt. "I expected it. I felt all along that we would be unable to get a fair and just trial in Honolulu. American womanhood means nothing, even to white people in Hawaii."

She would later tell a reporter, once she got back to the USS *Alton*, "We killed the wrong person. We should have shot William Heen and William Pittman, the attorneys for the rapists."

Some of the jurors were happy to explain their decision to the press. The *haoles* had been unwilling to consider the murder charges because they didn't believe the defendants had "malice aforethought." At the same time, they didn't buy into either of Darrow's theories: they didn't think Tommie was temporarily insane when he pulled the trigger, and most didn't believe that Tommie had fired the shot. They also didn't believe that Joe had confessed. They did believe that Thalia had been raped, though, but by someone else, so they were sympathetic to the Massies' ordeal. The manslaughter verdict ultimately came down as a compromise.

* * *

Pressure behind the scenes began to mount on the Territorial government, from not only the military in Hawaii, but also from private businesses and from Washington, D.C. The Navy threatened to cancel all shore leaves and to boycott the employers of any of the jurors, so those employers and other business owners called constantly, pressuring Governor Lawrence Judd for some kind of relief. Over one hundred United States congressman sent a jointly signed letter to Judd, demanding that he pardon the defendants. Even President Herbert Hoover got into the act, under pressure from his old friend Walter Dillingham, meeting with his cabinet to discuss whether to declare martial law in Hawaii unless Judd pardoned the defendants. Judd ultimately reached a decision as to what to do, and some said after he received a call from the White House, though he always denied it.

On Wednesday, May 4, two days earlier than scheduled, the defendants and their lawyers gathered back in Judge Davis's courtroom at 10:30 a.m., along with John Kelley and Barry Ulrich for the prosecution. Governor Judd had announced that he would have a statement to make to the press at Iolani Palace at 11:00 a.m., immediately following the pronouncement of the sentences, so a large contingent of press people gathered in the courtroom, ready to dash across to Iolani Palace once the Judge had completed sentencing.

All in the courtroom rose at precisely 10:30 as Judge Davis entered and took his position on the bench. "Be seated," he said.

All sat but John Kelley. "Your Honor, the Territory of Hawaii formally requests that sentence be pronounced."

He sat down.

"I'll ask that each of the defendants approach as I call your name," Judge Davis said. "Albert O. Jones."

Jones stood and approached alone. Darrow and Leisure remained at the table behind him. Jones looked up at the judge, his face expressionless.

"It is the judgment and sentence of the Court that you, Albert O. Jones, be confined in Oahu Prison, at hard labor, for the term of ten years."

Jones didn't blink.

"Do you have anything to say, Mr. Jones?"

"No, Your Honor."

"You may be seated."

One by one, Judge Davis called the other defendants before him, ending with Grace Fortescue. In each instance, he pronounced the same sentence: confinement in Oahu Prison, at hard labor, for the term of ten years.

Yet, like Jones, none of them showed any emotion while Judge Davis spoke. Once sentence had been pronounced on all four, Major Ross, the high sheriff of Honolulu, escorted the defendants and their attorneys out of the courtroom and across the street to Iolani Palace. After they had left, Judge Davis dismissed the members of the press, who all shared one common question: The defendants had no reaction when they were sentenced, so why were they smiling as they left the courtroom?

At Iolani Palace, Governor Judd greeted the defendants and their counsel when they arrived at his office. Darrow handed Judd a document. Judd opened it and read what was on its pages. Then he took a stack of envelopes from a nearby table. He shook hands with the defendants, handed each of them an envelope, and motioned them into the governor's suite. Inside, pots of tea and assorted cookies and pastries had been assembled on a table. When all were inside, they tore open the envelopes and read the contents of the single page inside of each.

Judd emerged about ten minutes later and walked down the hallway to where a lectern had been set up and members of the press waited. At approximately 11:10, he read a brief statement to the reporters.

"The four defendants in the so-called Fortescue case were sentenced this morning in accordance with Territorial law to ten years in prison. Acting on a petition of the four defendants, joined by counsel for the defendants and in view of the recommendation of the jury, I am commuting the sentence to one hour in custody of the High Sheriff."

By commuting the sentence, Judd had not given the defendants an outright pardon, which would have erased their convictions. Instead, he had simply exercised authority that the trial judge lacked, but which he, as governor, had to shorten the term of imprisonment. Since the sentences had been handed down at 10:30 a.m., the defendants had about twenty minutes left to serve for killing Joe Kahahawai. They spent those twenty minutes drinking tea and nibbling on cookies while "imprisoned" in the governor's suite.

Later, a statement was issued on Thalia's behalf that began:

> Mrs. Massie is quite willing to do anything she can in bringing to justice the men who made the assault upon her. She realizes that they can be convicted only in the event that she remains here to testify against them on a second trial and because of that fact has informed the City and County Attorney's office that she is willing to be subjected again to the embarrassment of describing the sordid details of the attack upon her, if upon a new trial an impartial and unbiased jury can be secured. She has learned from experience in the last trial that without an impartial jury a conviction is impossible.

Apparently Thalia concluded that a fair and impartial jury, as she defined it, could not be secured because, four days after Judd commuted the sentences, Tommie and Thalia Massie, Grace Fortescue, Clarence and Ruby Darrow, and

George Leisure boarded the Matson liner *Malolo* and set out for San Francisco, never to return. Jones and Lord left the next day on a Navy ship for new assignments outside of the Hawaiian Islands.

The Massie case was over.

PART FIVE

EPILOGUE

Chapter Thirty-one

The Pinkerton Report

"It has been shown that the five accused did not have the opportunity to commit the kidnapping and rape described by Mrs. Massie."

Although the Massie trial was over, that wasn't quite the end of matters. After all, there was still a retrial looming of the surviving Ala Moana Boys—but John Kelley had no taste for it, particularly if Thalia Massie was not going to be available to testify. He also had his own doubts about the guilt of the Boys in the first place. As he reviewed the record from the rape trial, he developed serious questions about the prosecution's handling of the whole thing and began to question whether the evidence actually supported the charges. But he also believed that the Boys were entitled to clear their names with an acquittal, if they truly were innocent. To simply leave things as they were, and not pursue a retrial, would leave the unanswered question of guilt or innocence hanging over their heads.

At Kelley's strong suggestion, Governor Judd and the mayor of Honolulu prevailed upon the Territorial legislature and the city's board of supervisors to fund an exhaustive independent investigation into the Ala Moana case by the most famous detective agency in the world: The Pinkerton National Detective Agency of New York, New York.

On June 9, 1932, Kelley met with J. C. Fraser, Pinkerton's California Division Manager, in Honolulu to kick off the investigation. Also present at that meeting were Governor Lawrence Judd, Hawaii's Attorney General Harry Hewitt, and Deputy Attorney General Raymond C. Brown. At that meeting, simple ground rules were set—leave no stone unturned in getting to the truth—and the Pinkertons were hired.

The investigation consumed three months and, indeed, turned over every stone, as investigators interviewed witnesses, studied police and hospital records and reports, and scoured through the trial transcripts of both trials. The starting point was "Mrs. Massie's statements, made immediately following alleged rape"—not only statements made to the police, but also to her rescuers on Ala Moana Road. From there, the investigation delved into the evidence, or lack of evidence, to support her claims. The Pinkerton Report, as did the defense in the Ala Moana trial, placed considerable importance on the timeline of events for the night of September 12–13, as well as on Thalia Massie's evolving memory of what had occurred.

The table of contents for the report listed the following topics:

- Number of assailants
- Nationality of assailants
- Kind of auto used by assailants
- License number of auto used by assailants
- Names mentioned by assailants
- As to rape having occurred
- Mrs. Massie's ability to identify assailants
- Identifying auto used by accused
- Arrest of suspects
- Identification of suspects
- Other evidence opposing Mrs. Massie's recital
- Time factor, re Mrs. Massie
- Time factor, re the accused
- Miscellany

One of the points of emphasis was Thalia's initial inability to identify her attackers, an inability that morphed into certainty by the time of trial that Henry Chang, Horace Ida, Joe Kahahawai, and Ben Ahakuelo had been her assailants. Certainty that included a brown jacket and a gold tooth. Remarkably, to the very end, she never identified David Takai as one of her attackers, but he had been prosecuted under the "judged by the company you keep" rationale.

Neither Mrs. Clark nor George Clark Jr., who had been in the car that picked up Thalia Massie that night on Ala Moana Road, testified at the rape trial. They did, however, both give statements to the Pinkerton Detective Agency. On June 22, 1932, Mrs. Clark offered these additional details about Thalia Massie's appearance the night of the attack to supplement the testimony her husband and Eustace Bellinger had given at trial:

Mr. Bellinger slowed up and as the woman approached the car she said, "Are you white people?" Someone said "Yes," then she came up to the car, opened the front door and got in next to my son. When asked what happened, she said some Hawaiian boys had beat her. Her face about the lips was badly swollen and she had a mark on her cheek which might have been caused by a ring. I suggested, or someone did, that we take her to the police station so she could report the matter, but she said, "I don't want to go there. Take me home, please, and my husband will take care of me." . . . Her hair was down. She wore an evening gown (green) with fur trimmings on short sleeves; am not sure of any at neck or gown. I asked her if she had been hurt any other way, she said No, and asked us not to ask any more questions, as her jaw hurt her so badly. As we were strangers, she perhaps did not want to tell us what had occurred. My attention was drawn to her as she stood in the road waving her arms, as she looked like my daughter Ramona, who was out that night.

I had a good look at her from the light in the car, and could see that she was badly hurt. I am sure she was not drunk or had she been drinking as I sat right back of her and was leaning forward and there was no liquor on her breath.

We all noticed her evening gown seemed to be in good condition and after reading of the assault wondered how it could be if four or five men assaulted her.[1]

In his statement, George Clark Jr. added an interesting comment about Tommie Massie, even though he had never met him. He said that, after Mr. Bellinger had arrived at the address given to him by Thalia, "Mother wanted me to go to the house with the woman, but I did not think it advisable as her husband might take a shot at me."[2]

The Pinkertons noted Thalia's remarkable ability to later recall the license plate number of the assault vehicle—one she initially repeatedly denied having seen—after she had been clued in as to what it was. Several witnesses corroborated this fact.

Police officer William Seymour told the Pinkerton Agency:

There were several parties or people who came to the Emergency Hospital with Massie and during the discussion between Massie and

---

1   Pinkerton Report at pages 5–6.
2   Pinkerton Report at page 6.

Jardine a radio car stopped in front of the Emergency Hospital. Shortly thereafter a dispatch was broadcast from headquarters in regard to automobile 58–895 having been picked up, said number having been given by Mrs. Peeples to the police due to an argument in a near collision whereby one of the boys in the car slapped her face. This number was broadcast several times and the signals from the car could be heard at least fifty feet from the car. Several members of the Massie party heard this broadcast and appeared to be much interested in same. I did not overhear their conversation.[3]

Dr. Liu, who examined Thalia that night, said that the license plate number wasn't mentioned in his office during the examination, "but they were talking about some number on the porch outside."[4] A. W. Mackenzie, a member of the United States Navy, and who had been among those gathered outside the Emergency Hospital that night, gave a statement as to what had happened after Thalia was brought out of the hospital to a patrol car: "First I tried to get information from the doctor. He also told me the case could not be discussed. Then Mr. Massie came out and told us what had happened and one of the detectives standing there said they had the number of the car they were looking for that had assaulted another woman." When asked whether the detective mentioned the actual number, Mackenzie said, "I think he did but I don't know."[5]

As for the incident involving Agnes Peeples that set in motion the events leading to the trial of the Ala Moana Boys, the report blamed poor police procedure.

At this point in this review it is well to mention the occurrence involving five local youths in an altercation with Mrs. Peeples, also a local resident, transpiring the same night and presenting situations which obviously were misinterpreted and apparently inexpertly handled by various ones participating in the investigation of the alleged rape case, the identification of suspects and their personal property.[6]

---

3   Pinkerton Report at page 41.
4   Pinkerton Report at page 41.
5   Pinkerton Report at page 42.
6   Pinkerton Report at page 8.

On October 3, 1932, Asher Rossetter, Vice-President and General Manager of the Pinkerton Detective Agency, sent his preliminary report to Governor Judd. That report concluded that the evidence adduced in the investigation:

> . . . makes it impossible to escape the conclusion that the kidnapping and assault was not caused by those accused, with the attendant circumstances alleged by Mrs. Massie. We can only assume that the reason Mrs. Massie did not give to the authorities, immediately after the alleged offense, the same details of information she was able to furnish by her testimony at the trial is because she did not possess it at the time she was questioned by those she came in contact with immediately after the alleged offense.

* * *

> Our investigation embraced a careful examination into the alibi of the accused and we failed to discover any important circumstance disproving in any manner any portion of the statements which they made immediately upon their arrest, their examination by the police and prosecution subsequently and their testimony at the trial. In other words, the movements of the accused on the night of the alleged assault remain precisely as they were originally accounted fo [*sic*].

Less than two weeks later, on October 14, Rossetter submitted Pinkerton's final report, an exhaustive 279-page analysis of the evidence, testimony, and witness interviews. It contained, among others, these conclusions:

> It seems that the more opportunity afforded Mrs. Massie to view the accused the more details she remembered of the identifying marks of her assailants corresponding with similar characteristics of the accused. The record indisputable [*sic*] shows that prior to seeing the five accused youths, Mrs. Massie could furnish absolutely no description of her assailants to the police . . . .[7]

* * *

---

7   Pinkerton Report at page 23.

Mrs. Massie alleged that she was raped by five men a total of six times. These men had previously handled her very roughly, according to her statement, beat her with their fists about the head and face. It is therefore improbable that any consideration would be taken by these men while ravishing her. Mrs. Massie stated one of these men savagely struck her in the jaw while he was raping her. They were all young and athletic and naturally would have been hurried and violent in their operations. The approximate minutes available for these raping incidents as determined by a check of the movements of Mrs. Massie and of these boys as far as can be determined would require very considerable haste in their accomplishing, so much so that it is highly improbable six rapists could have accomplished their purpose in the space of time Mrs. Massie states or within the time available for the accused, were they the rapists.[8]

* * *

It is a debatable point whether the rape of a woman of Mrs. Massie's size and strength is possible by one man or several men unless she be rendered helpless beforehand, without the clothing of herself and the clothing of her assailants clearly showing the effects of her struggle to prevent the rape. . . . A careful examination of the clothing worn by Mrs. Massie on the night of the assault failed to show any evidence of an attack such as she described, the garments being in perfect condition, no rips or tears, except on one stocking. It seems improbable that an attack such as described by Mrs. Massie would not show some evidence on clothing of such flimsy material, and if the clothing were to have been turned up above the hips, there would certainly be some indications of some nature caused by the character of the ground on which she lay.[9]

* * *

We have found nothing in the record of this case nor have we thru [sic] our own efforts been able to find what in our estimation would be

---

8 Pinkerton Report at page 46.
9 Pinkerton Report at page 48.

sufficient corroboration of the statements of Mrs. Massie to establish the occurrence of rape upon her. There is a preponderance of evidence that Mrs. Massie did in some manner suffer numerous bruises about the head and body but definite proof of actual rape has not in our opinion been found.[10]

* * *

The testimony of Mrs. Massie at the trial of the accused, with respect to her opportunities to see and identify them while in their control and the apparent close and careful observation she took of these details, in view of her lack of knowledge of these same important details when interviewed by numerous persons immediately after the alleged rape, must of necessity give rise to grave doubt as to the accuracy of any of her statements with reference to the accused and it seems to be entirely within reason to believe that Mrs. Massie's knowledge of the appearance, dress and other identifying marks of the accused was acquired through events in the interim.[11]

* * *

Notwithstanding Mrs. Massie's denial that she had been furnished with the license number of Ida's car, saw it while the car was at police headquarters at the time she also was there, 3:30 a.m. September 13th, 1932 [*sic*], or heard it mentioned by others or broadcast over police radio while she was in the Emergency Hospital shortly before 3:00 a.m. September 13th and while a police car with loud receiver was standing outside hospital, receiving this broadcast, it has been established that the license number of Ida's car was known to a number of persons who were in contact and conversation with Mrs. Massie prior to Mrs. Massie giving her statement to Inspector McIntosh at 3:30 a.m. September 13th, 1931, at which time she told Inspector McIntosh the license number of her assailant's car was 58–805.[12]

---

10 Pinkerton Report at page 67.
11 Pinkerton Report at pages 71–72.
12 Pinkerton Report at page 85.

The Report then concluded that the original prosecution had been doomed to failure from the start, a clear warning about any future prosecution.

> It seems fair to assume that the prosecution of the accused was forced upon the Territory by reason of Mrs. Massie's story and her identification of these boys. No other course appears to have been possible in view of the circumstances, than to try the case which had its basis and support exclusively upon Mrs. Massie's narrative and identifications. That the prosecution failed for want of corroboration of essential parts of Mrs. Massie's story and the alibi of the accused was inevitable.[13]

Based on the Pinkerton Report, Prosecutor John Kelley had no choice as to how to proceed. He didn't have Thalia Massie available to testify, and the Pinkertons were telling him that, even if he did, she wasn't believable. So he did the only thing he could possibly do: on February 13, 1933, he dismissed the case against the remaining Boys. In the Motion for *Nolle Prosequi*,[14] he stated:

> A careful analysis of the evidence adduced at the former trial indicates clearly the following principal weaknesses in the prosecution's case:
>
> (a) The methods employed in securing the identification of the defendants by the complaining witness.
> (b) The lack of medical, physical and material evidence of the alleged rape upon the complaining witness.
> (c) The lack of evidence to overcome the alibi presented by the defendants.

After tracking many of the conclusions from the Pinkerton Report related to (a) and (b), the motion concluded:

> Since the former trial of this cause exhaustive examinations have been made by the office of the Attorney General of the Territory of Hawaii, the office of the Public Prosecutor of the City and County of Honolulu and the Pinkerton National Detective Agency Inc. of New York City. Every known fact and circumstance of the case has been reviewed and

---

13 Pinkerton Report at page 279.
14 Latin for "we shall no longer prosecute."

no effort has been spared to secure evidence additional to that presented at the former trial which would tend to strengthen the case of the prosecution particularly with reference to the two foregoing matters and which would also aid the prosecution in overcoming the alibi presented by the defendants. All of these investigations embraced a careful examination and analysis of the alibi of the defendants presented at said trial and they have failed to discover any circumstances disproving or tending to disprove any portion of the statements made by the defendants immediately upon their arrest, their examination by the police and the prosecuting officials subsequently, and their testimony and the testimony of the witnesses called on their behalf at the trial. The movements and whereabouts of the defendants on the night of the alleged assault remain precisely as they were originally accounted for by them.

The evidence adduced at the trial of said defendants was such that it is not surprising that a verdict of conviction was not obtained, and, in view of the fact that the above mentioned investigations uncovered no new or additional evidence, there certainly is not more likelihood that a conviction could be obtained on a retrial of the case.

Chapter Thirty-two

What Really Happened?

"Blasted careers, ruined lives, tragedy, and death."

So what happened to the key players in this sordid story? Did they live happily ever after? Or was real life uglier than that?

John Kelley and Clarence Darrow

Let's start with the two courtroom heavyweights, John Kelley and Clarence Darrow, who, coincidentally, both died in 1938. Kelley continued as Honolulu's top prosecutor after the Massie trial, but the white and military establishment never really accepted him. After all, he had convicted some of their own, and then had refused to prosecute the natives that so many still believed had raped and beaten Thalia Massie. As it turned out, the whites and the military did not need actual facts to justify their racism; they came by that naturally. Kelley died quite suddenly of heart failure at the age of fifty-two, likely the victim of working—and drinking—too hard for the bulk of his relatively short life.

Darrow, on the other hand, lived to the ripe old age of eighty, leaving behind a legacy as champion of the underdog and standing up for the rights of unpopular minorities—the "attorney for the damned," as he was called in some circles. But as far as the Massie case goes, in which he appeared to have sold his soul for a big fee, he might well have been called simply a "damned attorney."

Even to his dying day, Darrow defended his clients in the Massie case and their actions, even though he clearly had doubts of his own. His doubts did not extend to the question of the guilt of the Ala Moana Boys, though, an opinion he formed without the benefit of the facts that had been developed at the rape trial. As he wrote in his memoir, *The Story of My Life*:

> Of course, all the attorneys for the prosecution, and those for the defense, as well as the judge, knew that legally my clients were guilty of murder. Yet, on the island, and across the seas, and around the earth,

men and women were hoping and praying and working for the release and vindication of the defendants. As in similar cases, everyone was talking about "the unwritten law." While this could not be found in the statutes, it was indelibly written in the feelings and thoughts of people in general. Which would triumph, the written or the unwritten law, depended upon many things which in this case demand the most careful consideration.[15]

He asserted that he deliberately avoided making an issue of race in the trial, although he noted, "It was unfortunate that all the men who assaulted Mrs. Massie were brown."[16] In a disturbing example of self-imposed, selective observation, he expressed an opinion that racial prejudice in Hawaii was one-sided, directed by the natives against the whites, but not in the other direction.

No lawyer on either side raised the question of color or race, and I knew it would have been fatal to our side to let anything of that sort creep in. I was morally certain that the majority of the jury would be brown men. I knew that the white men had no prejudice against the brown ones, nevertheless the brown men were prejudiced against the white. I was quite sure that had I been a brown man, and a native living under the circumstances that they met in Hawaii, I should have felt as our Indians do about the "pale-faces" who now own the land over which their ancestors reigned so long.[17]

He even attributed the jury verdict to the racial makeup of the jury, concluding that, "A jury of white men would have acquitted."[18]

Admiral Yates Stirling

Yates Stirling spent two more years at Pearl Harbor and then served out his distinguished career in the United States Navy in other posts. In his memoir, he continued to hold to the notions that the Ala Moana Boys were guilty, that Tommie Massie was justified, and that Hawaiians were a subordinate race. For him, a clear miscarriage of justice had occurred, but it was the hung jury in the

---

15 Darrow, Clarence, *The Story of My Life*, p. 468 (Charles Scribner's Sons, 1932).
16 *Ibid.* at p. 471.
17 *Ibid.*
18 *Ibid.* at p. 479.

Ala Moana case and the subsequent convictions of Grace Fortescue, *et al*, that he found repugnant to his sense of right and wrong. He bemoaned:

> The criminals are brought to trial and conviction found impossible. The criminals go free. The family of the martyred woman invoke the unwritten law for the crime of rape. They fail to kill all five, but succeed in sending to his God the most brutal and unfeeling. For this, four people are tried and convicted. [19]

Stirling's friendship with Governor Judd suffered as a result of the case, particularly Judd's act in commuting the sentences of the defendants instead of granting them an outright pardon:

> According to what I had been told by the defense lawyers, Judd had promised pardons to all. Instead, it was not a pardon that was handed out, which would have given them back their citizenship, but only a discharge after an hour in the sheriff's custody, the same that he had given Kahahawai[20] to permit him to attend for Hawaii an athletic contest in New York.

Stirling also had some interesting notions of what had and had not happened in the house rented by Grace Fortescue in Manoa. Picking up on a suggestion to him from Ann Kluegel, whom he identified as a "splendid type of patriotic woman who was the head of a civic organization for better government," Stirling held to the possibility, if not the outright belief and desire, that Grace Fortescue, and not Tommie Massie, had pulled the trigger and fired the bullet that killed Joe Kahahawai. In his memoir, he described his thoughts this way:

> When the mother heard the Hawaiian's confession, spoken, as it was testified, in a spirit of bravado, instead of everything going black around *her*, I believe she would see all the more clearly, not a human being, but a scorpion or centipede to be exterminated. Does it not seem logical

---

19 Stirling, Yates, *Sea Duty: The Memoirs of a Fighting Admiral*, p. 269 (G.P. Putnam's Sons, 1939).

20 Stirling likely meant Ben Ahakuelo, who had been convicted in the "assault to ravish" matter along with Henry Chang. Ben boxed for Hawaii in the AAU championships in New York.

that a loyal mother would have hoped for this moment? The confessed ravisher of her baby standing arrogantly before her. Would our world blame a mother if she had failed to resist the temptation to deal out a deserved punishment which the courts had been impotent to give? Even though the taking of a life was repugnant to her every principle, did Mrs. Fortescue seize the revolver and kill Kahahawai? I have always hoped so.[21]

Governor Lawrence Judd wrote in his memoir that Stirling told him that he actually believed that Grace had fired the fatal shot. This is how Judd described a conversation over cigars and brandy with Stirling and several others in New York a few years after the events in question:

> We shook hands all around. Stirling and I, once friends, later adversaries, regarded each other steadily. There was small talk until I arose and went to a table for the cigar box.
>
> Stirling arose and followed me. He touched my sleeve and said: "There's one question I want to ask you about that unfortunate Massie case."
>
> "Go ahead."
>
> "Who do you think killed the Hawaiian, Kahahawai?"
>
> "Who do you think killed Kahahawai?" I parried.
>
> "I think Mrs. Fortescue killed him," said the admiral.[22]

Stirling, in a display of distorted reasoning, would even pat himself on the back for having taken quick action to protect the Ala Moana Boys from military personnel following the hung jury. He wrote:

> The reaction among Navy personnel, intensely bitter against this travesty on justice, might have been more alarming if all had not been held under strict discipline. Knowing that the five accused men were as free as air, I had half expected, in spite of discipline, to hear any day that one or more had been found swinging from trees by the neck up Nuuanu Valley or at the Pali.

---

21 *Ibid.* at 264.

22 Judd, Lawrence M., *Lawrence M. Judd & Hawaii [An Autobiography]*, as to told to Hugh W. Lytle, p. 215 (Charles E. Tuttle Co., 1971).

Through their officers, I issued a warning to all naval personnel at the Navy Base that they must conduct themselves in a manner to permit the law to take its course and that severe punishment could be expected if anyone acted otherwise.

After the mistrial I am convinced that this warning had its effect in preventing Navy men from taking summary action on the five defendants at large in the community of Honolulu.[23]

As for the beating that Horace Ida had received, Stirling offered this explanation, in effect taking credit for sparing Horace's life: "When Ida, one of the defendants was seized and severely beaten, I believe that the warning and the discipline our men were under prevented more drastic action upon him."[24]

His ultimate conclusion as to the legacy of the Massie case and the plight of the Ala Moana Boys was that the miscarriage of justice, as he saw it, might defeat any aspirations the native populace entertained about ultimate statehood. Unless ill feeling against the military could be curbed, "our National Congress may become convinced that, after all, self-government in Hawaii is a menace to the nation's naval security in the Pacific Ocean and the sooner curtailed the better for the nation."[25]

His parting tribute as to his own legacy was far more optimistic and, again, somewhat distorted. Perhaps that was the result of a natural astigmatism caused by not viewing himself from a distance, but only from within the confines of his self-protective ego. Protesting too much that he was not doing so "boastfully," he quoted at length from glowing editorials in Honolulu newspapers of his tenure, closing with these words from the *Honolulu Times*: "Hawaii will remember Admiral Stirling as a fine naval officer, a competent executive, and an outstanding American."[26]

Governor Lawrence Judd

Lawrence Judd continued to serve as Territorial governor of Hawaii until early 1934. In 1947, he became superintendent of the Kalaupapa Settlement on the Hawaiian island of Molokai, the so-called "leper colony" most commonly associated with Belgian priest Father Damian. Part of Judd's legacy is his tireless

---

23 Stirling, *Sea Duty supra* at p. 253.
24 *Ibid.*
25 *Ibid.* at p. 269.
26 *Ibid.* at p. 271.

humanitarian effort on behalf of the occupants of the settlement, not only during his tenure as superintendent, but also before and after. He later served as governor of American Samoa, appointed by Secretary of the Interior Douglas McKay, an appointment that was approved by President Dwight Eisenhower.

But notwithstanding his legacy as a humanitarian and a public servant, the Massie case and the plight of the Ala Moana Boys haunted him the rest of his life. In fact, it plagued him greatly at the time the events played out. Referring to the allegations of rape when they were first made by Thalia Massie, he later wrote:

> From this beginning were to come blasted careers, ruined lives, tragedy, and death. I was the forty-four-year-old governor of Hawaii, appointed by President Hoover to serve at his pleasure. Before the case was closed I wished devoutly that I was back in private business, or could change place with a carefree motorman on one of the open-sided tramcars that clanked from Honolulu to Waikiki.[27]

At the height of the debacle, no one was under more pressure, from both within the Territory of Hawaii and from the mainland, than Governor Judd—pressures that included concerns about the long-term future of Hawaii, whether as a territory, a state, or a military protectorate. He noted in his memoir that Hawaii was:

> [A] creature of Congress, which could turn it into an outpost ruled by a military committee, or even could return it to the Hawaiians, if it chose. Hawaii was as completely at the mercy of the Congress as were the raw Indian lands of the west when they were made territories. All depended upon the judgment, or the whim, of the Congress, and the tenor of the feeling in Washington had been apparent for some time. Many summed it up in these words: "Hawaii's chief value to America is as a fortress."[28]

And so he was torn between local justice and the broader issue of governance of the Islands. Interestingly, the decision to commute the sentence for the Massie defendants from ten years at hard labor to one hour in the custody of the sheriff earned him no friends on either side of the argument, and ultimately tore apart

---

27 Judd, *Judd & Hawaii*, *supra*, p. 166.
28 *Ibid.* at p. 200–210.

his friendship with Admiral Yates Stirling. Stirling and the military establishment were adamant that the defendants should be pardoned, leaving them with no criminal records, but Judd felt that it was vital that the convictions stand, even if the sentence was commuted.

He told one of his military aides, Lieutenant Colonel Frank Boyer, "I'll commute their sentences to time served. They'll remain felons. Commutation does not condone the crime, but merely expiates the servitude imposed by law. Then we'll retry the assault case and clear the air. Remember the jury recommended leniency."[29] He acknowledged in his memoir, though, that in hindsight he regretted doing even that, stating, "I acted under the heaviest congressional pressure and against my better judgment. Had I possessed facts which I later learned, I doubt if I would have commuted the sentences."[30]

He also described a conversation with Clarence Darrow in which Darrow demanded pardons for his clients, but Judd refused. When Darrow accused him of "breaking a pledge" if he did not pardon the defendants, Judd snapped, "Whose pledge? Not mine certainly." Then, in his memoir, Judd added this observation:

> I did not admit to him, nor have I admitted to anyone else until now, the full extent of my feeling of personal guilt in granting commutation in the face of threats by scores of congressmen and assorted public officials and newspaper publishers from coast to coast. I felt I should scrub my hands afterwards, even though the jury recommended leniency.[31]

Although he conceded that he acted under great pressure, Judd ultimately accepted all blame for the commutation. He told his friends and advisors while contemplating his decision, "Whatever I do will be my own responsibility. On my own head be it."[32] And the one person he said *did not* pressure him was the man who had appointed him as Territorial governor of Hawaii in the first place.

> Never at any time did President Hoover give me any instructions in connection with the Massie case or on any other matters. During a

---

29 *Ibid.* at p. 203.
30 *Ibid.* at p. 168.
31 *Ibid.* at p. 203.
32 *Ibid.* at p. 200.

conversation with the President, just before he left office, he made a remark that touched me so deeply it remains indelibly in my memory: "You handled the Massie case to my entire satisfaction."[33]

The Ala Moana Boys

The surviving Ala Moana Boys lived out the rest of their lives in obscurity. Ben Ahakuelo had one more brief chance at acclaim when he won the Hawaiian amateur boxing championship. Later he became a firefighter in rural Oahu. Horace Ida became a storekeeper. Henry Chang and David Takai bounced around from job to job, just trying to get by. Only Henry had any further problems with the law—it seems he developed a drinking problem.

The Massie Case Defendants

Edward Lord and Albert Jones went on to undistinguished careers in the Navy. Tommie and Thalia Massie had some real problems, though. They divorced two years after the trial—in fact, Thalia went to Reno on the second anniversary of Joe Kahahawai's death to file for divorce, claiming "extreme cruelty" as grounds. One has to wonder if that pact she had with Tommie that called for divorce if she didn't shape up, and which was one of the reasons why she went with him to the Ala Wai Inn that night in the first place, played any role in that claim.

Tommie remarried—twice more—and moved from one duty station to another. While serving aboard the USS *Texas* in 1940, he inexplicably erupted in uncontrollable rages, claimed to hear music in his head, hallucinated, and became violent. Preliminarily thought to be schizophrenic, he was hospitalized as psychotic and ultimately discharged from the Navy, diagnosed as suffering from manic depressive psychosis. He lived out the rest of his life in San Diego on his disability pension and doing various odd jobs. He died, at the age of eighty-one, on January 8, 1987—the fifty-fifth anniversary of Joe Kahahawai's murder.

Thalia fared even worse. She survived a series of failed suicide attempts, starting with the night her divorce from Tommy was officially granted, on February 23, 1934, when she was hospitalized for swallowing poison. Later that year, she tried again on the cruise ship *Roma*, where she slashed her wrists and, surviving that, attempted to jump from the ship's bridge, but other passengers stopped her in time. Following those dual attempts, she spent a month

---

33 *Ibid.* at p. 216.

in a sanitarium in Genoa, Italy, and then disappeared from public view for a while. Years later, she resurfaced in Los Angeles, where she became a bit of a notorious drunk, with a number of court appearances for being drunk in public or driving while intoxicated. In 1950, her pregnant landlady sued, accusing a drunken Thalia of physically beating her.

Thalia married again, but that marriage was short-lived. On July 2, 1963, she finally succeeded in ending her tortured life, dying alone on the floor of her apartment, just a few miles from her mother's house in Palm Beach, after taking an overdose of barbiturates. One has to wonder whether guilt over the Ala Moana case drove her to drink and ultimately to commit suicide.

Grace Fortescue was another story altogether. She finally came into some money—an inheritance from her father. She gave Thalia an allowance, and she and Roly, together again, bought a house in the Bahamas. Later, she had a home specially designed and built for her on Lake Worth in Palm Beach, Florida. She called it her "Isle Home" because it captured the flavor of Hawaii. She took up waterskiing at the age of seventy-five, parasailed in Acapulco at eighty-seven, and died at the ripe old age of ninety-five. The downside to living to that age was that she outlived her daughter, and so she was able to experience what Esther Anito, Joe's mother, had lived through: the tragic loss of a child.

What Really Happened

Two questions from the whole debacle survived the events in 1931–1932 Honolulu, one of which may have been later answered, while the second remains unclear. The first question is: Who shot Joe Kahahawai that morning in Grace Fortescue's house in Manoa? At trial, Tommie Massie testified that he held the gun when the fatal shot was fired, while Admiral Yates Stirling, in his memoir, made a case for Grace as having been the shooter. But in the early 1960s, a more plausible version of events was revealed, when Albert Jones, one of the murder defendants, gave an interview to Peter Van Slingerland of *Look* magazine.

Up to a point, Jones's account corresponded with Tommie Massie's testimony, at least until the critical question of who pulled the trigger. Then it veered off in a direction of its own. Here is how Van Slingerland reported that portion of the interview:

Q: You say Massie was questioning him. Then what happened?
A: Massie asked him a question and Kahahawai lunged at him. I say, "lunged." Somebody else might say he just leaned forward.

Q: And then?

A: I shot him.

Q: *You* shot him?

A: You're God damn right I did. I shot him underneath the left nipple and to the side. When that slug hit him he just went over backwards on the *chaise longue*. The bullet didn't go through him. It stayed in his body. That was the climax right there.

Q: Did you know what you were doing?

A: When I shot that son-of-a-bitch, I knew what I was doing.[34]

Von Slingerland, good journalist that he was, asked all the right questions, including the one he knew his readers wanted the answer to: Did Darrow know?

Q: Did Clarence Darrow ever quiz you about what happened that morning in Mrs. Fortescue's house?

A: No, he never did, although he knew what happened there.

Q: How do you know?

A: I told him.

Q: When?

A: At the very end of the trial; just about the last day or two.

Q: Under those circumstances, how did you feel in court?

A: I didn't think nothing of it. That seemed to me Mr. Darrow's idea to let Tommie take the rap, because, if it had been either Lord or I that was up there, they'd say, "What in hell was he doing in it, anyway?" But Tommie had a motive and a reason. After all, it was his wife.[35]

Jones's story strikes a chord as being honest. It's questionable whether Tommie Massie had the nerve, and it seems unlikely that Grace would have dirtied her hands. But Jones as the shooter has a ring of authenticity to it.

The second question that survives the events of 1931–1932 is bigger and with more ramifications: What actually happened that night to Thalia Massie on Ala Moana Road? Was she really raped and beaten, or was it merely a tryst that went wrong? The Clarks and the Bellingers testified that Thalia appeared to have been struck in the face, but later reports suggest that when the police

---

34 Van Slingerland, Peter, *Something Terrible Has Happened*, p. 318 (Harper & Row, 1966).

35 *Ibid.* at p. 322.

arrived at her home, her condition was worse than what it had been when she was picked up on Ala Moana Road. Had her husband administered a second, fiercer beating after she got home that night? Did she concoct a story about rape to try to satisfy him and to salvage her miserable marriage? We may never know. The only person who can say for sure is the woman who took her secret to her grave when she overdosed on barbiturates in 1963.

However, there are four conclusions that can be drawn with some certainty:

(1) *Something* happened that night on Ala Moana Road.
(2) Whatever happened, it's almost a dead certainty that the Ala Moana Boys had nothing to do with it.
(3) Whatever secret Thalia Massie was trying to hide with her lies, whether it was an affair that went bad or simply a one-night stand that ended in violence, it set events in motion that led directly to the death of Joseph Kahahawai.
(4) Whatever happened, and whatever the secret was, the ultimate result was a colossal miscarriage of justice that tarnished the legacy of one of our country's greatest legal minds.

Source Notes

As I mentioned in the Introduction, I first became aware of this story when I picked up a copy of Theon Wright's *Rape in Paradise* (Mutual Publishing). Since that time, I have tried to find every possible source I could to help me understand exactly what happened in 1931–32 Honolulu that led to this miscarriage of justice. I have come across six nonfiction books that tell this story, although three of those are decades old—those three were published in 1966. In addition to *Rape in Paradise*, the two others published in 1966 are *The Massie Case: The Most Notorious Rape Case of the Century* (Bantam Books) by Peter Packer and Bob Thomas, and *Something Terrible Has Happened* (Harper & Row) by Peter Van Slingerland. Told in the typical "reporting" style of journalists, each of these books is very informative and well written. Van Slingerland has the added benefit of having interviewed Albert "Deacon" Jones about what really happened the morning that Joe Kahahawai was killed. Wright, on the other hand, was a reporter in Honolulu who covered the Massie murder trial, so he had firsthand knowledge of much of what actually transpired during that proceeding.

The three more recent books are *Hawaii Scandal* (Island Heritage, 2002) by Cobey Black; *Honor Killing* (Penguin, 2006) by David E. Stannard; and *Local Story: The Massie-Kahahawai Case and the Culture of History* (University of Hawaii Press, 2014) by John P. Rosa. Black, who passed away in 2014, was a journalist and a resident of Hawaii. Stannard is a professor of American Studies at the University of Hawaii, and Rosa is an assistant professor of history at the University of Hawaii. These three works rely heavily on media reports from the time, as well as on court documents. *Honor Killing* is perhaps the most complete and thorough of these six nonfiction works, and certainly appeals to the serious reader, whereas *Local Story* is the thinnest (literally, at only 108 pages of narrative).

Other books that were invaluable to my research include memoirs and autobiographies of some of the key players. Clarence Darrow's autobiography, *The Story of My Life* (Charles Scribner's Sons, 1932), has an addendum chapter, tacked on to the end of the original publication, that addresses the Massie Case. Darrow's account is generously colored to justify his actions in the case (including his invoking of the unwritten law, which required him, questionably, to put the gun in the hands of Tommie Massie).

Likewise, Honolulu police detective John Jardine, in his memoir *Detective Jardine: Crimes in Honolulu* (University of Hawaii Press, 1984), devoted a chapter to the Massie Case, with what appears to be even less concern for accuracy than Darrow. Admiral Yates Stirling also contributed his take on the story in a chapter of his memoir *Sea Duty: The Memoirs of a Fighting Admiral* (Putnam, 1939). If Darrow's and Jardine's versions periodically veered off the road toward fiction, in my opinion Stirling's took a hard turn into fantasy. A noted racist, he viewed events through the prism of that racism. When first told of the alleged assault on Thalia, he said, "our first inclination is to seize the brutes and string them up on trees." He believed that the hung jury in the rape trial was a miscarriage of justice "which could have been avoided if the Territorial Government had shown more inclination to sympathize with my insistence upon the necessity of a conviction," and he justified the killing of Kahahawai by stating that "[t]he dark-skinned citizens have been taught how far the American white man will go to protect his women from brutal assaults by them." Still, fantasy or not, it offers an interesting insight into a man who was arguably one of the villains in the whole affair.

In my view, the most accurate memoir, at least as relates to the Massie case, is that of Territorial Governor Lawrence Judd, entitled *Lawrence M. Judd & Hawaii: An Autobiography* (Charles E. Tuttle Co., 1971). Although it offers very interesting insights into the political climate and the pressure brought to bear on Governor Judd to pardon the murder defendants, it, like the other memoirs, does not contain much detail, nor does it provide a purely objective view of the case. All of the memoir authors have their own separate agendas, more concerned with salvaging legacies than telling the true story.

Other books that I relied upon include *Horror in Paradise: Grim and Uncanny Tales from Hawaii and the South Seas* (Mutual Publishing, 1986), in which Gavan Daws, a writer and historian with a PhD from the University of Hawaii, contributes a chapter entitled "The Honolulu Martyrdom," about the Massie Case. And for the reference to the sad case of the murder of young Gill Jamieson, I relied on a fascinating book called *Jan Ken Po: The World of Hawaii's Japanese Americans* (University of Hawaii Press, 1973) by Dennis M. Ogawa.

To recount the events of the two trials, both the Ala Moana case and the Massie case, I had available considerable portions of the original trial transcripts to review. Some of the transcripts can be found online; I obtained others from the Hawaii State Archives. In fact, the interrogations of witnesses and arguments of counsel contained in the chapters set in the courtrooms during the respective trials ("Part Two: Territory of Hawaii v. Ben Ahakuelo, et al" and "Part Five: Territory of Hawaii v. Grace Fortescue, et al") are pretty much taken verbatim from the transcripts. Portions of Clarence Darrow's four-hour-and-twenty-minute closing can also be found in a compilation of closing arguments and speeches delivered by Darrow, entitled *Attorney for the Damned: Clarence Darrow in the Courtroom* (The University of Chicago Press, 1957), edited by Arthur Weinberg.

I found much of the factual detail that I included in the narrative chapters (such as the events of the night of September 12–13, 1931, the beating of Horace Ida, the kidnapping and murder of Joe Kahahawai, and the efforts to dispose of Joe's body) in witness statements given to police, trial testimony in the respective cases, and the incredibly detailed 279-page Pinkerton Report. Dialogue in interview scenes, such as those involving Thalia Massie and Captain John McIntosh, and Ben Ahakuelo and police officer D. W. Watson, come straight from transcripts of those actual interviews.

Other court records and documents, some of which I found online and others that I obtained from the Hawaii State Archives, proved invaluable. The transcripts of the interactions between Judge Albert Cristy and the grand jury proved not only to be valuable resources, but also made for fascinating reading, as did the transcript of the hearing on the motions to quash and to dismiss the indictments of Grace Fortescue, *et al.* As an attorney, I found the transcript of the hearing to be particularly fascinating, especially the sniping between Judge Cristy and attorney Montgomery Winn. I was also fascinated by pleadings and motions filed in the two cases—as a rule, papers filed with courts are incredibly dull, but the pleadings in these two cases proved to be exceptions to that rule.

One of the most valuable online resources I found is the University of Minnesota Law School's "The Clarence Darrow Digital Collection," found at http://darrow.law.umn.edu, which has a page on "Massie Case—1932," and which contains most of the trial transcripts from the Ala Moana trial as well as the Pinkerton Report and numerous other court documents. Another law school contribution is the University of Missouri-Kansas City Law School's "Famous Trials" website, which has a page on "The Massie ('Honor Killing') Trial," found at http://law2.umkc.edu.

This is not an exhaustive listing of all the sources I relied upon, as I found numerous other bits and pieces of information both online and in newspaper archives, but these are the major sources. I have tried to be as true to the historical record as possible. I have, obviously, taken some liberties with dialogue in scenes in which we don't have the actual record of the exact words that were spoken, but I have tried to stay true to the spirit of how those conversations and scenes were characterized in police statements or interviews, trial testimony, or the Pinkerton Report.

Bibliography

Published Materials

Baatz, Simon. *For the Thrill of It: Leopold, Loeb, and the Murder That Shocked Chicago*. New York: Harper, 2008.

Black, Coby. *Hawaii Scandal*. Honolulu: Island Heritage, 2002.

Darrow, Clarence. *The Story of My Life*. New York: Da Capo Press, 1996.

Daws, Gavan. "The Honolulu Martyrdom," in *Horror in Paradise: Grim and Uncanny Tales from Hawaii and the South Seas*, eds. A. Grove Day and Bacil F. Kirtley. Honolulu: Mutual Publishing, 1986.

Jardine, John. *Detective Jardine: Crimes in Honolulu*. Honolulu: University of Hawaii Press, 1984.

Journal of the House of Representatives of the Commonwealth of Kentucky and Journal of the Kentucky Senate. Resolution in the Matter of the Lawlessness in the Hawaiian Islands. (1932).

Judd, Lawrence M. *Lawrence M. Judd and Hawaii: An Autobiography*. Rutland, VT: Charles E. Tuttle, 1971.

Kotani, Roland. *The Japanese in Hawaii: A Century of Struggle*. Honolulu: The Hawaii Hochi, Ltd., 1985.

Linder, Douglas O. *The Massie Trials: A Commentary*. Kansas City: University of Missouri-Kansas City Law School, http://law2.umkc.edu (2007).

Ogawa, Dennis M. *Jan Ken Po: The World of Hawaii's Japanese Americans*. Honolulu: University of Hawaii Press, 1973.

Owen, Russell. "Hot Lands and Cold," in *We Saw It Happen: The News Behind the News That's Fit to Print*, eds. Hanson W. Baldwin and Shepherd Stone. New York: World Publishing, 1938.

Packer, Peter and Bob Thomas. *The Massie Case*. New York: Bantam Books, 1966.

Rosa, John P. *Local Story: The Massie-Kahahawai Case and the Culture of History*. Honolulu: University of Hawaii Press, 2014.

Stannard, David E. *Honor Killing: How the Infamous "Massie Affair" Transformed Hawaii*. New York: Viking, 2005.

Stirling, Yates. *Sea Duty: The Memoirs of a Fighting Admiral.* New York: G. P. Putnam's Sons, 1939.

University of Minnesota. "The Massie Trial" in The Clarence Darrow Digital Collection. http://darrow.law.umn.edu/trials.php?tid=5.

University of Missouri-Kansas City Law School. "Famous Trials: The Massie ('Honor Killing') Trials 1931–1932." http://law2.umkc.edu/faculty /projects/ftrials/massie/massie.html.

Van Slingerland, Peter. *Something Terrible Has Happened.* New York: Harper & Row, 1966.

Weinberg, Arthur (ed.). *Attorney for the Damned: Clarence Darrow in the Courtroom.* Chicago: University of Chicago Press, 1989.

Wright, Theon. *Rape in Paradise.* Honolulu: Mutual Publishing, 1966.

Zwonitzer, Mark (writer/director). *The Massie Affair* (documentary). Arlington, VA: PBS American Experience, 2005.

Unpublished Materials

Documents, and pleadings for Territory of Hawaii v. Ben Ahakuelo, et al. Hawaii State Archives, Papers of Governor Lawrence M. Judd, University of Minnesota Law School's "The Darrow Digital Collection." http://darrow .law.umn.edu.

Grand jury transcripts, documents, and pleadings for Territory of Hawaii v. Grace Fortescue, et al. Hawaii State Archives, Papers of Governor Lawrence M. Judd, University of Minnesota Law School's "The Darrow Digital Collection." http://darrow.law.umn.edu.

Pinkerton National Detective Agency, Inc. Report on Ala Moana case, 1932.

Police Booking Sheets, Honolulu Police Department.

Police Interview of Ben Ahakuelo.

Police Interview of Henry Chang.

Police Interview of Thalia Massie.

Proposition for Ala Moana Case laid before Chamber of Commerce Counsel, 1932.

Police Statements (various) related to kidnaping of Joseph Kahahawai and arrests of Fortescue defendants.

Trial transcripts for Territory of Hawaii v. Ben Ahakuelo, et al. Hawaii State Archives, Papers of Governor Lawrence M. Judd.

Trial transcripts (partial) of Territory of Hawaii v. Grace Fortescue, et al. Hawaii State Archives, Papers of Governor Lawrence M. Judd.

United States Senate, Committee on Territories and Insular Affairs. Hearings on Joint Resolution 81: A Joint Resolution for an Investigation of the Government of the Territory of Hawaii and for Other Purposes (1932).

Newspapers

Honolulu Advertiser
Honolulu Star-Bulletin
Honolulu Times
New York Times

Index